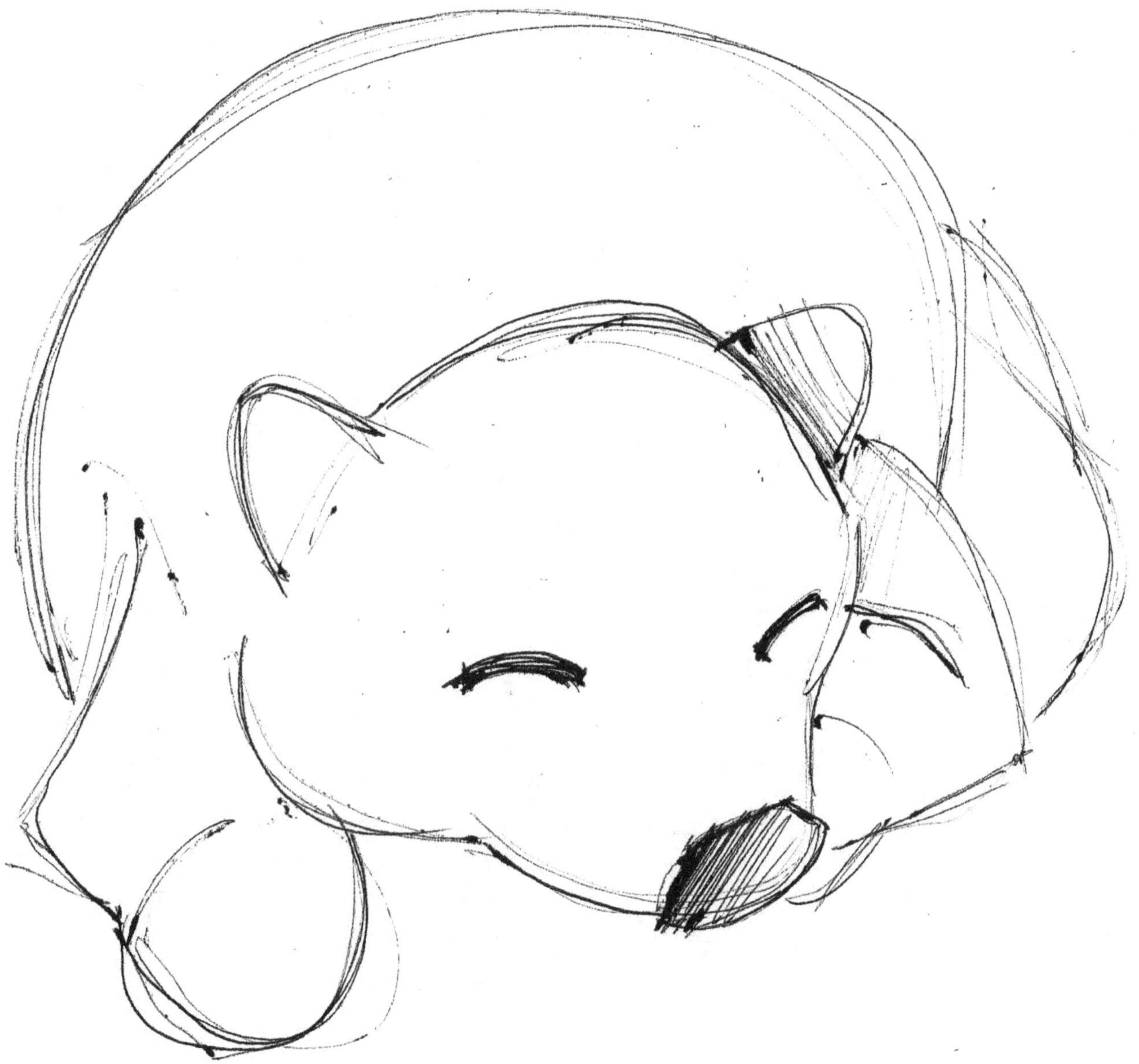

furry little dreams
marco aurelio galan henriquez

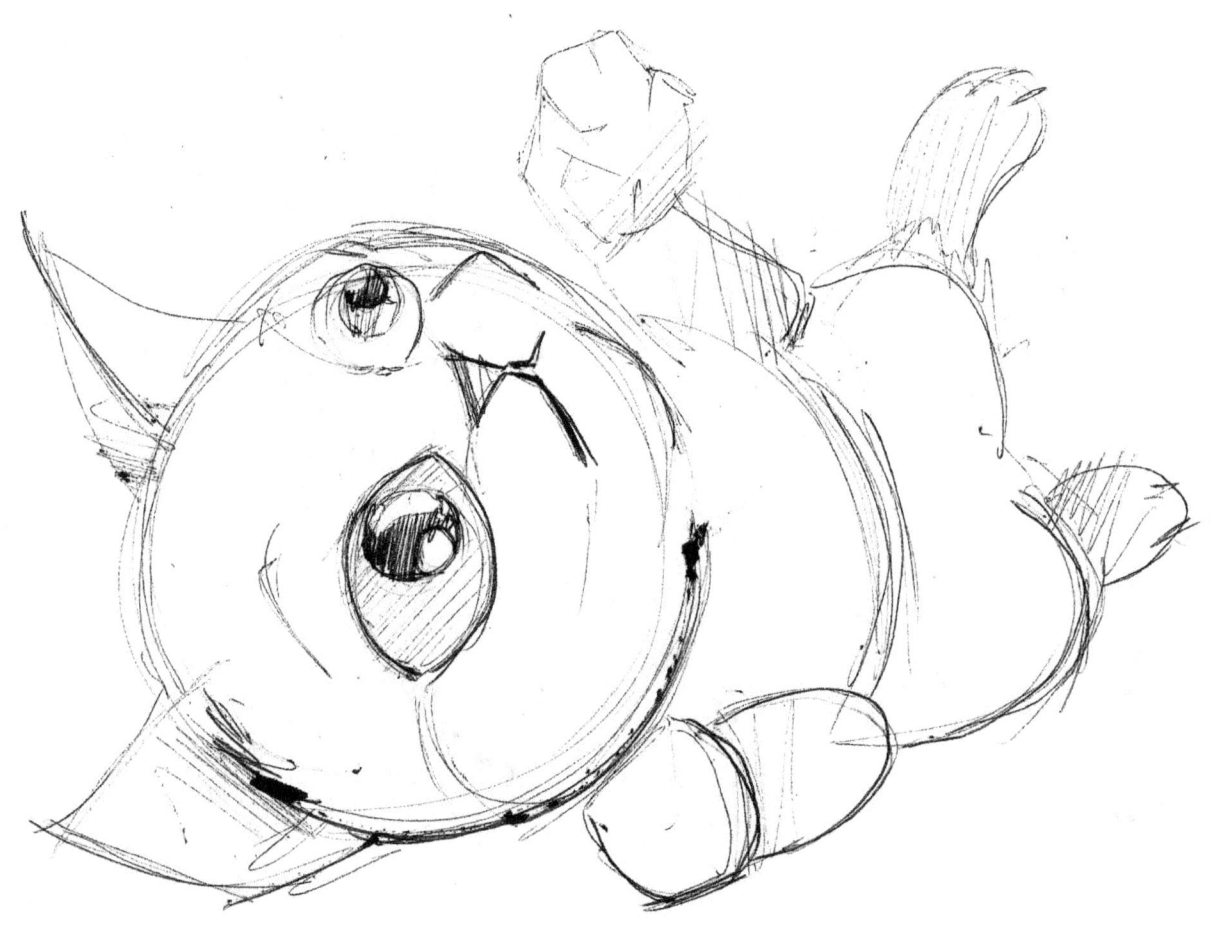

Copyright © 2013 MARCO AURELIO GALAN HENRIQUEZ

All rights reserved.

ISBN: 978-1494420796
ISBN-13: 1494420791

happy birthday Goyillita

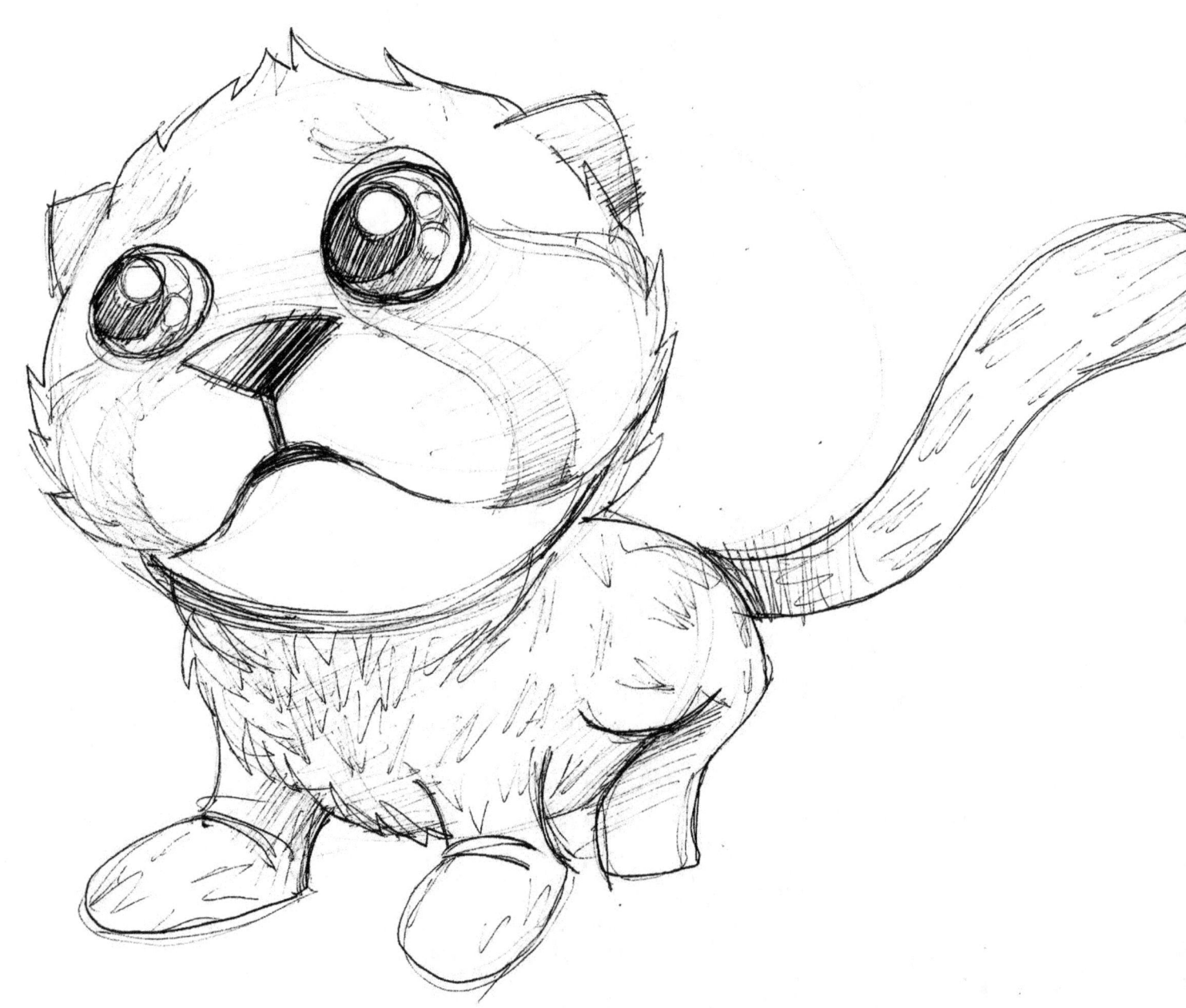

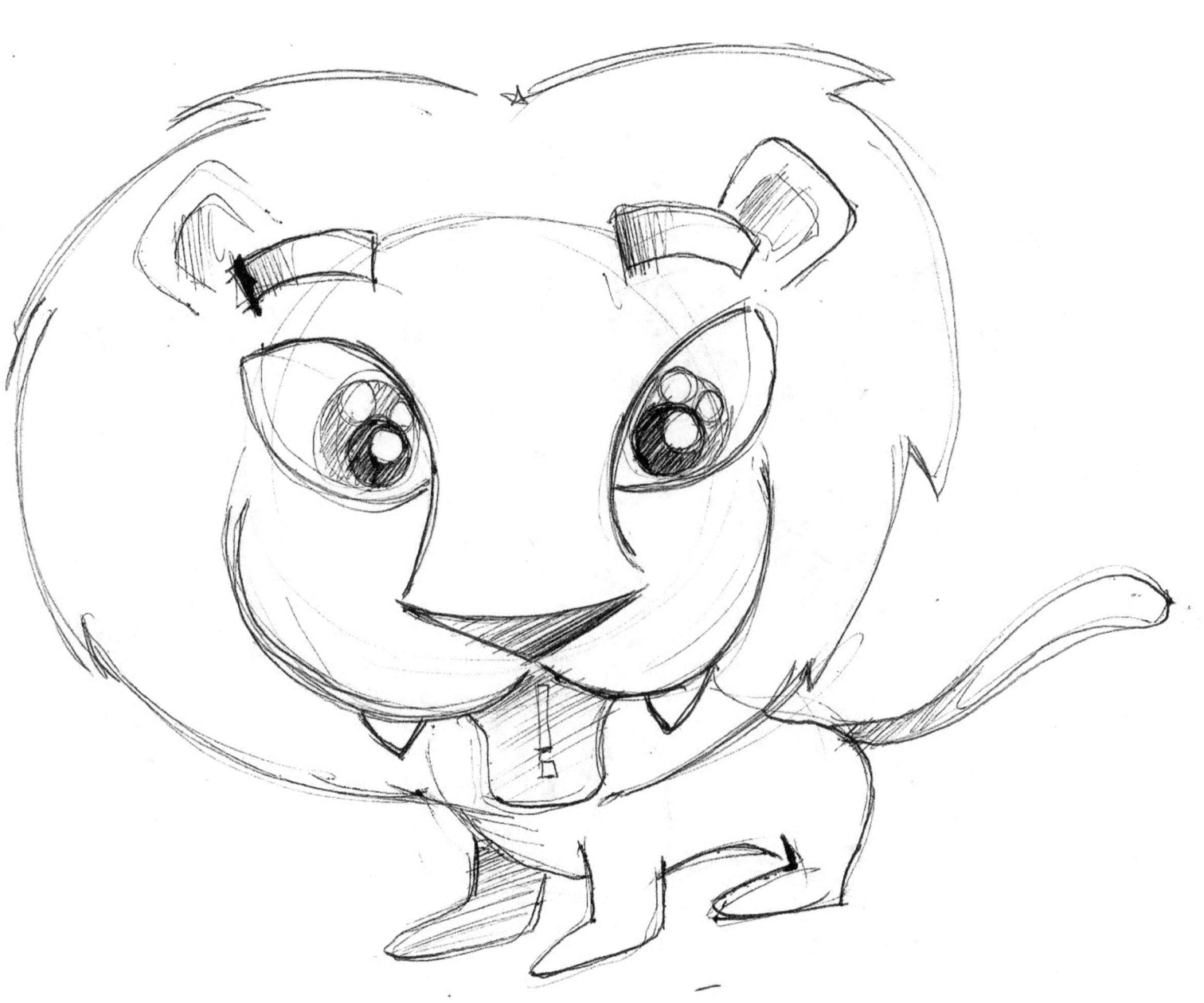

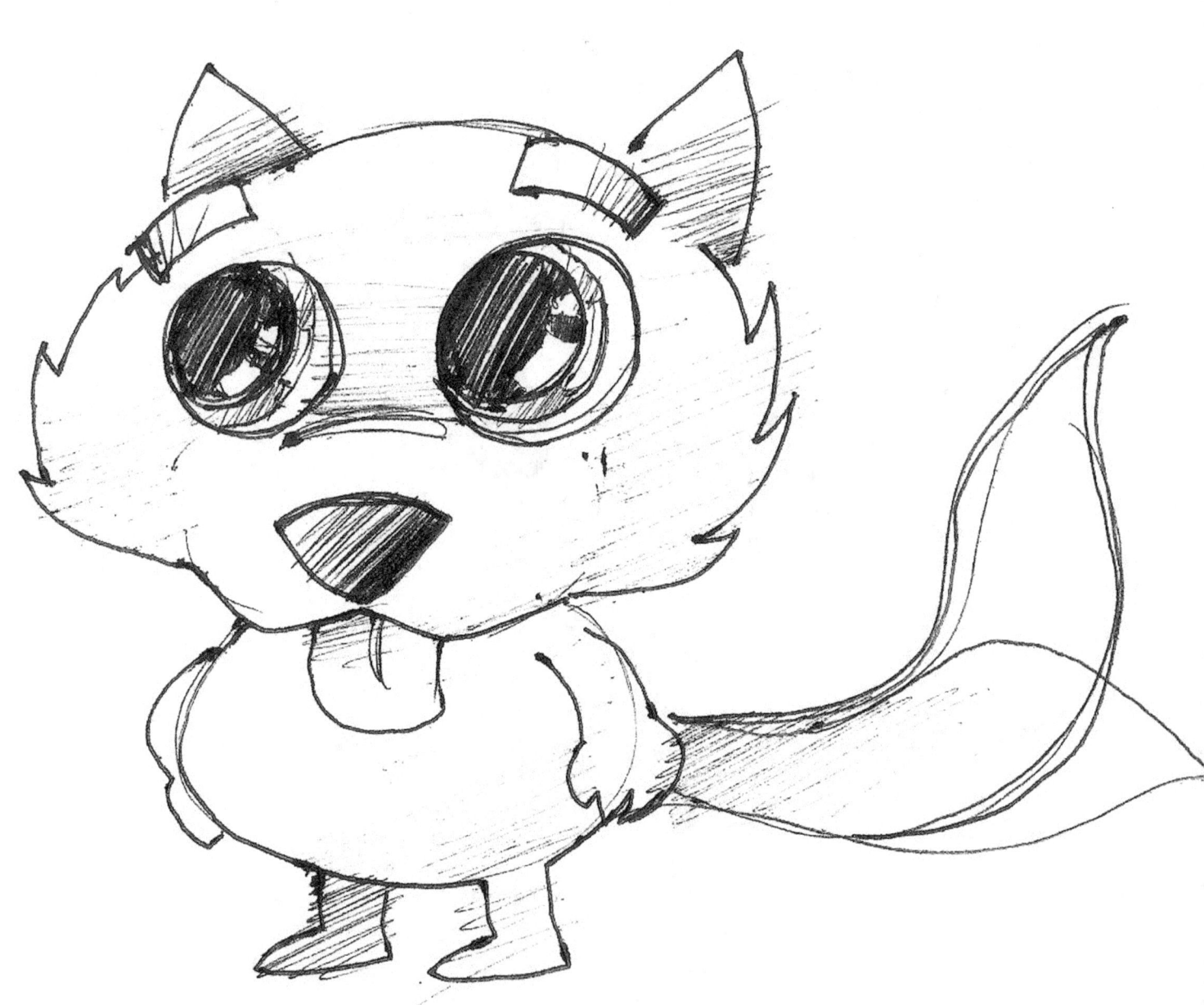

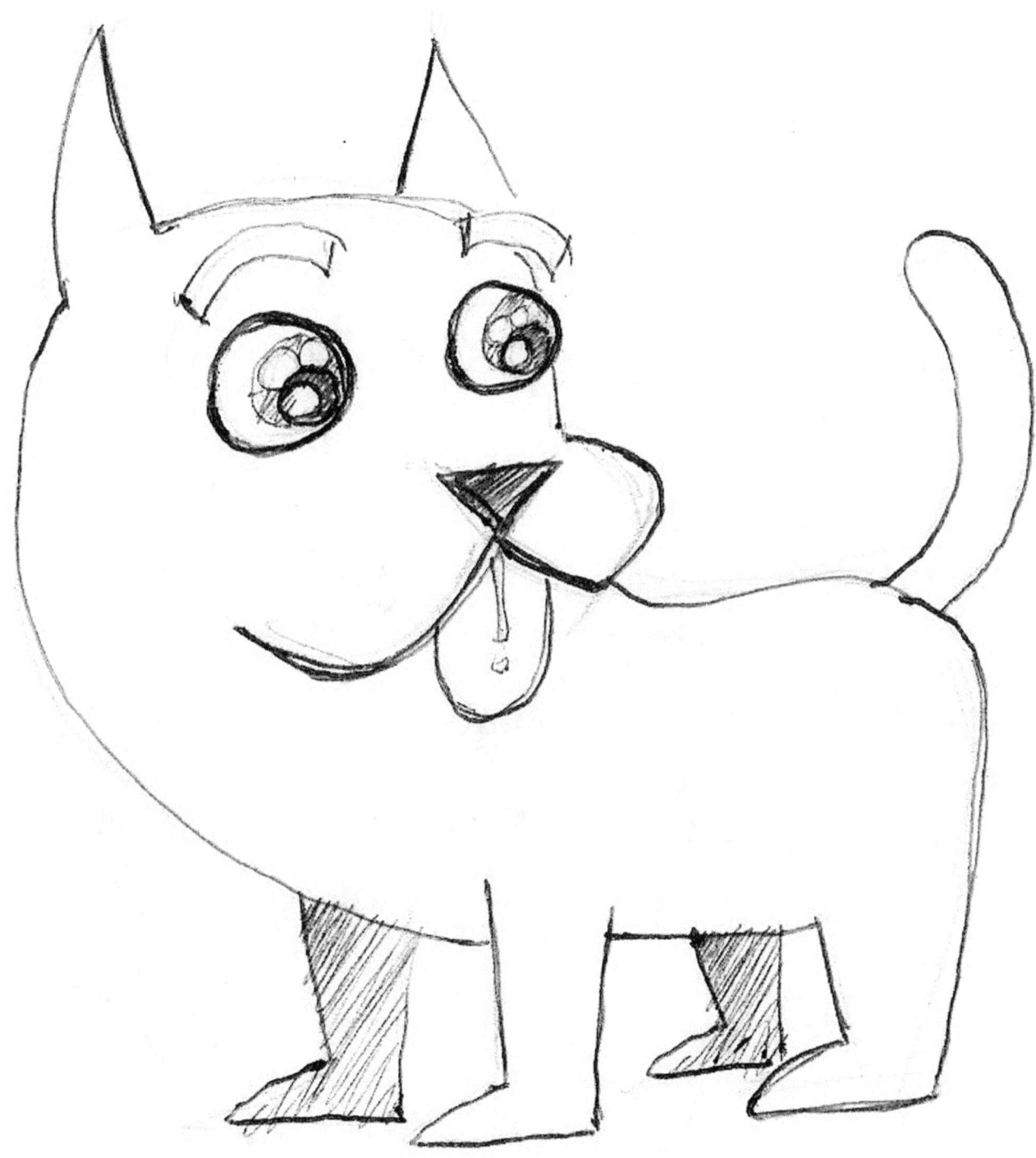

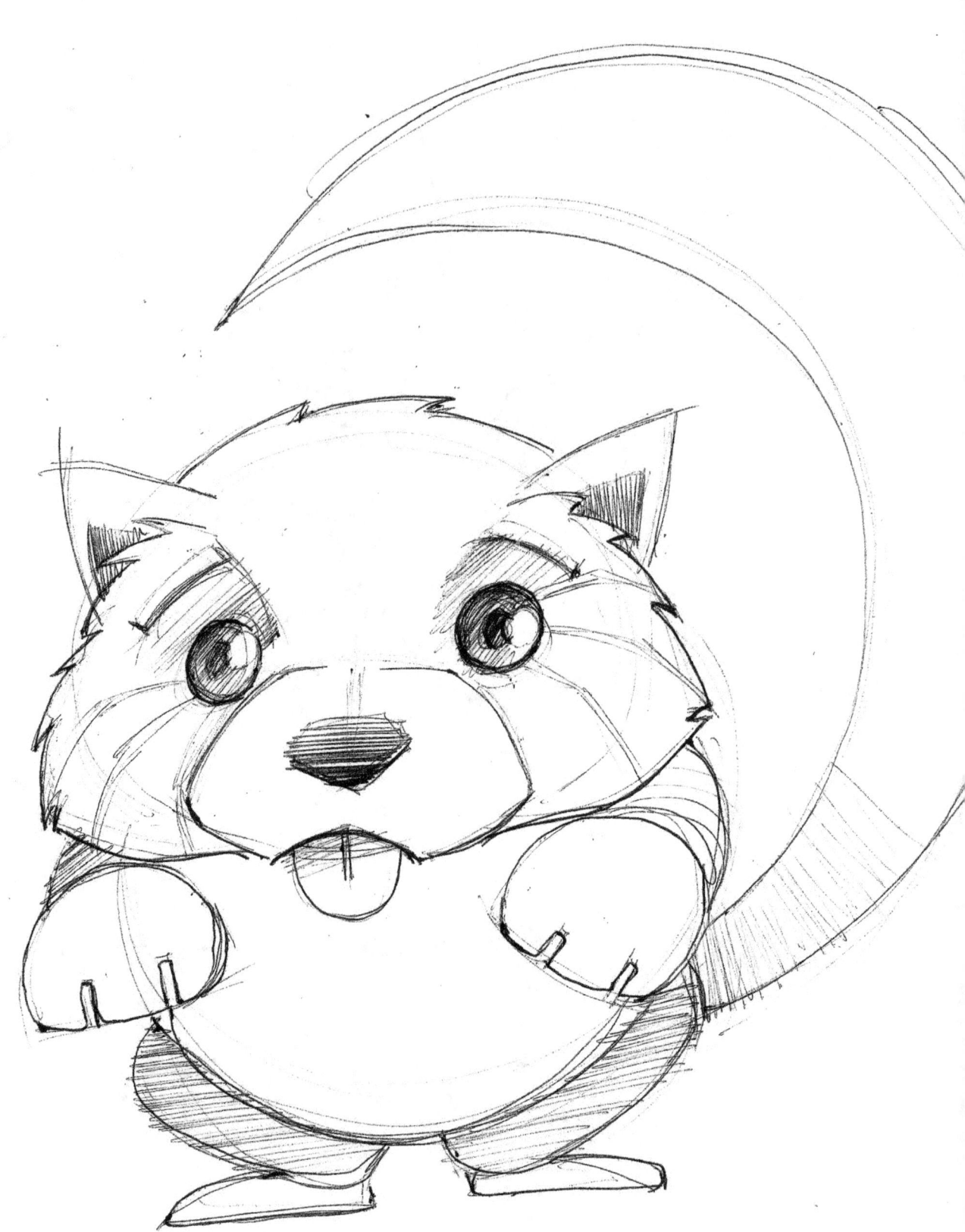

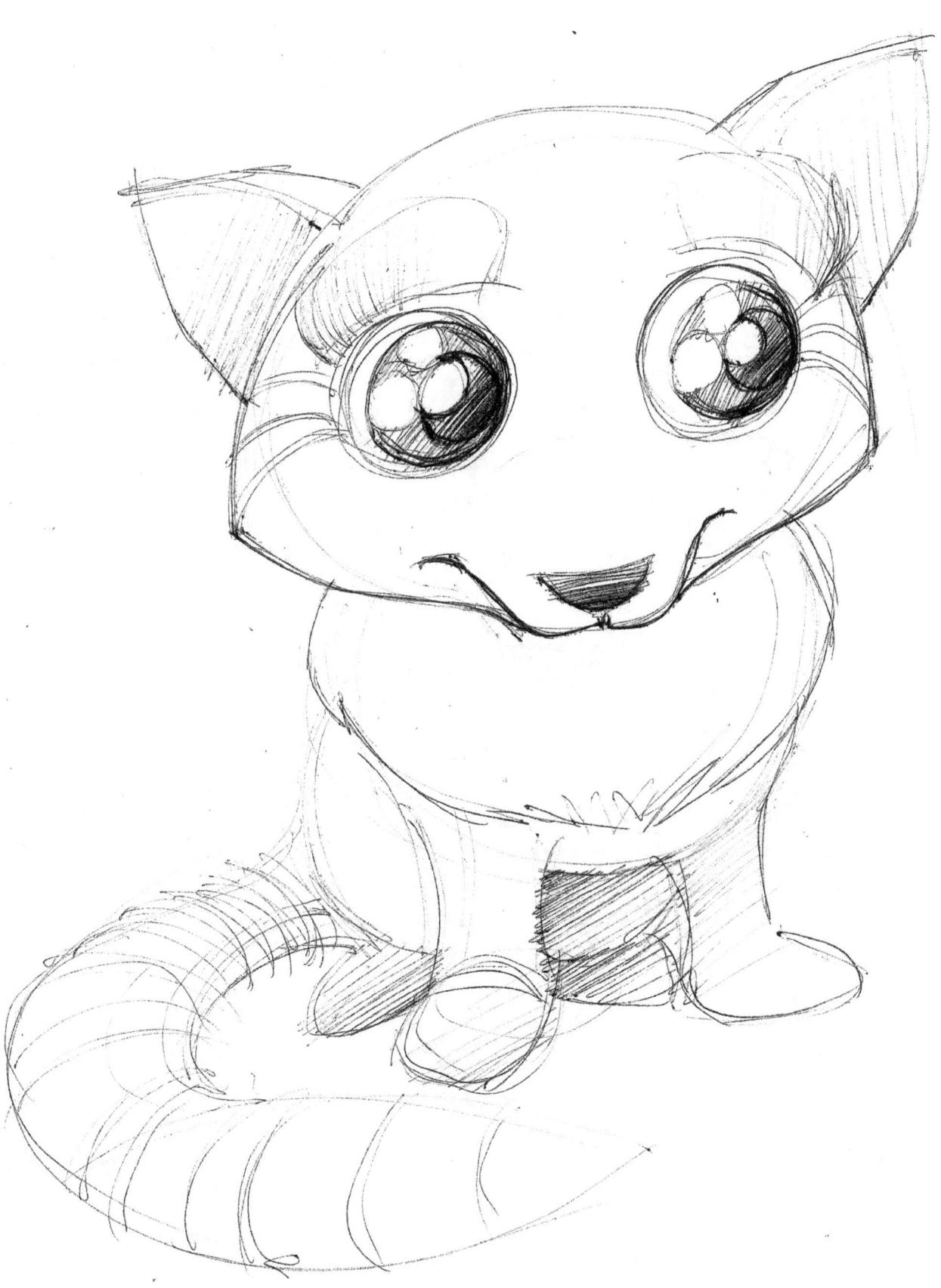

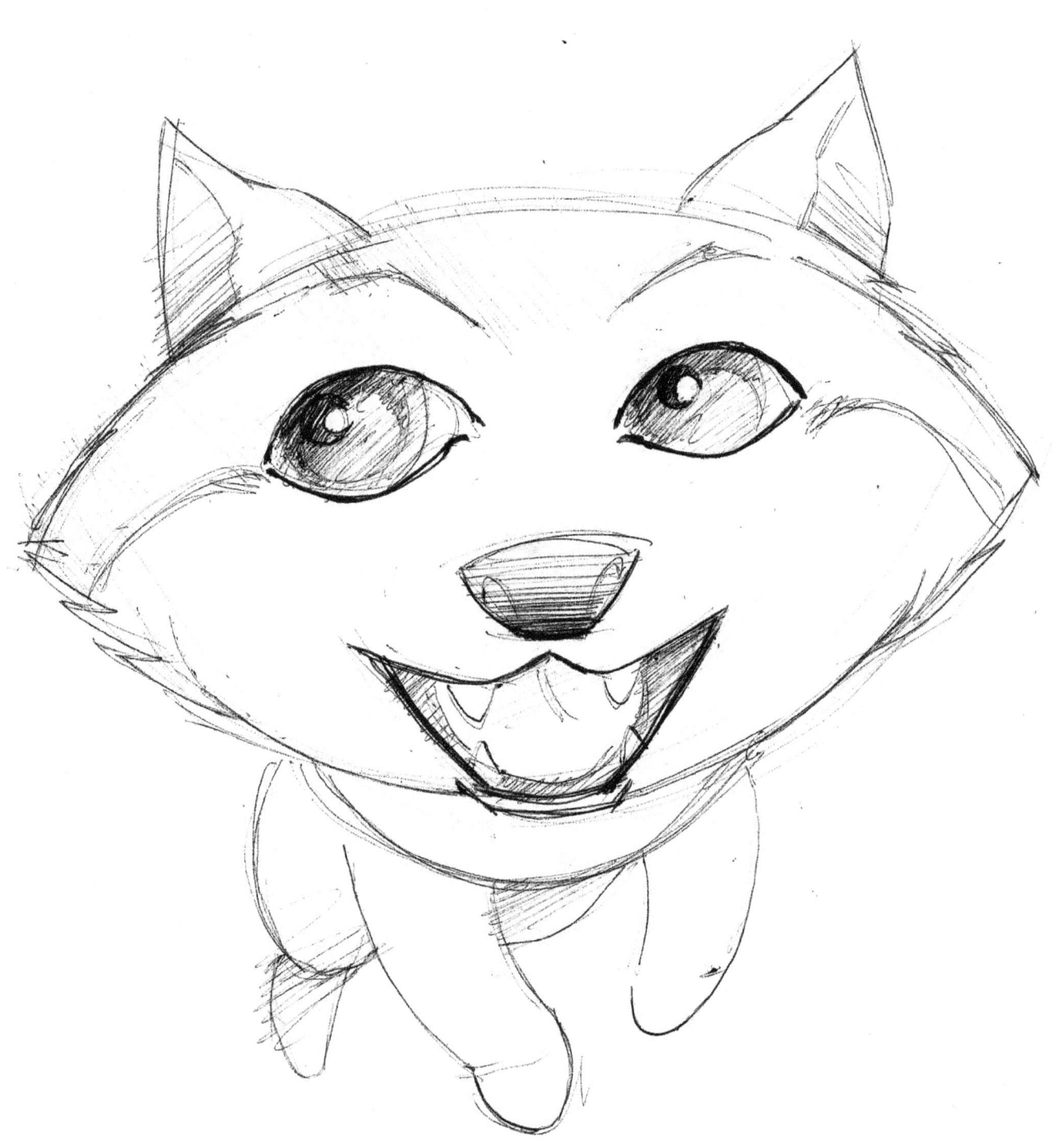

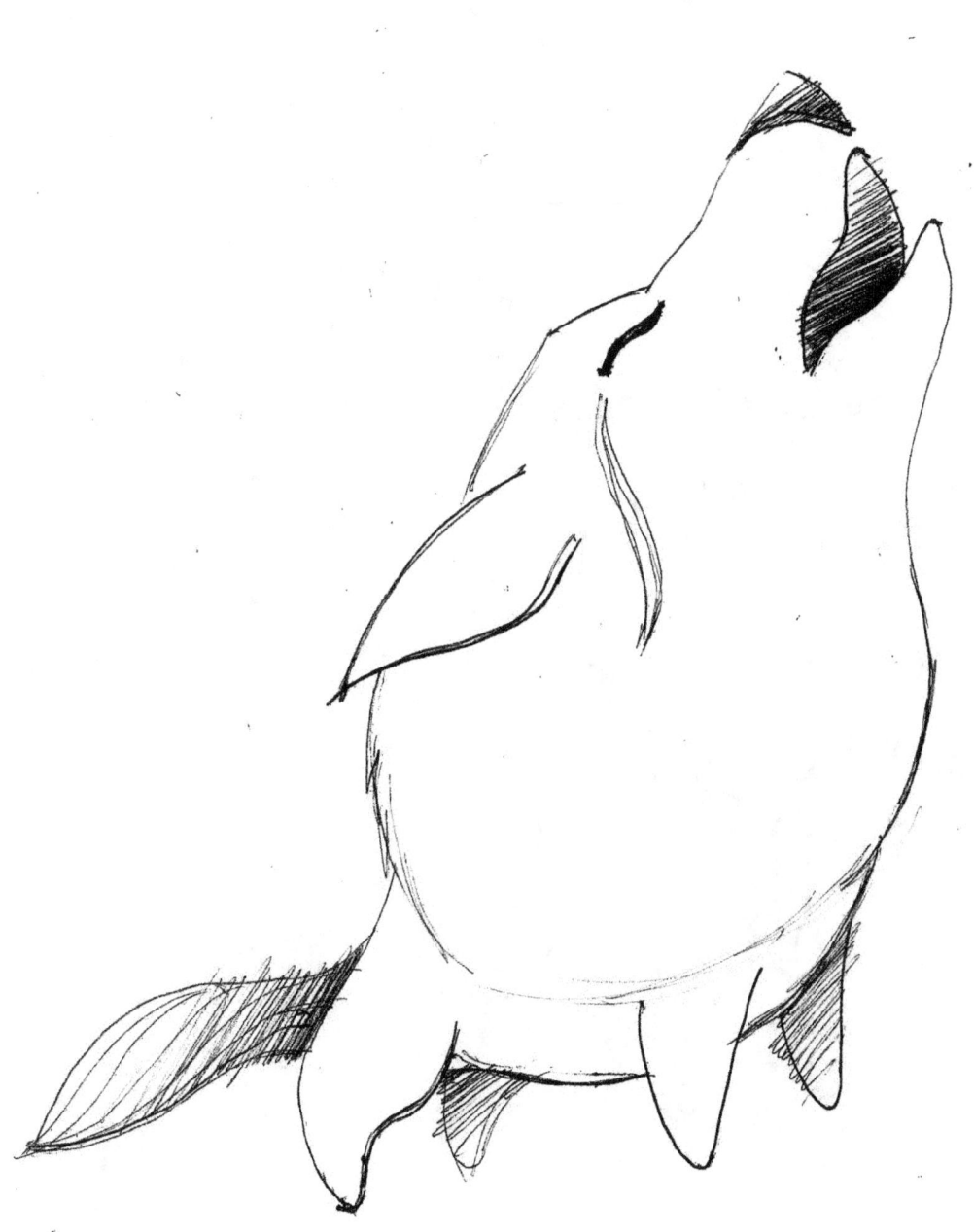

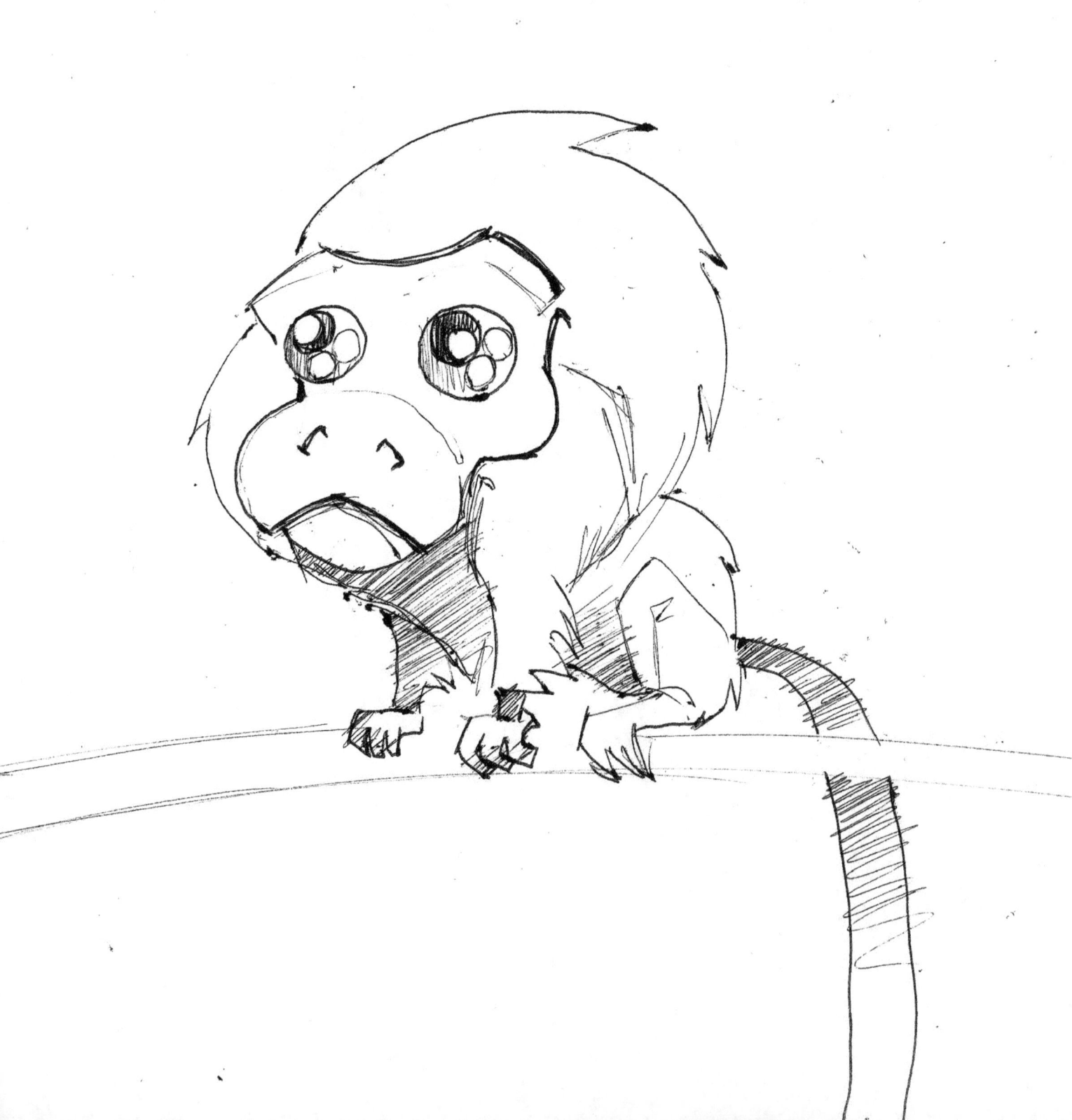

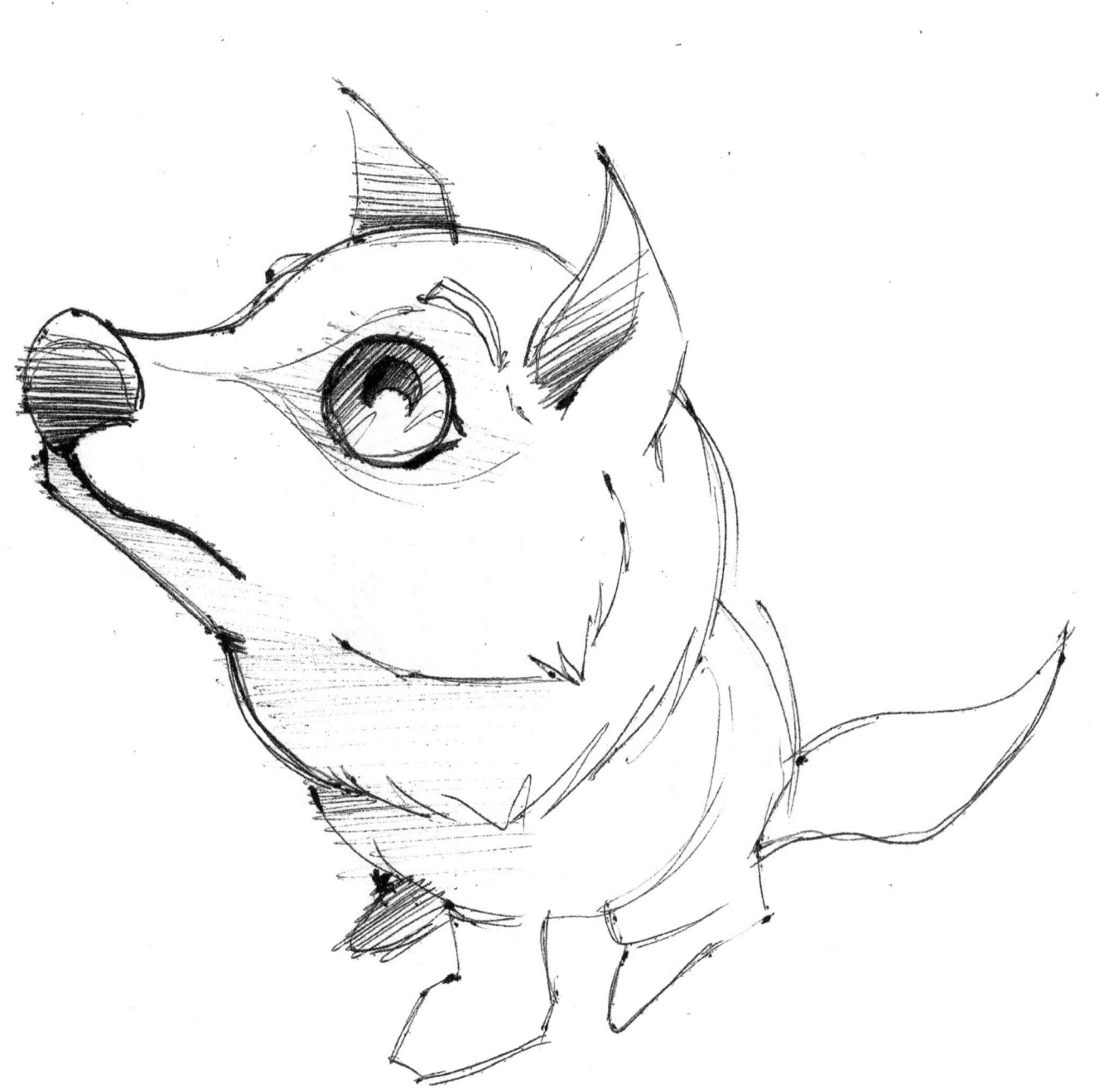

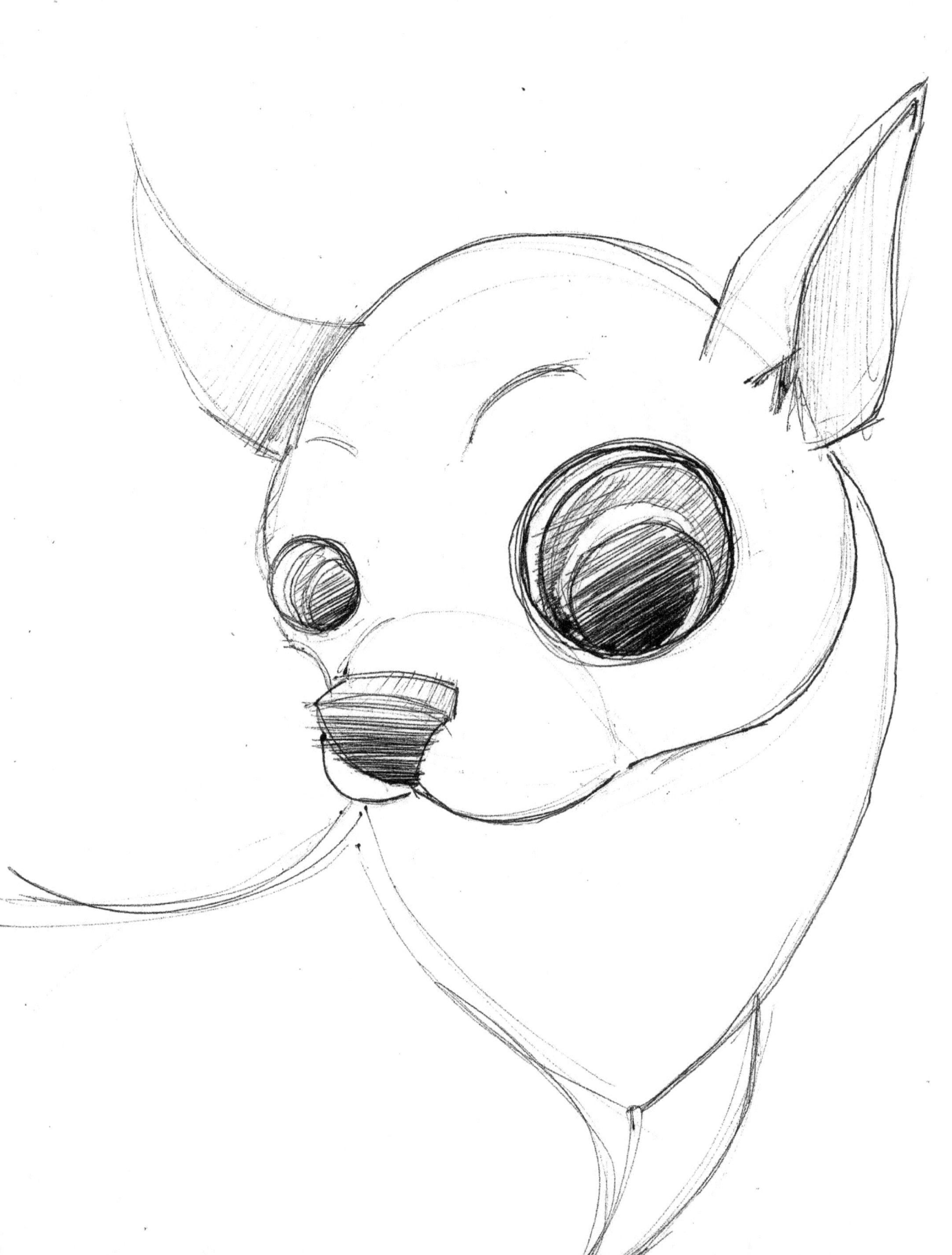

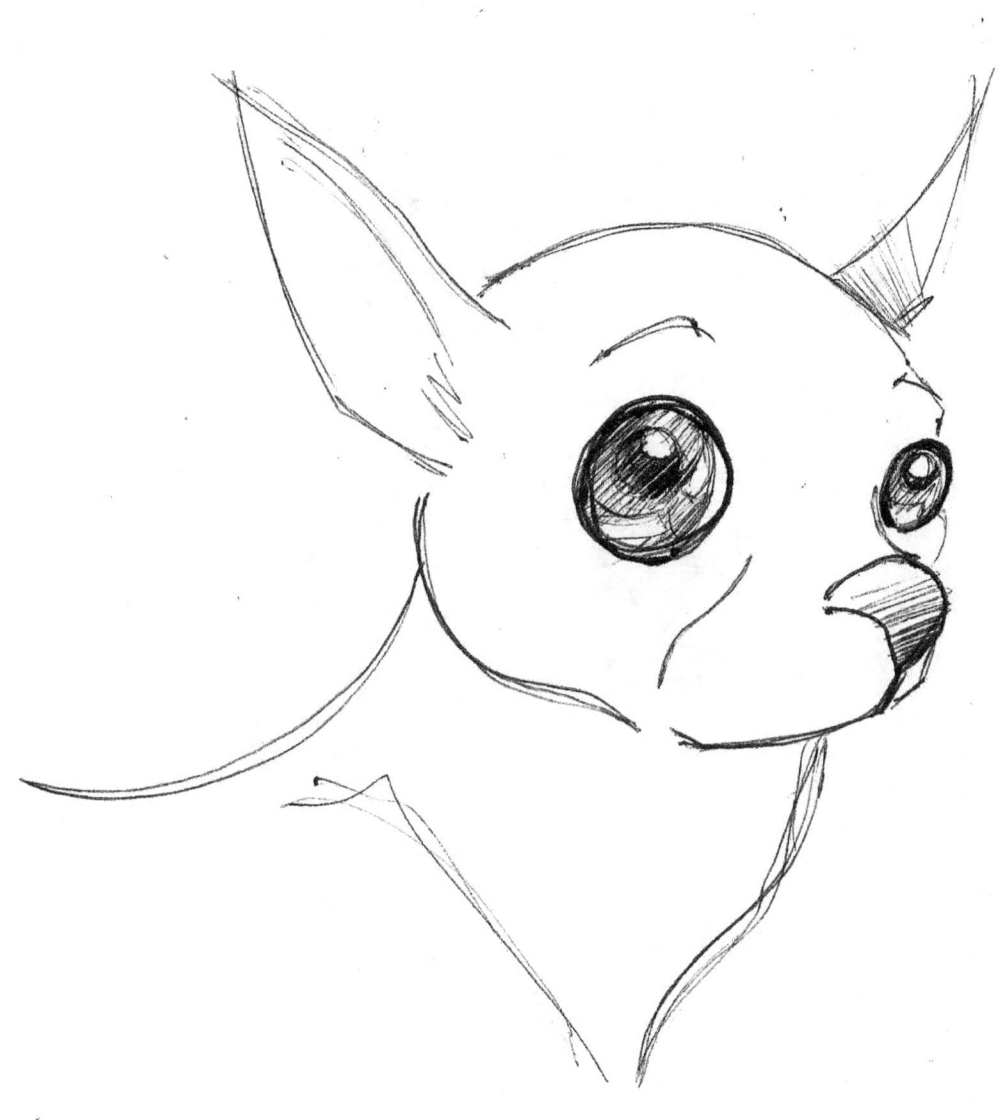

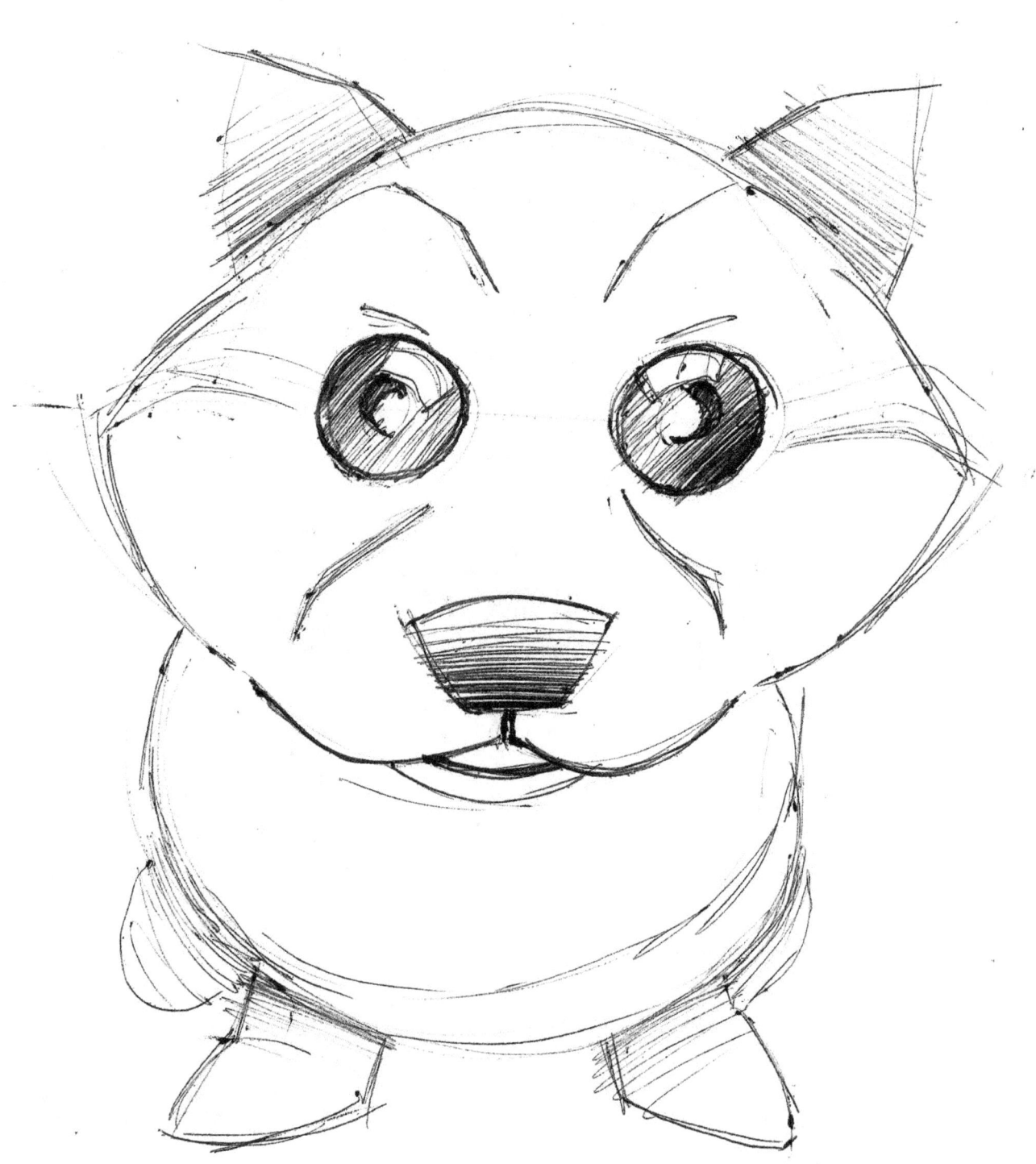

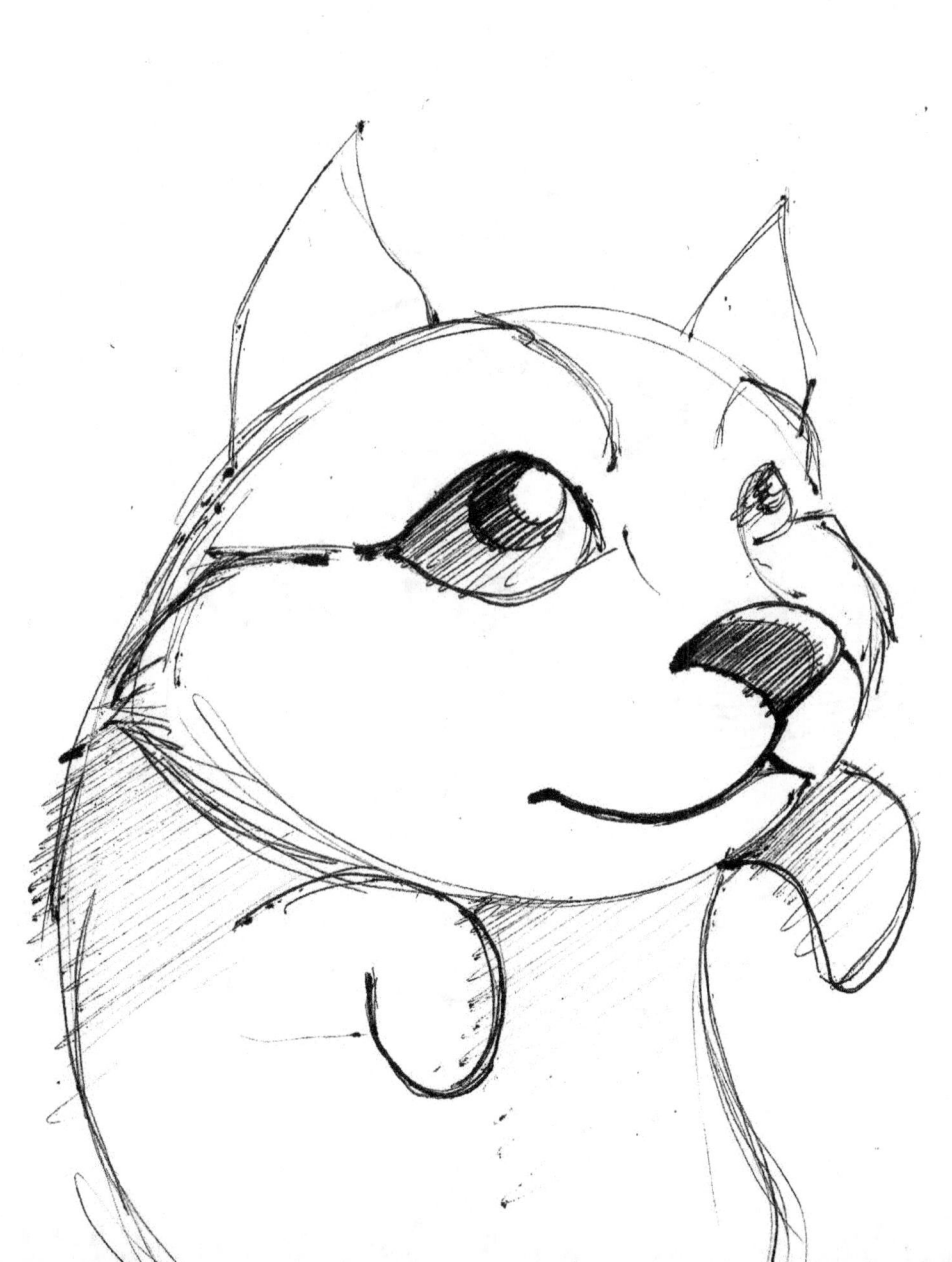

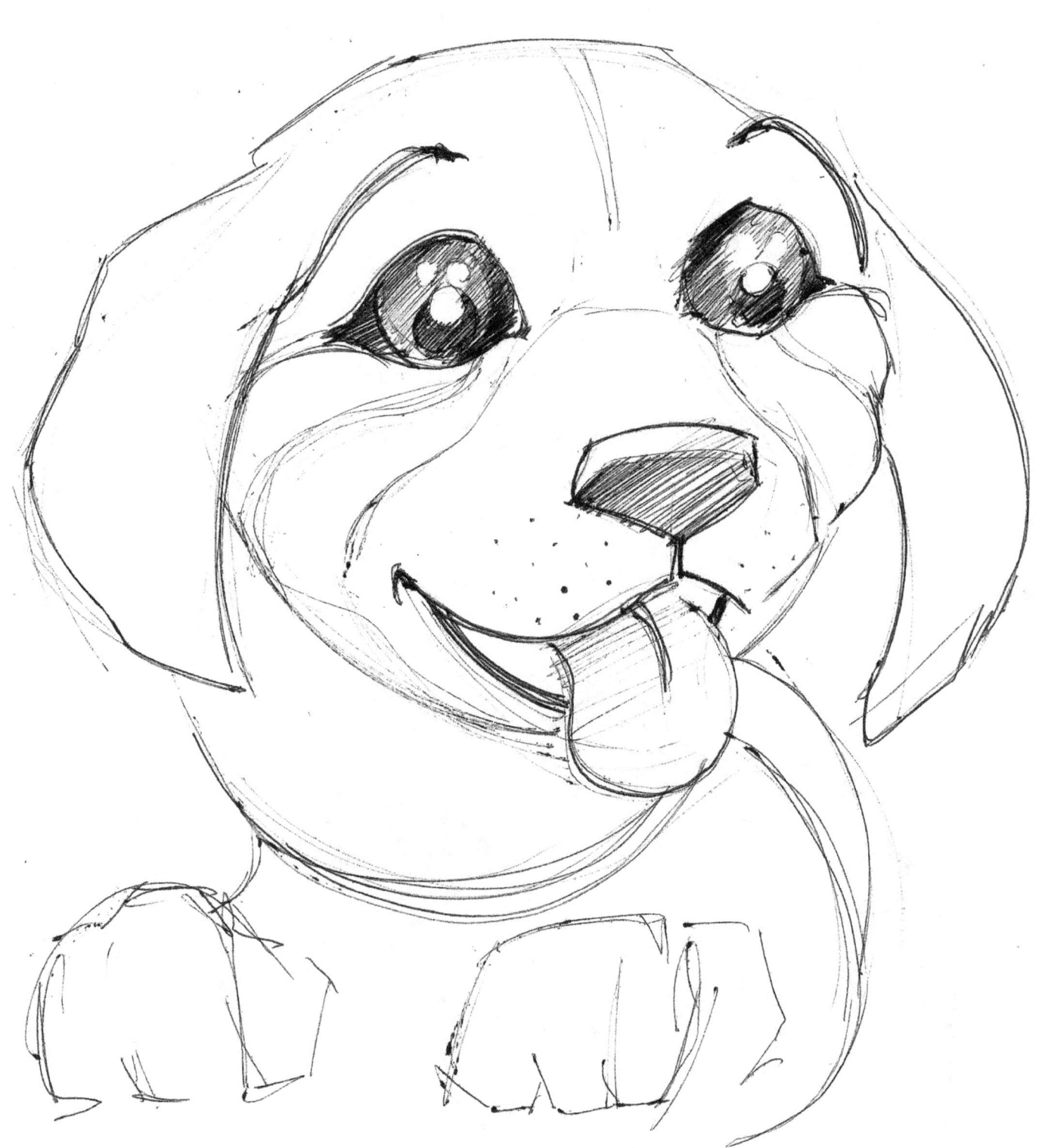

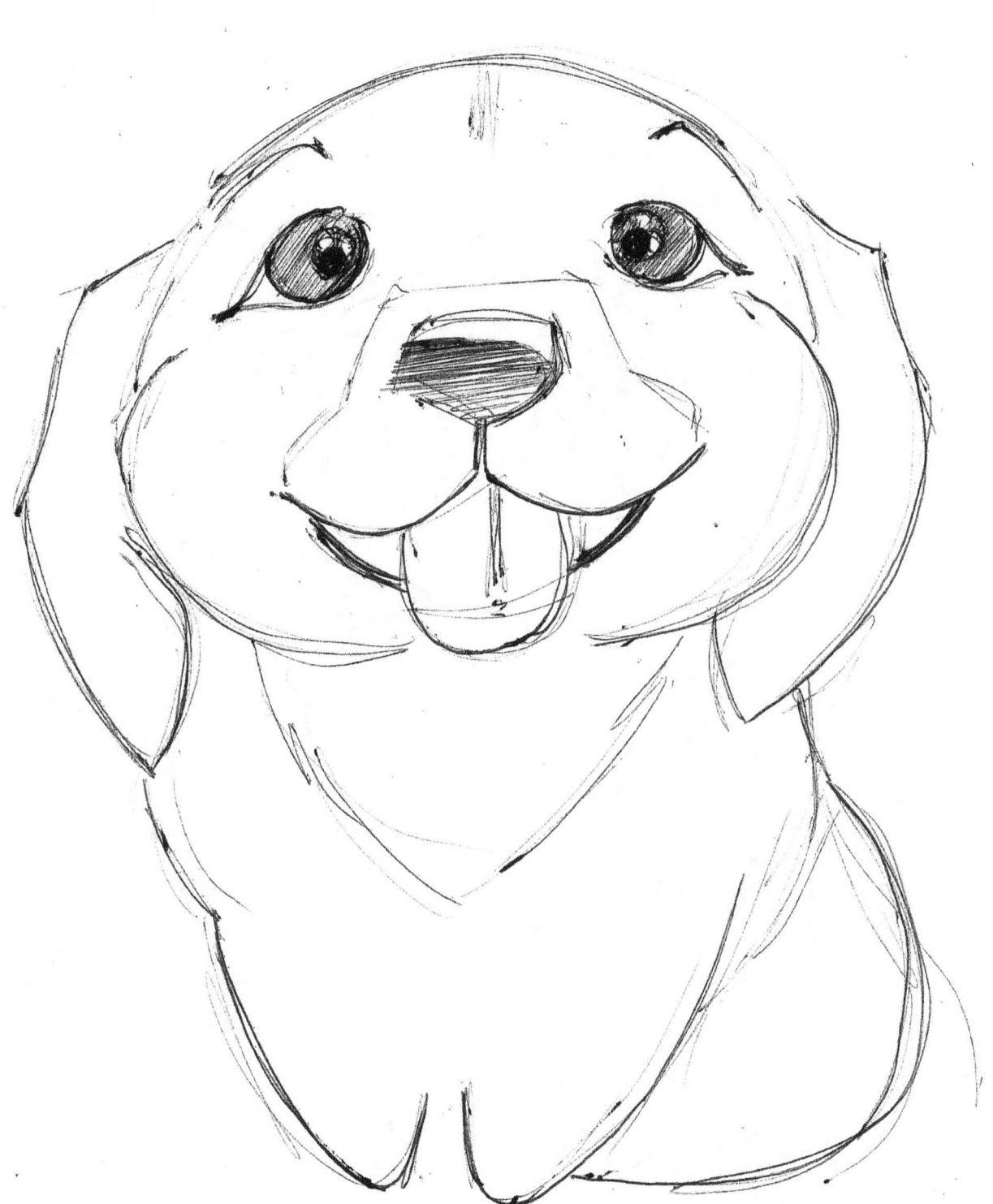

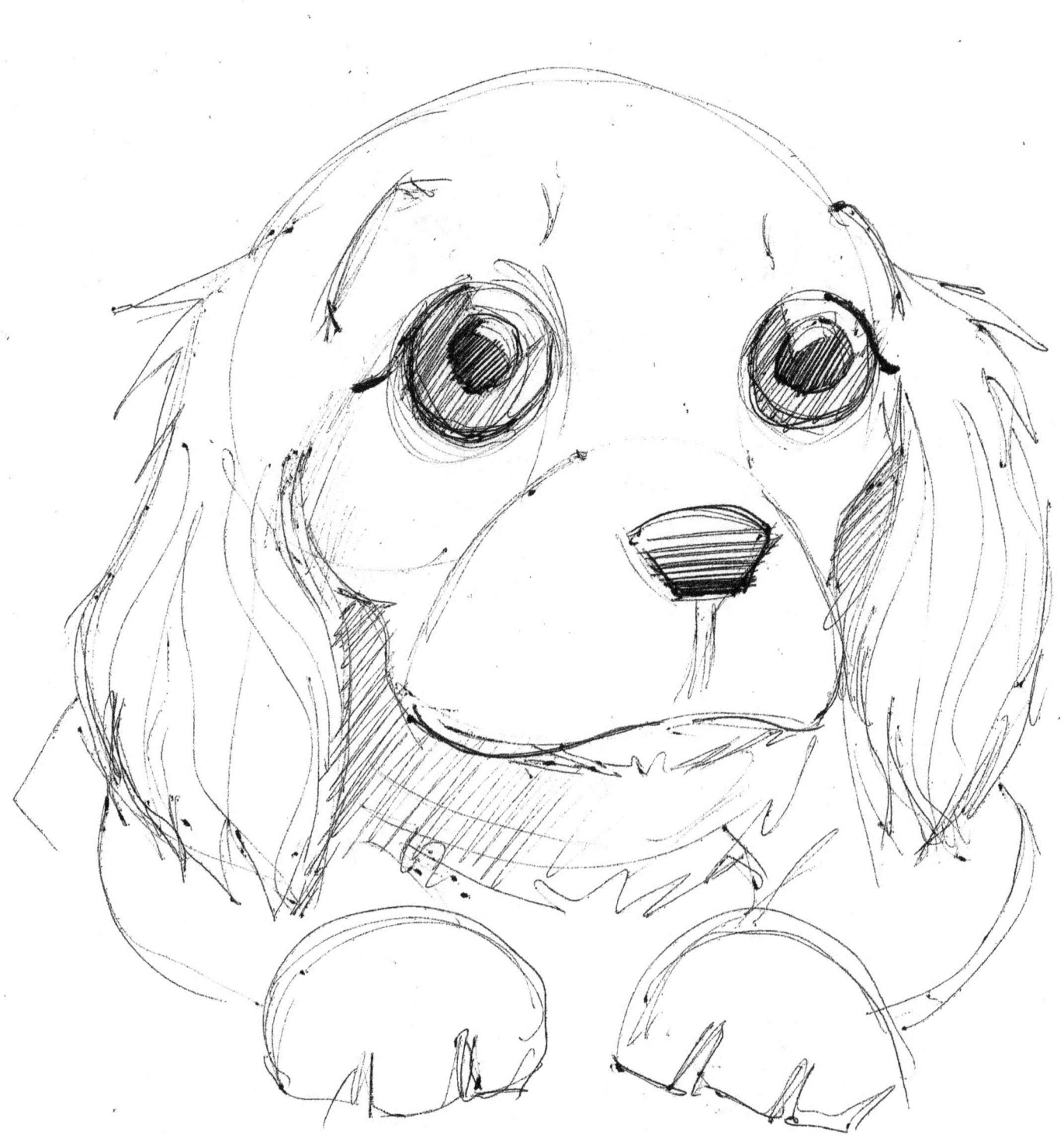

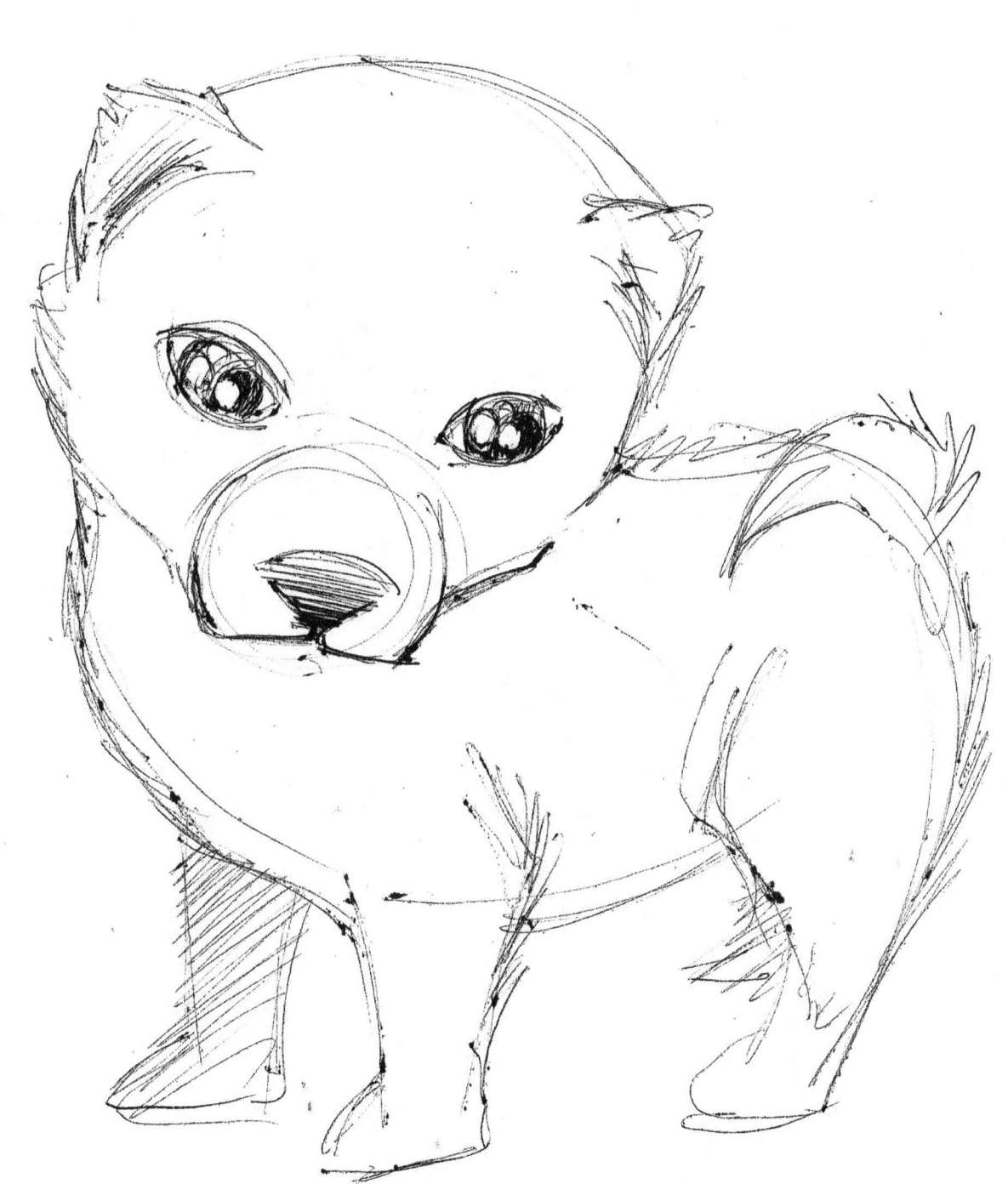

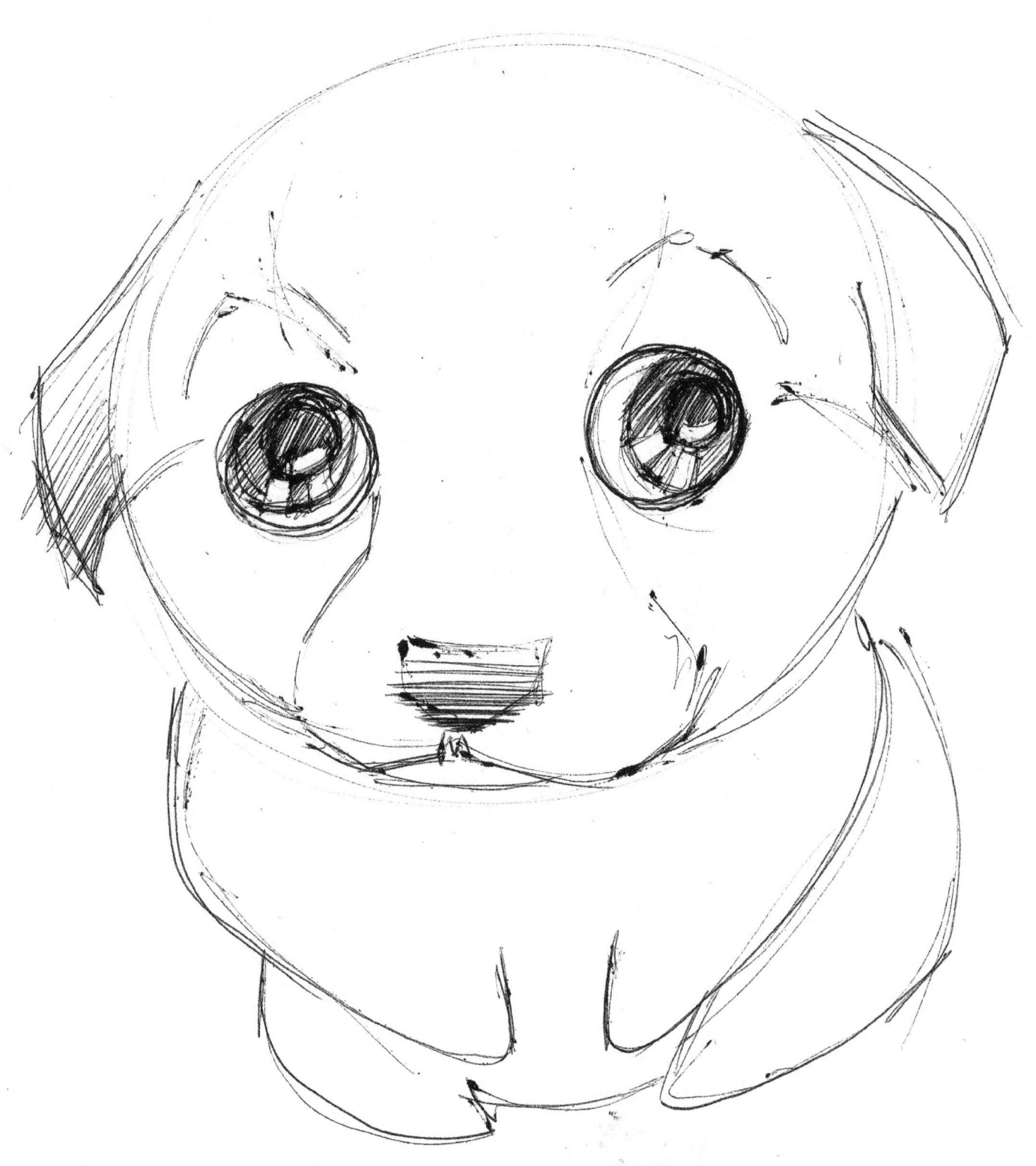

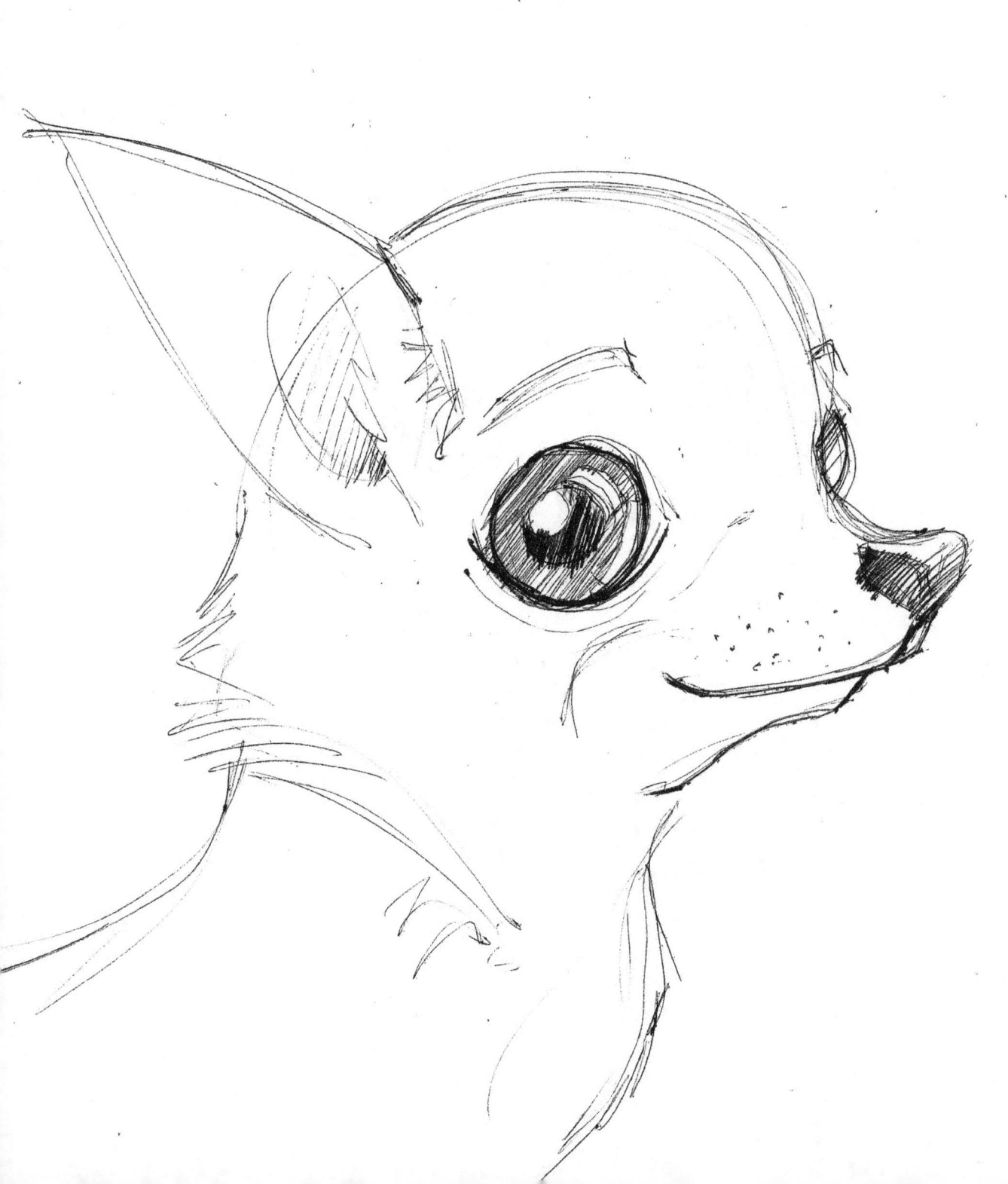

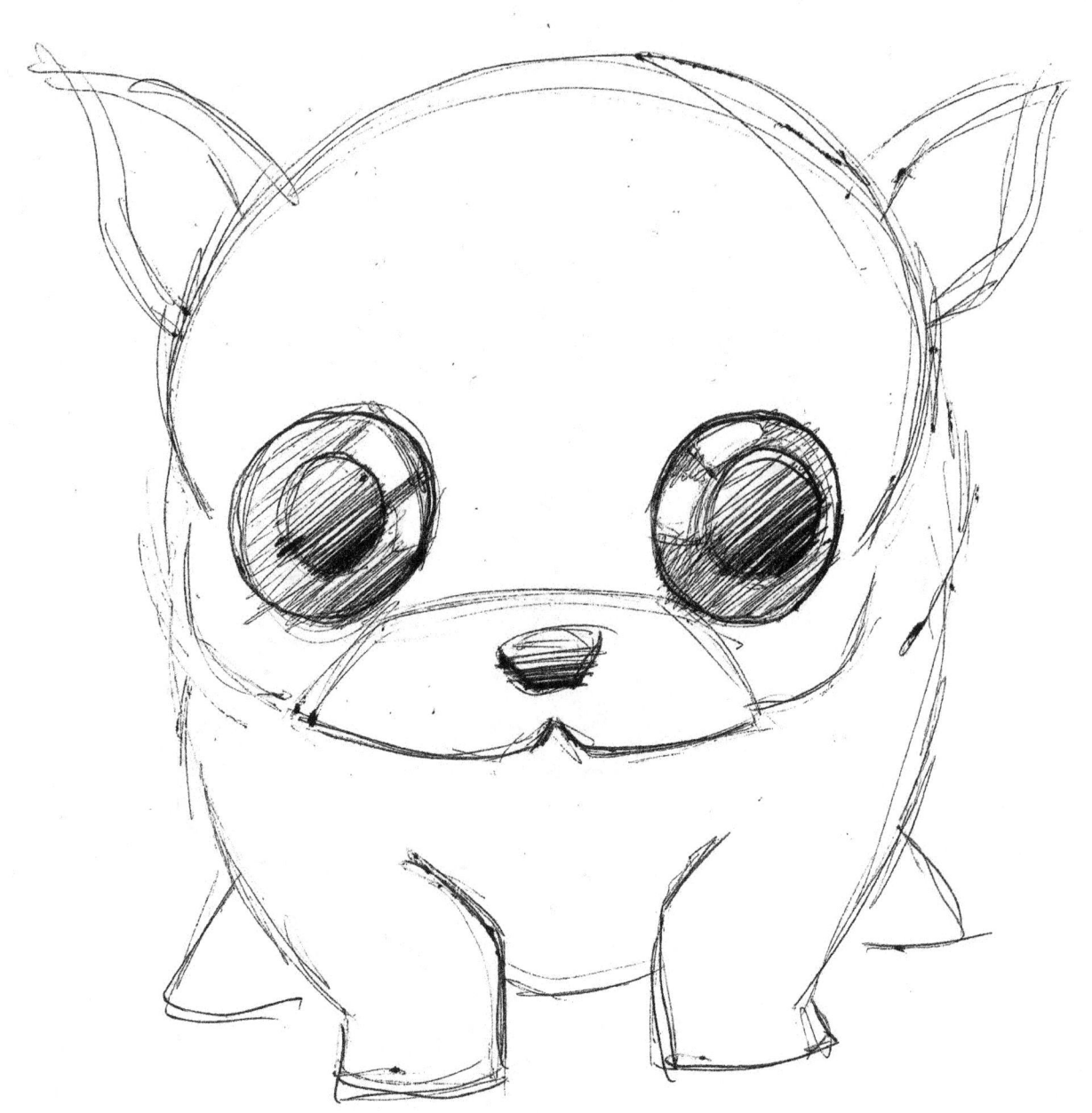

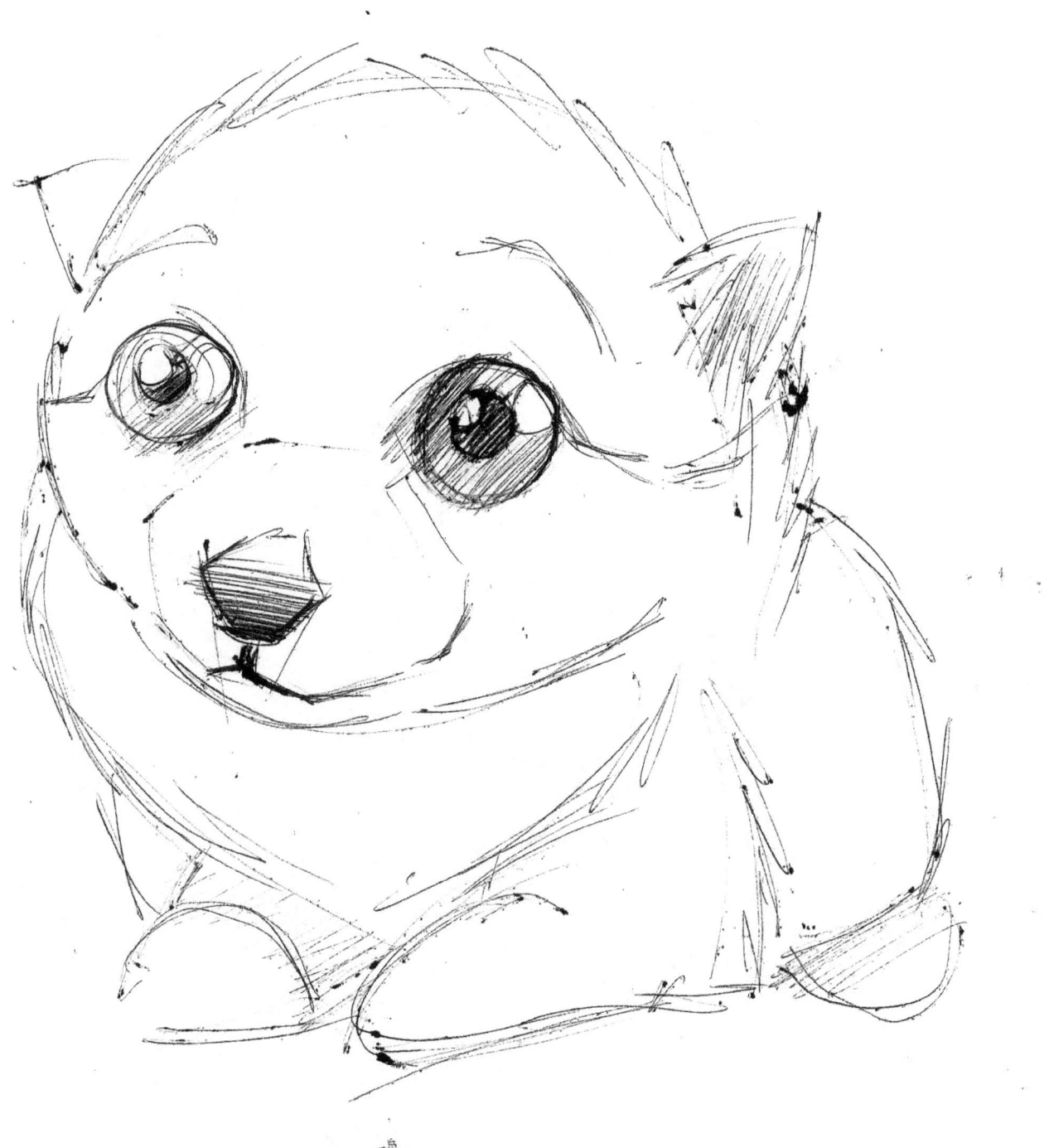

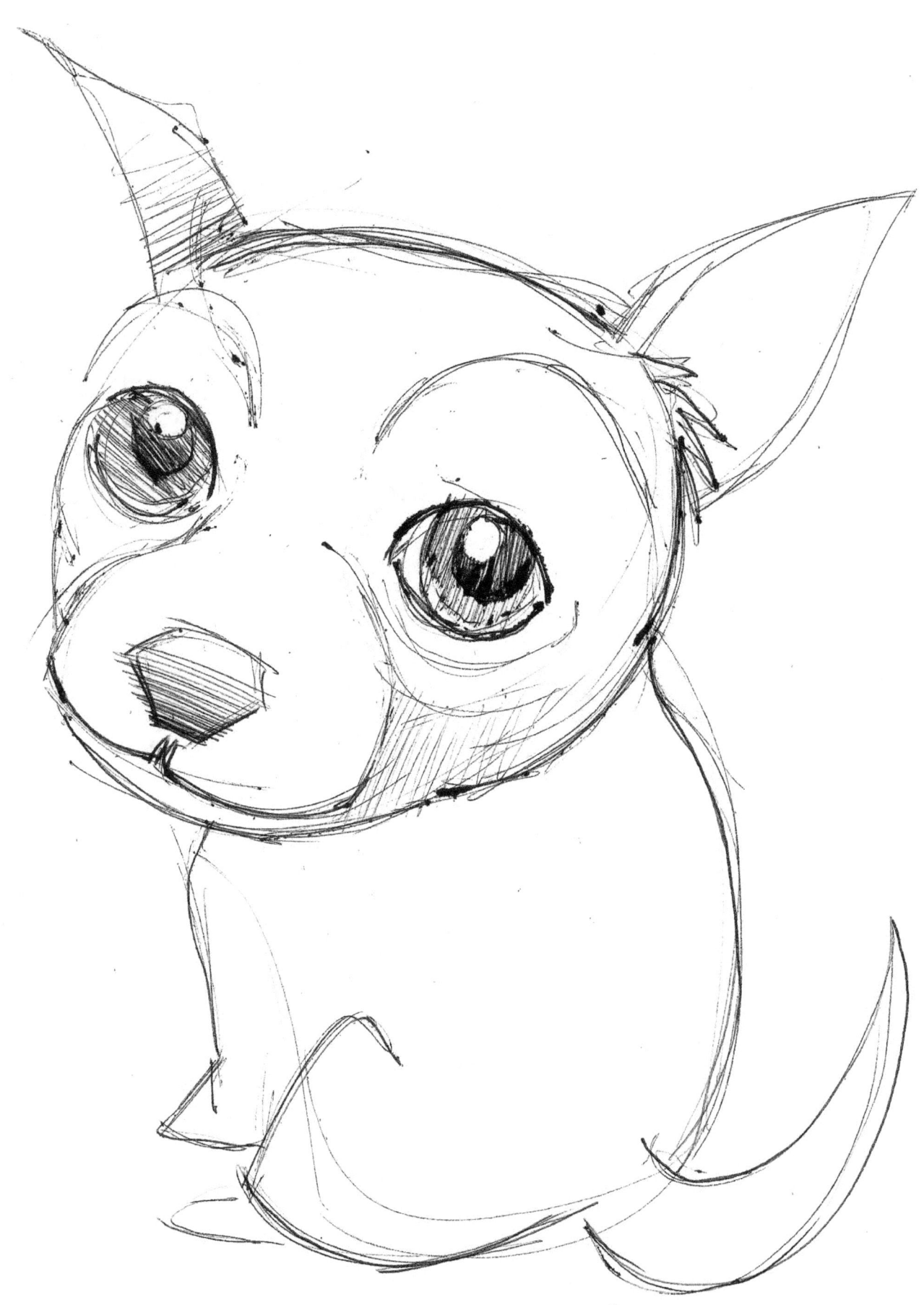

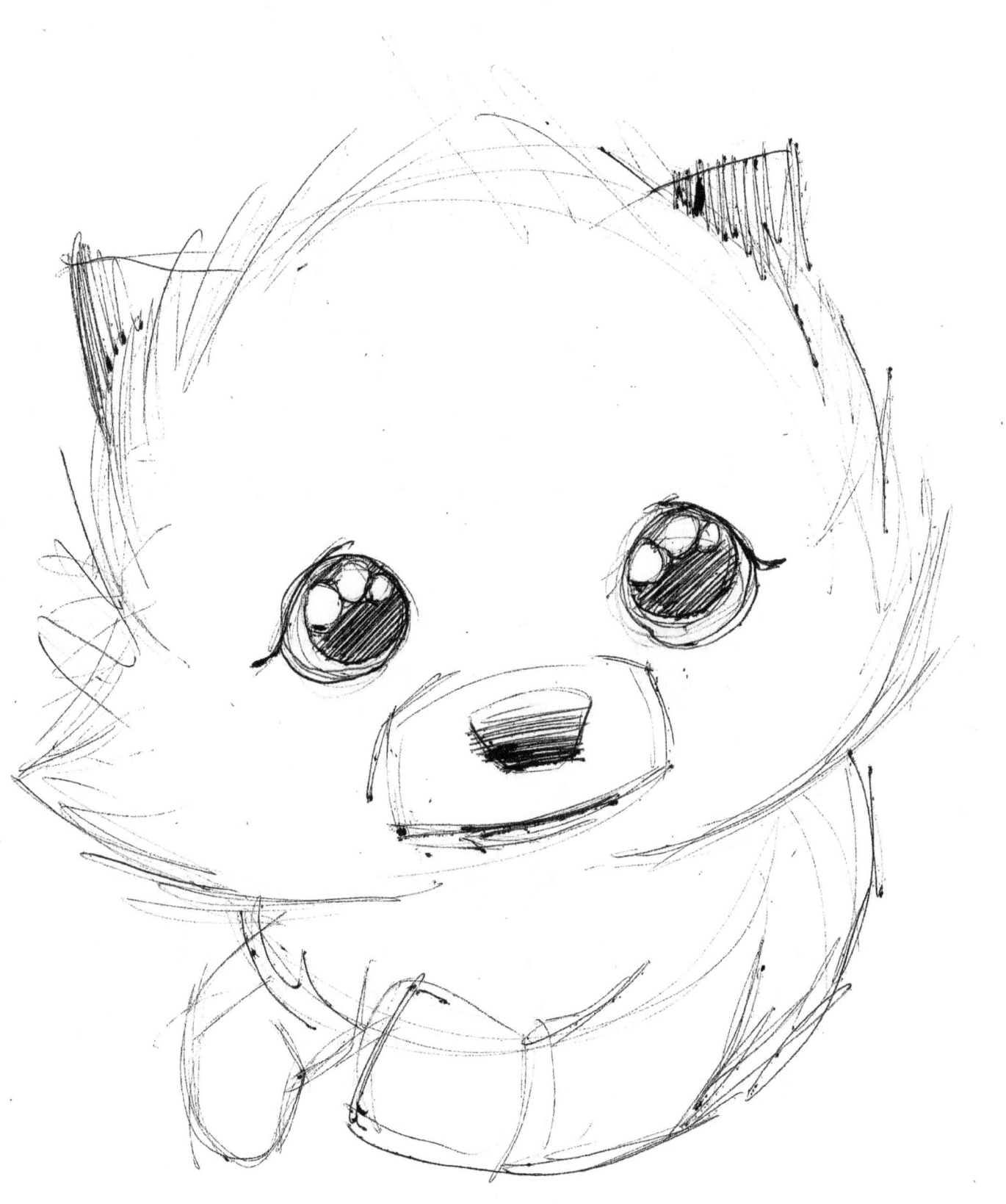

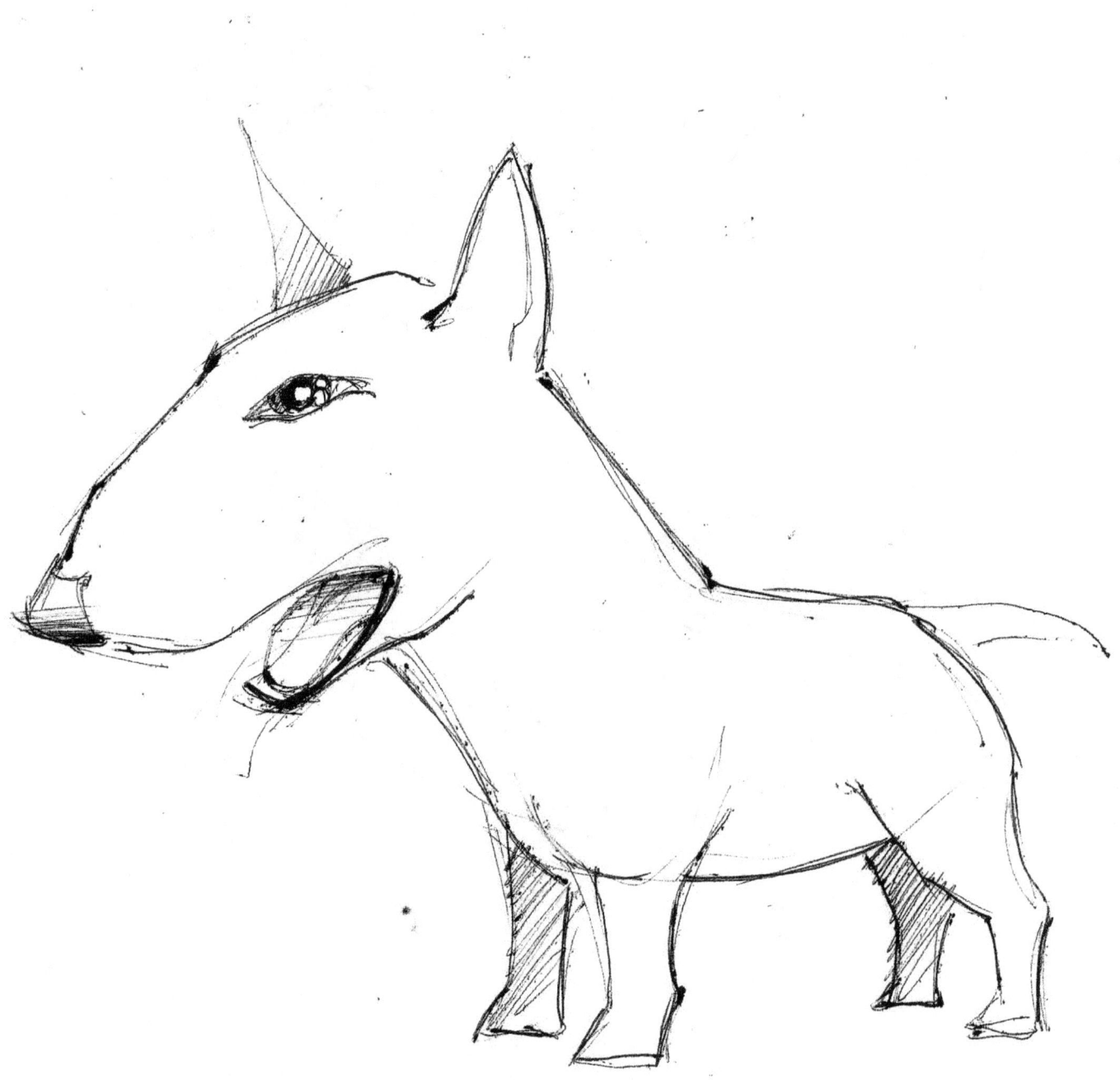

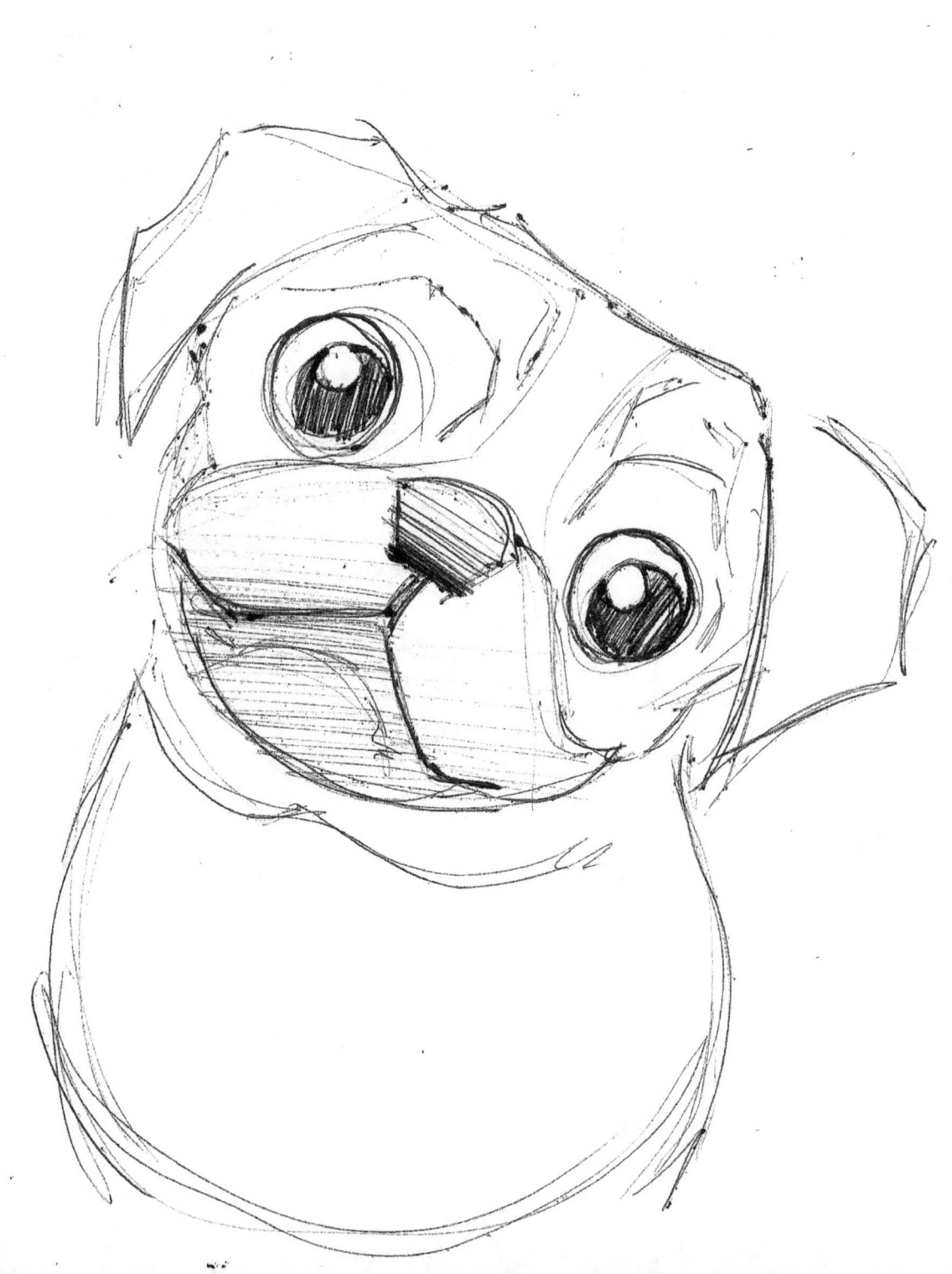

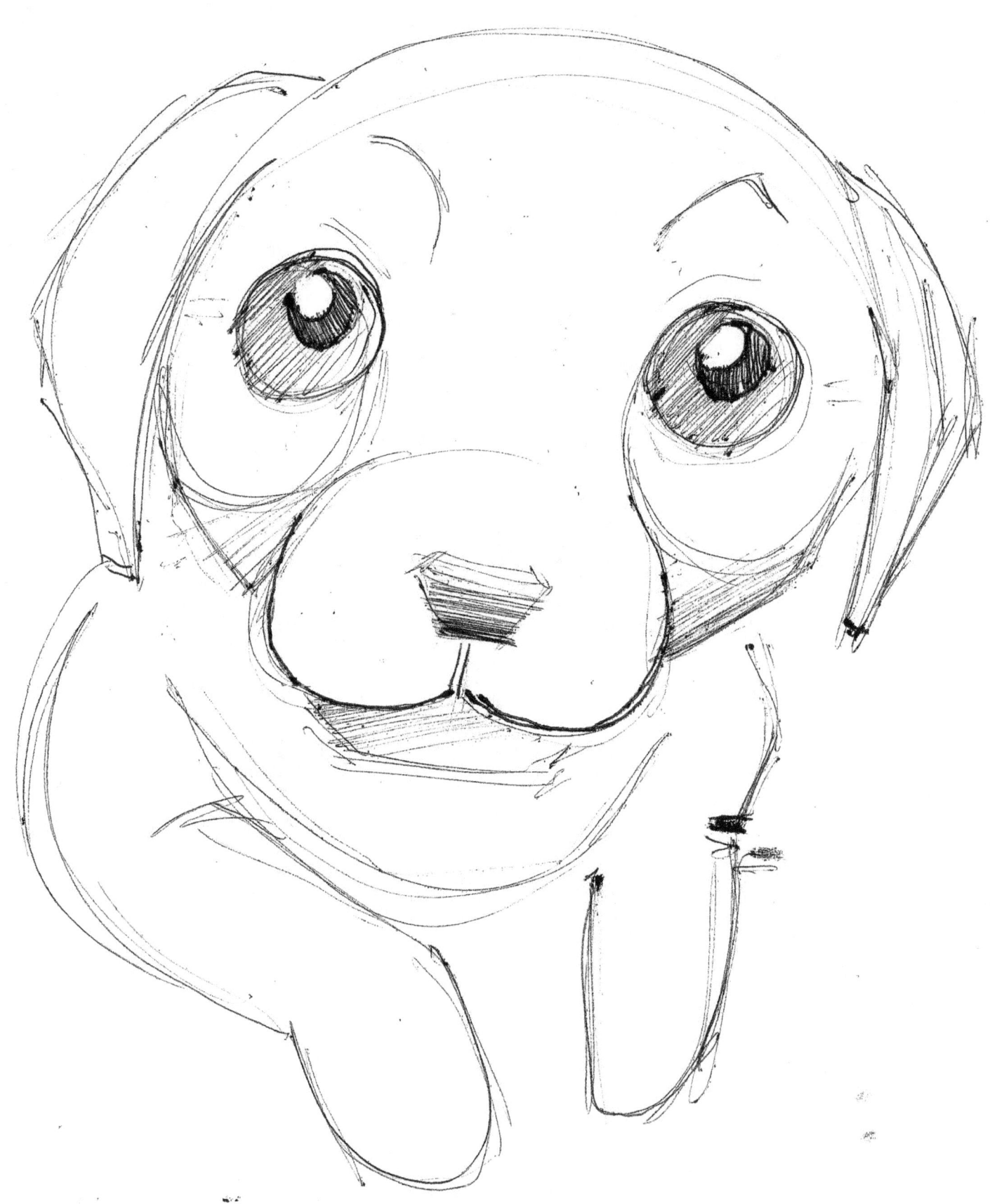

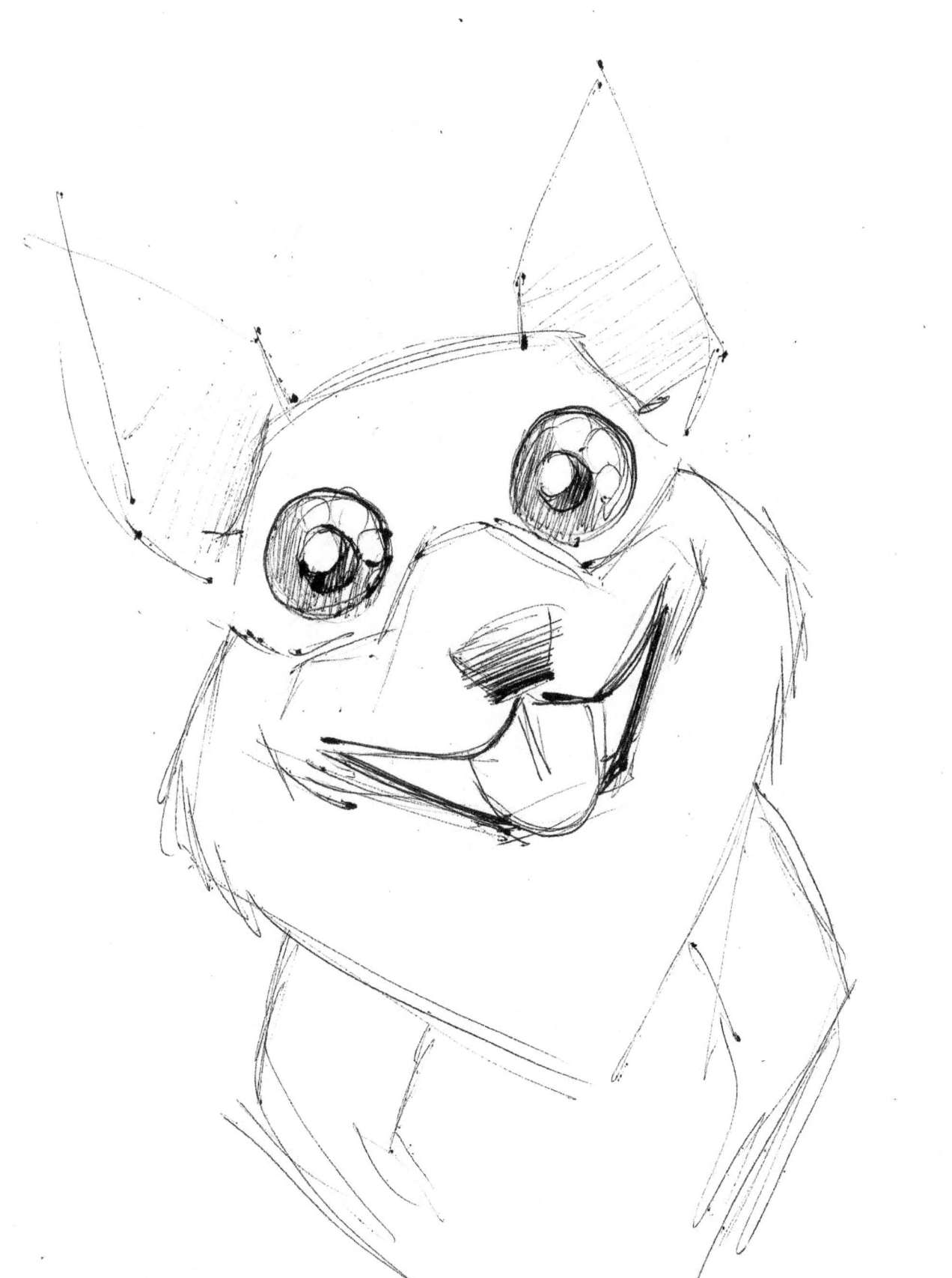

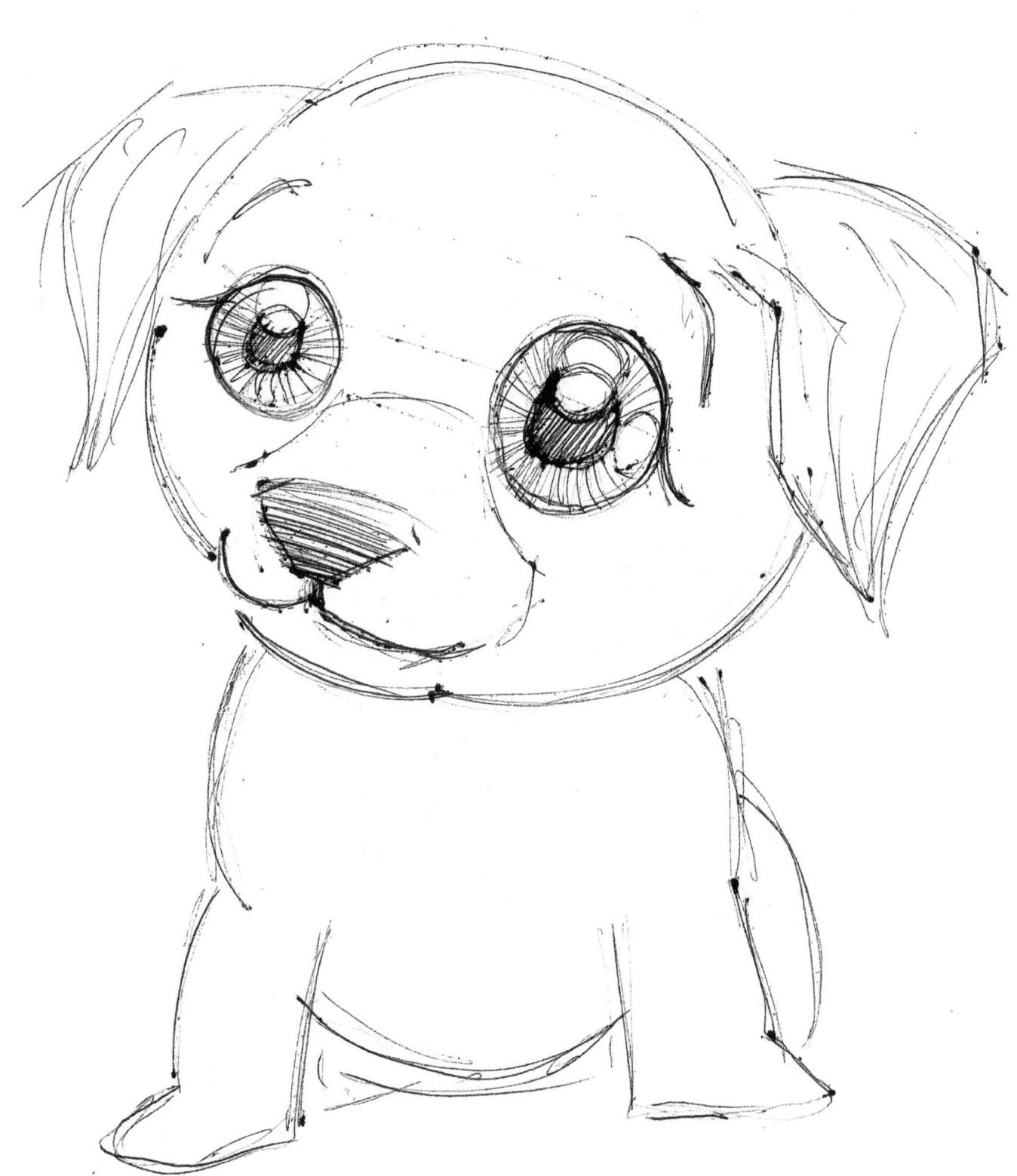

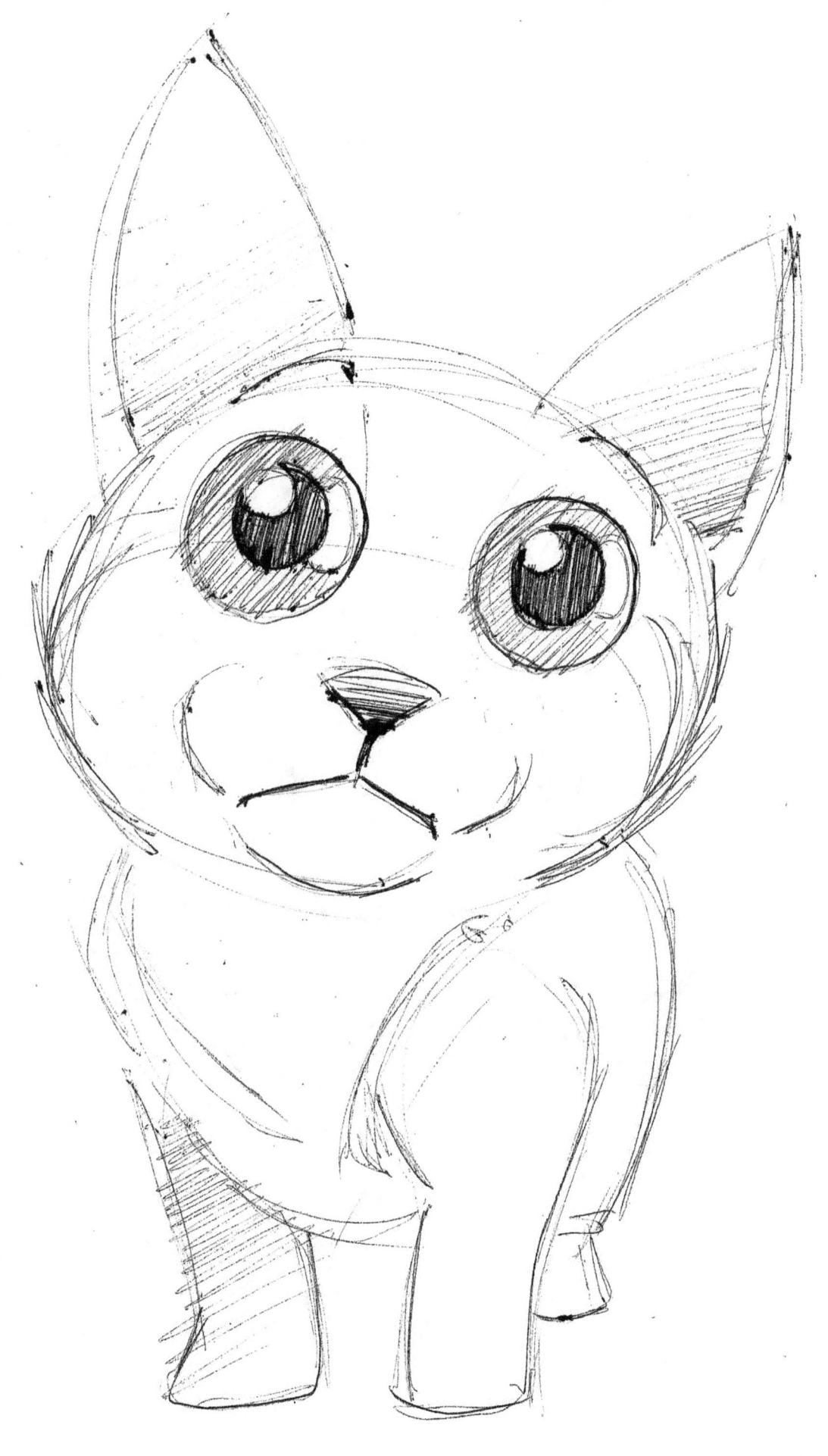

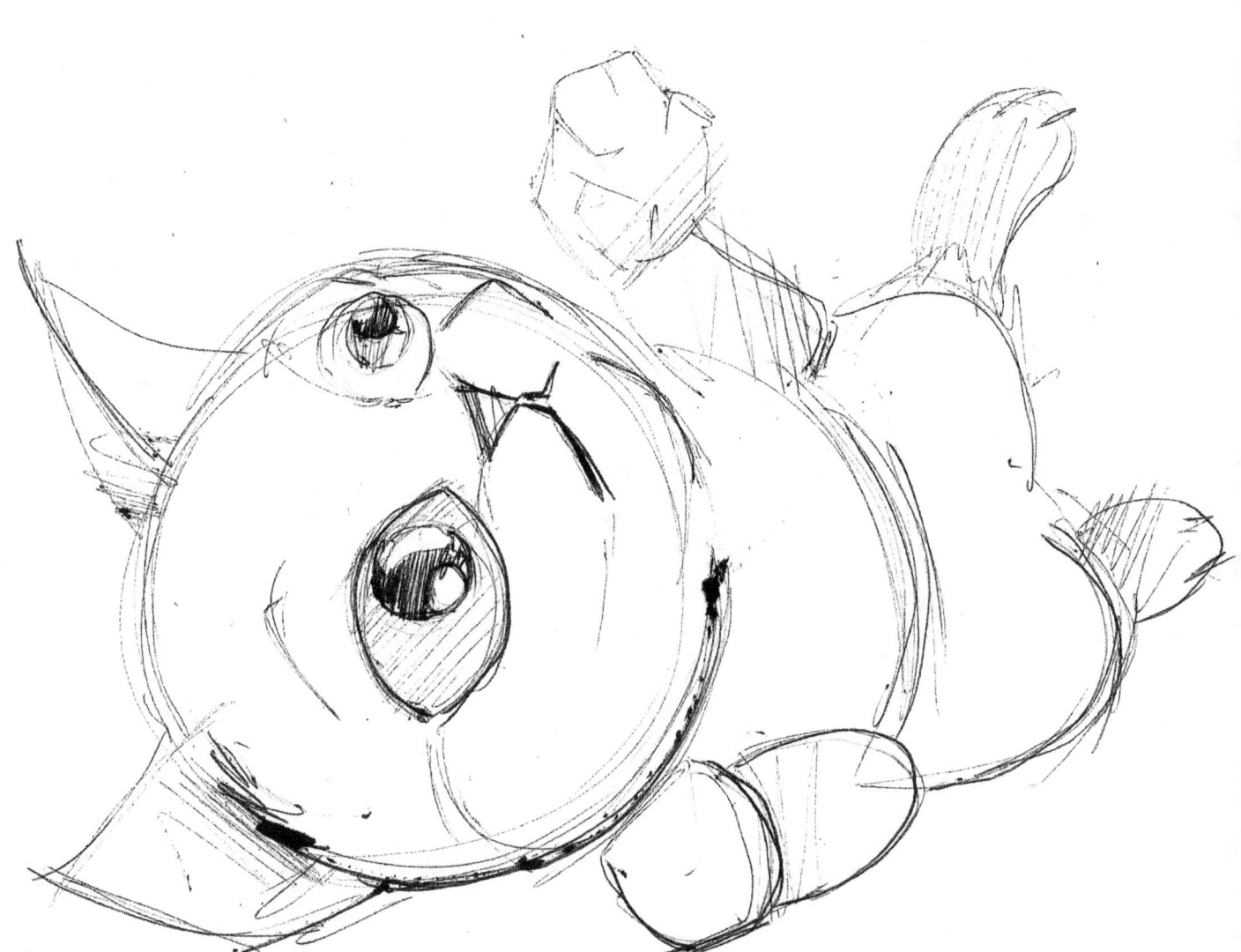

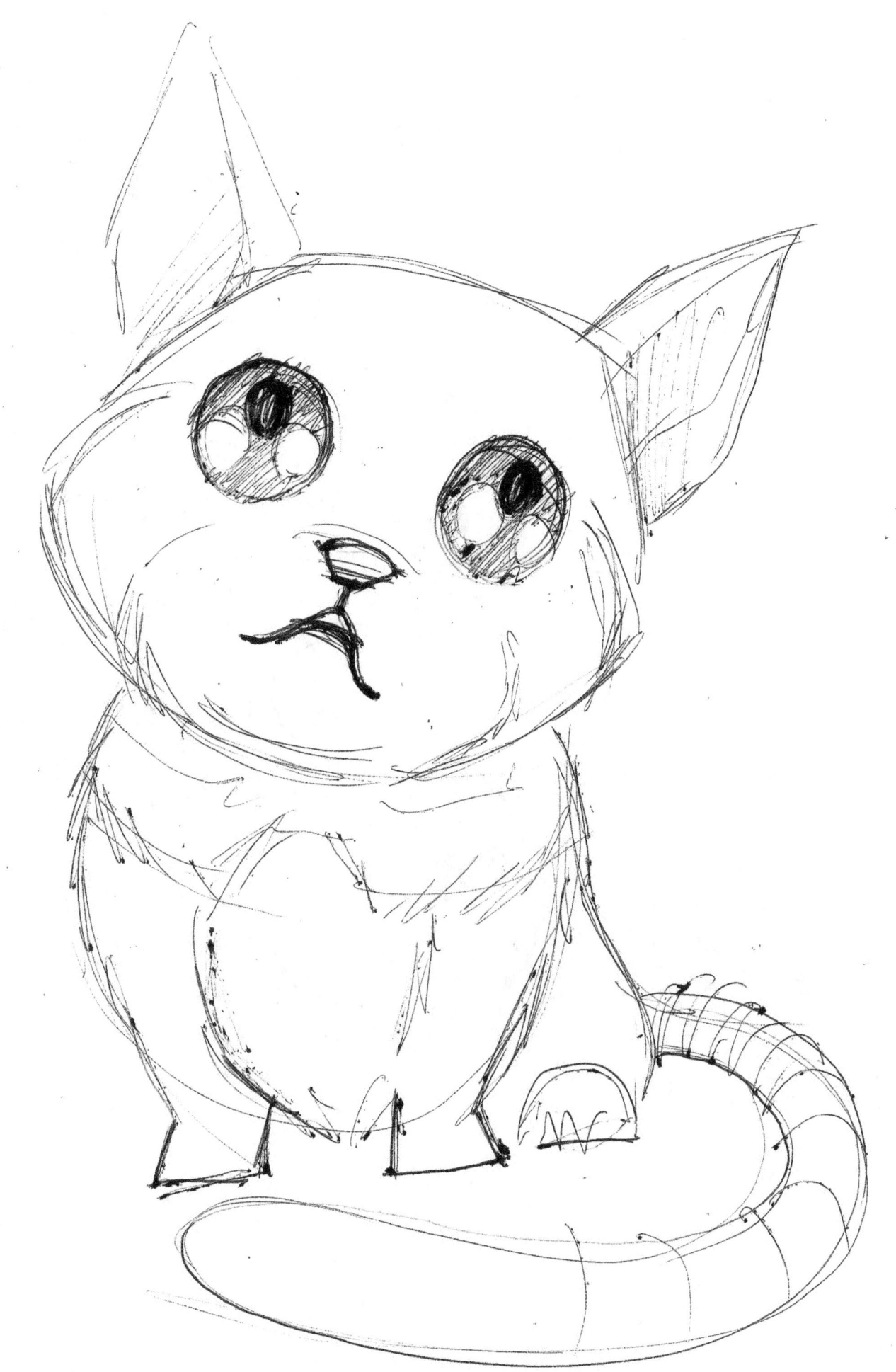

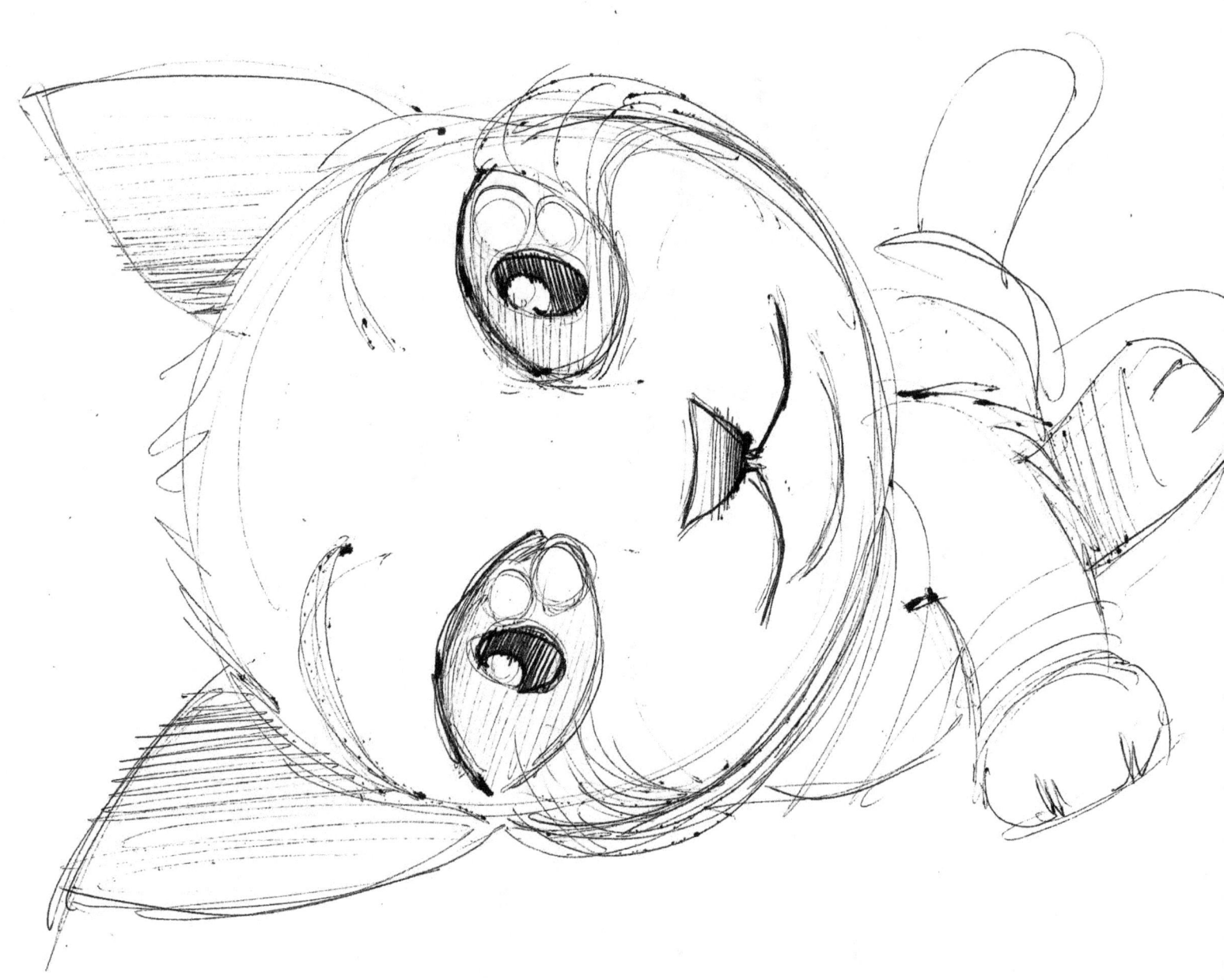

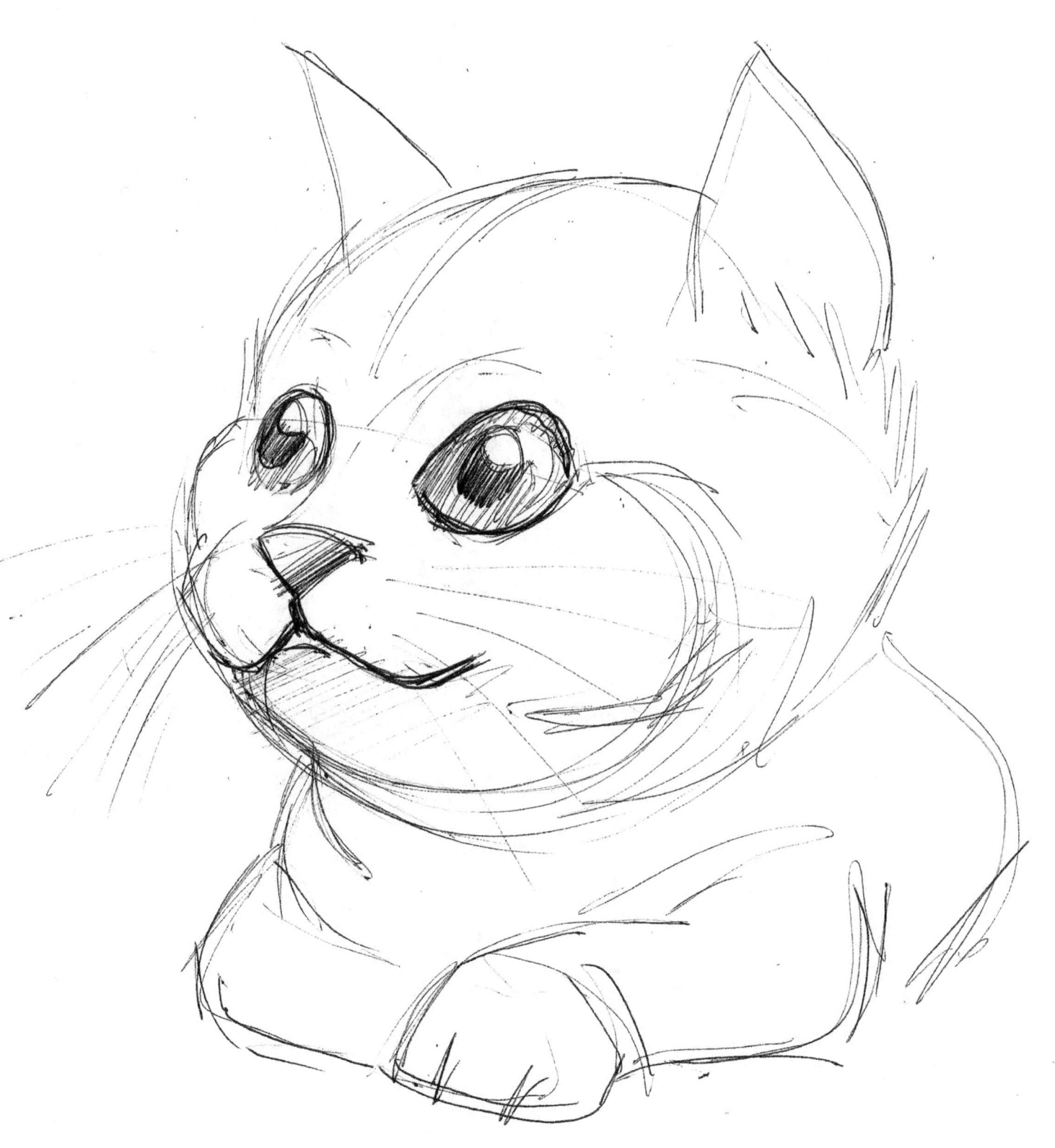

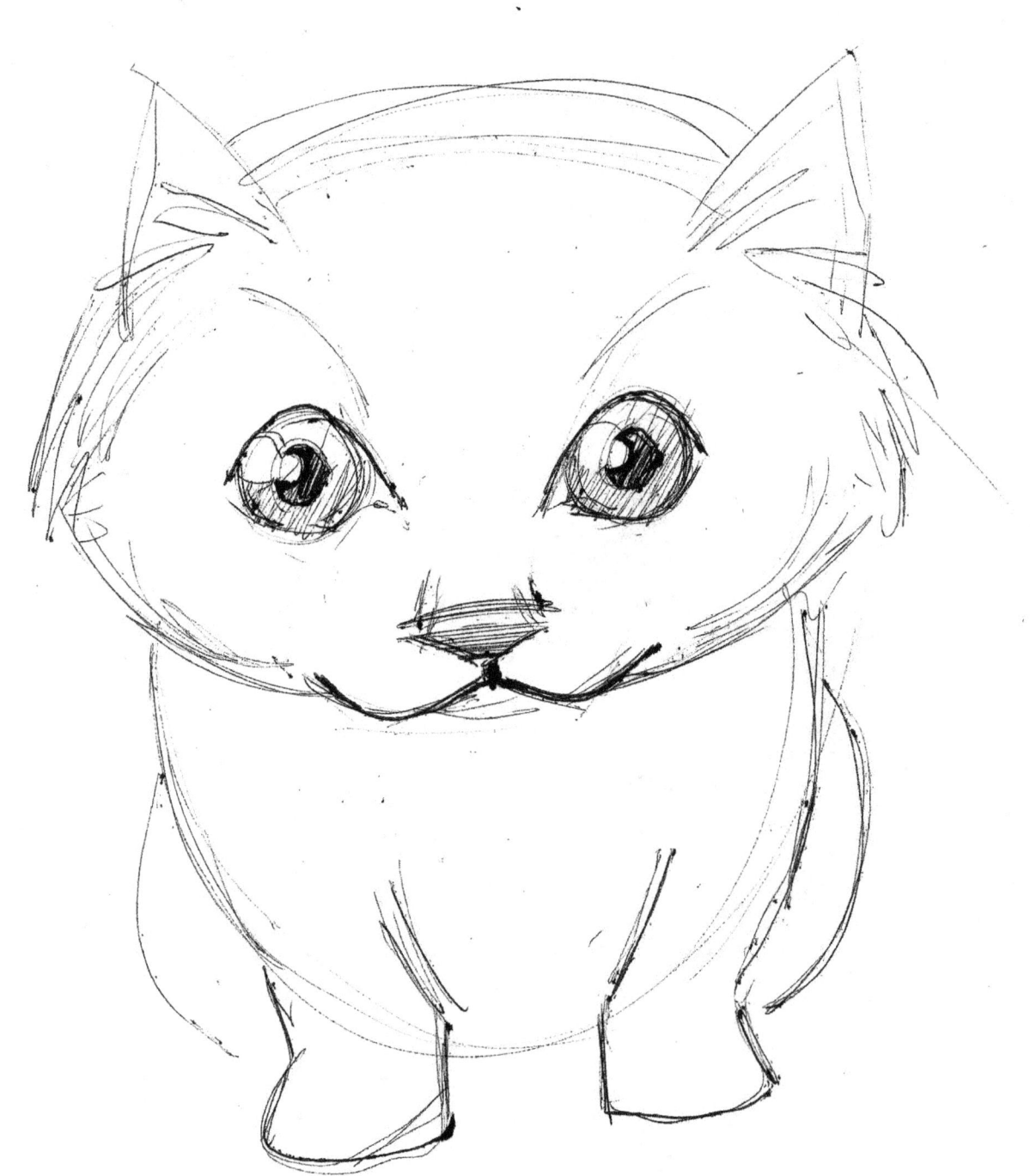

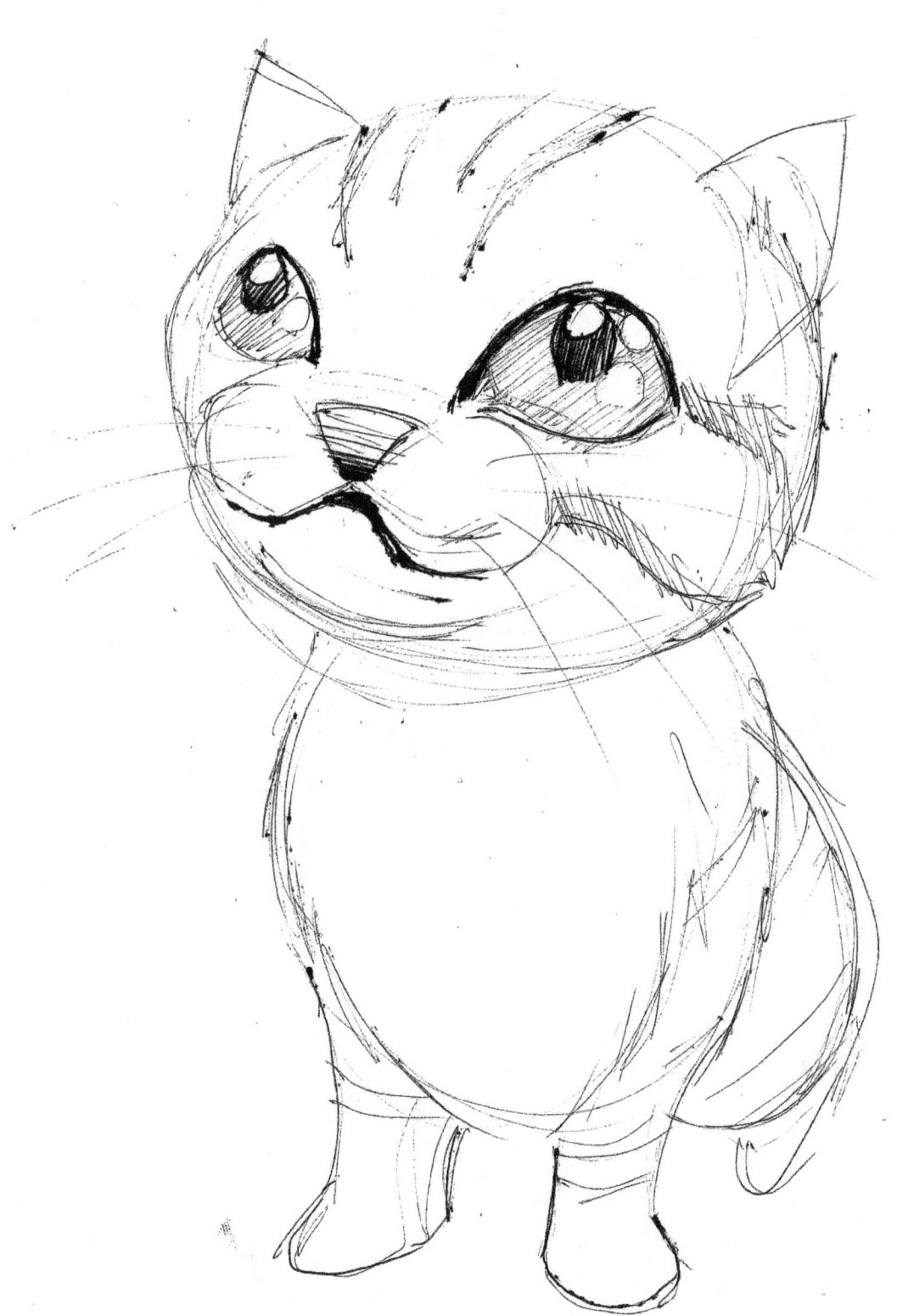

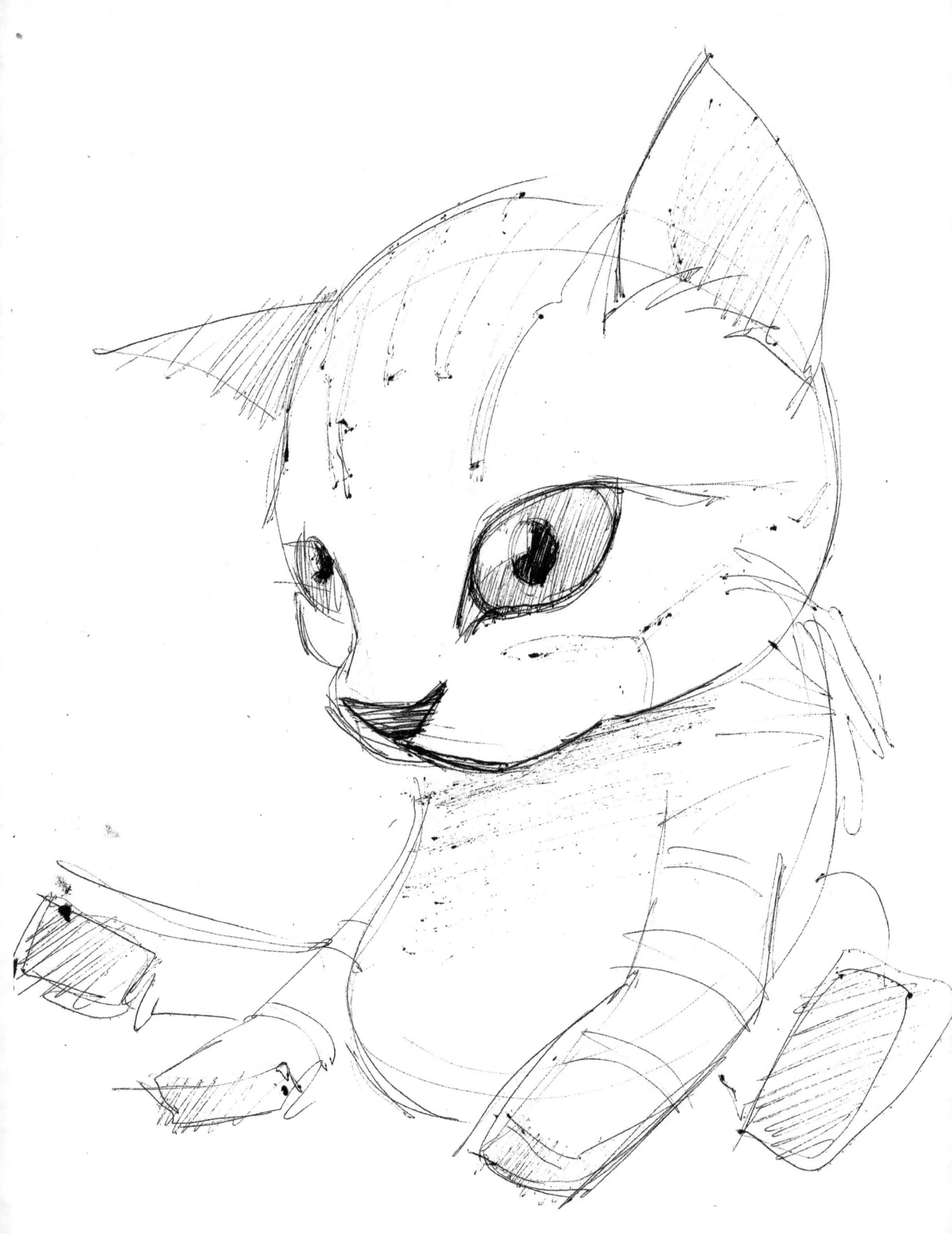

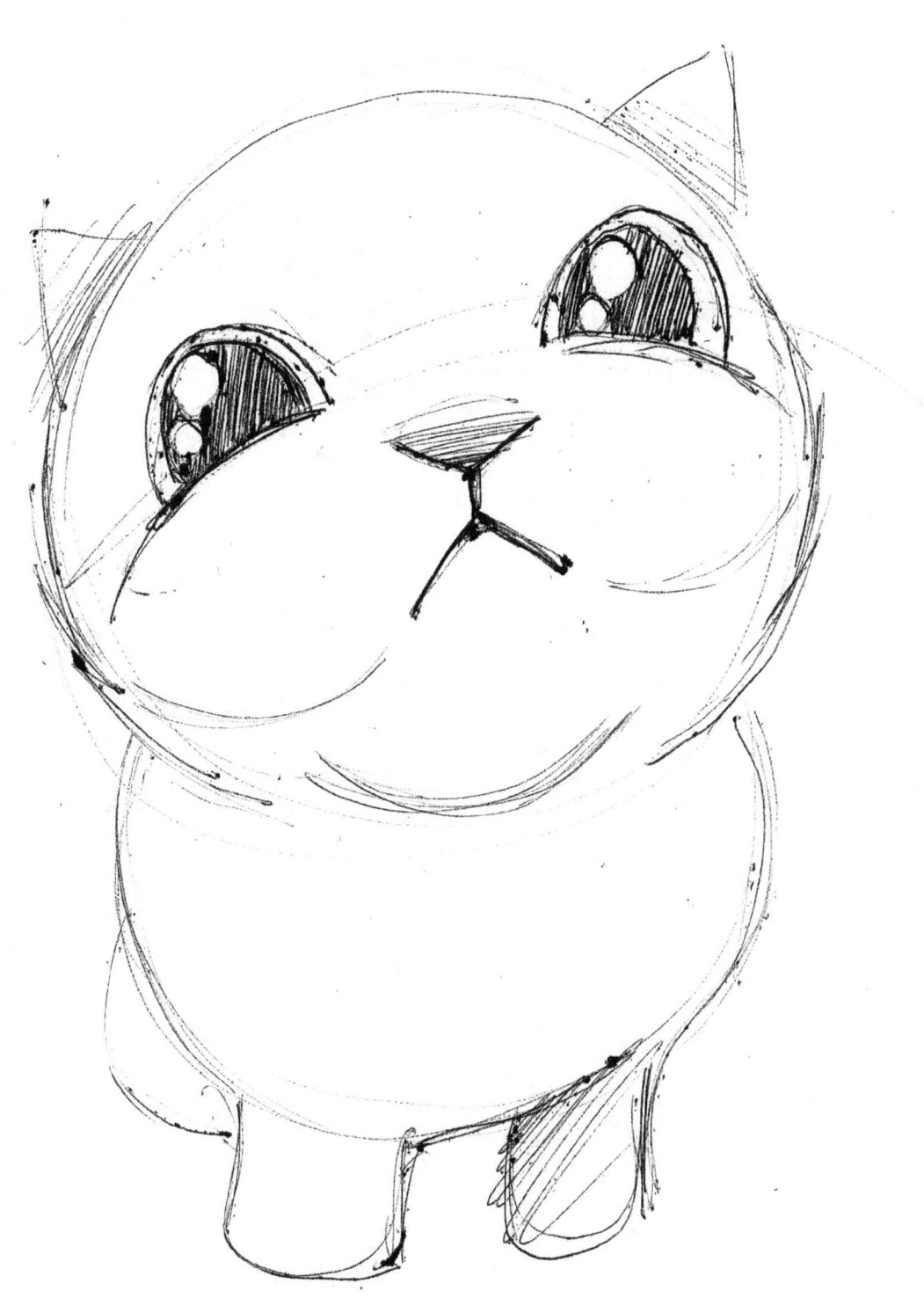

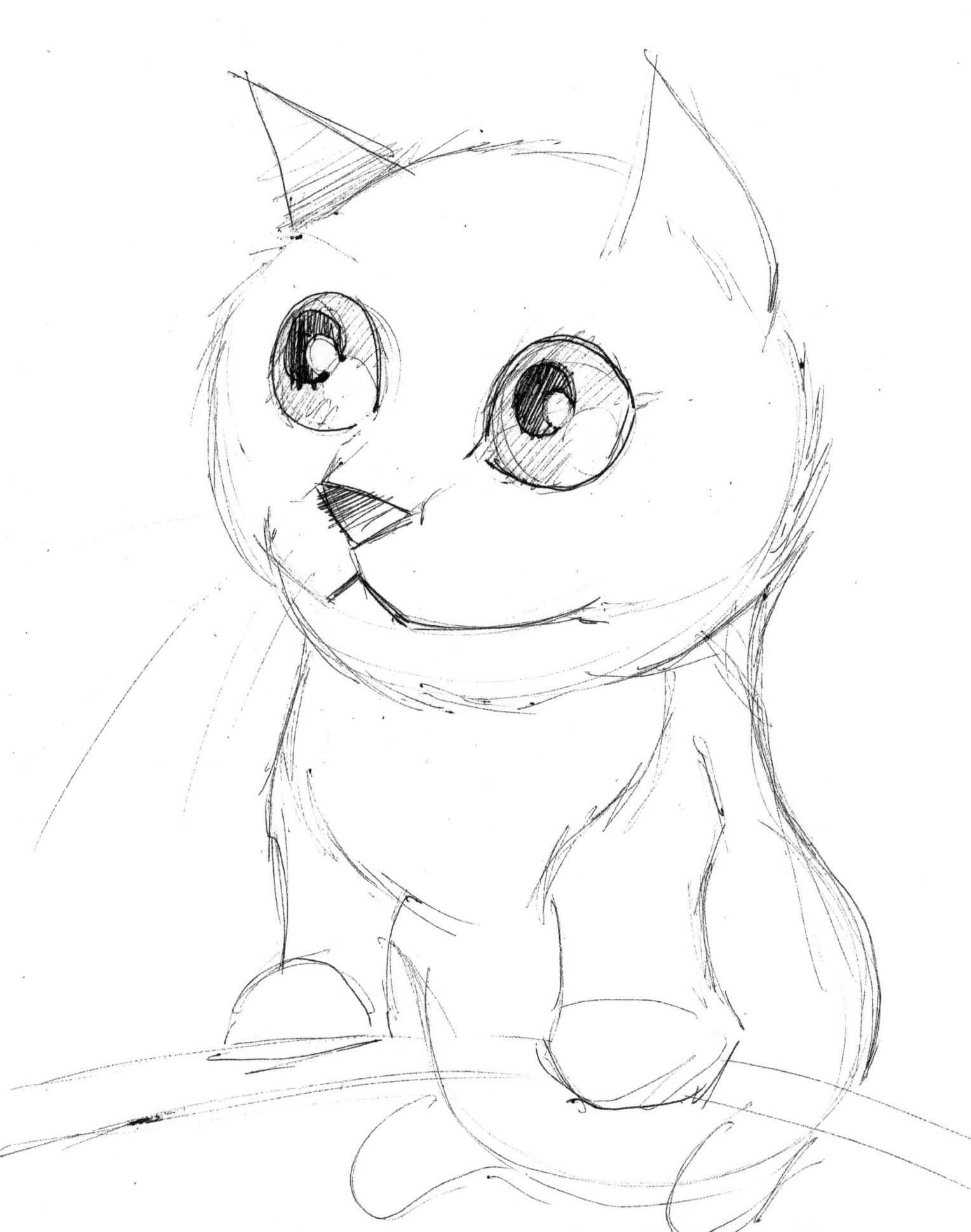

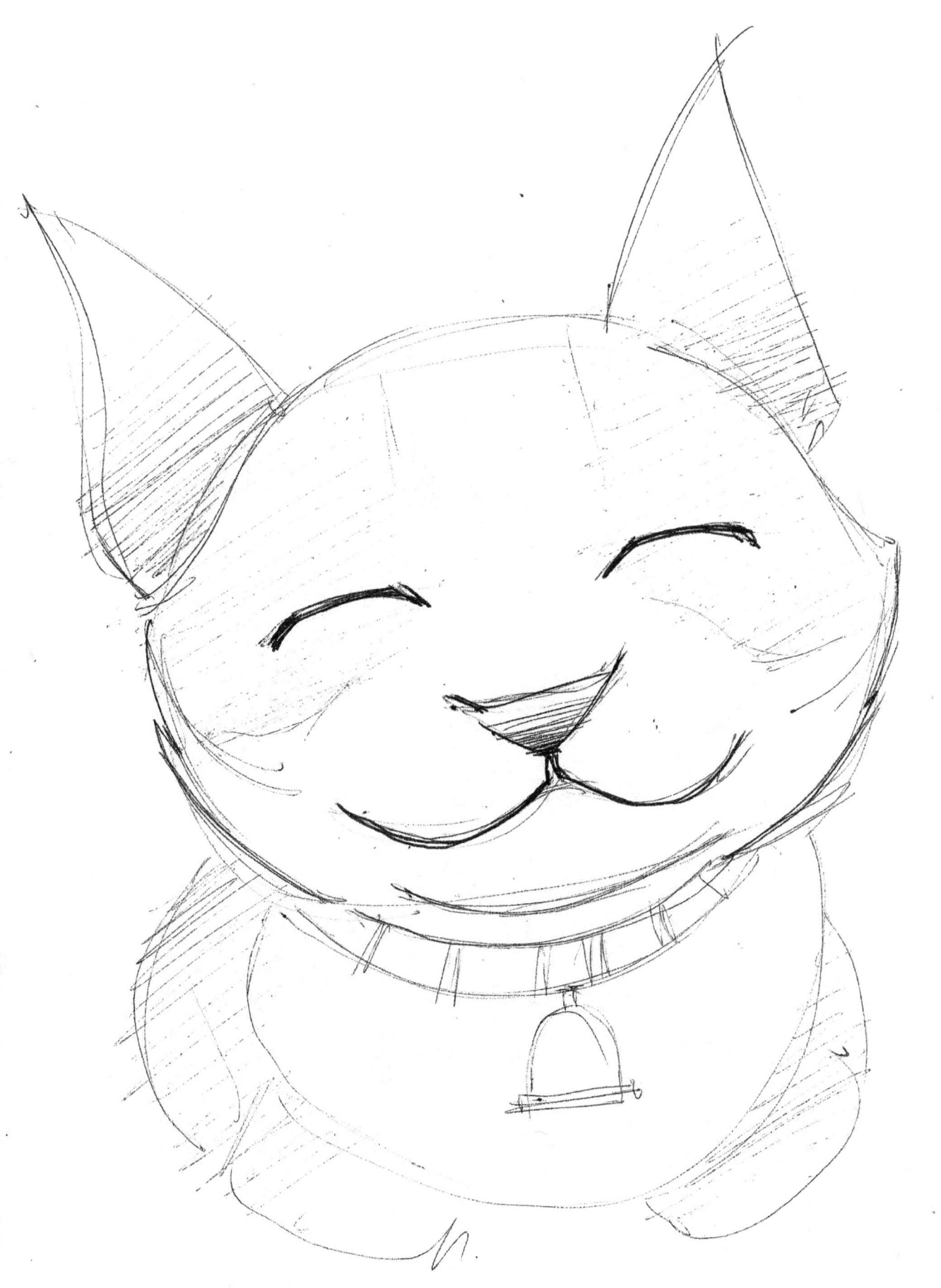

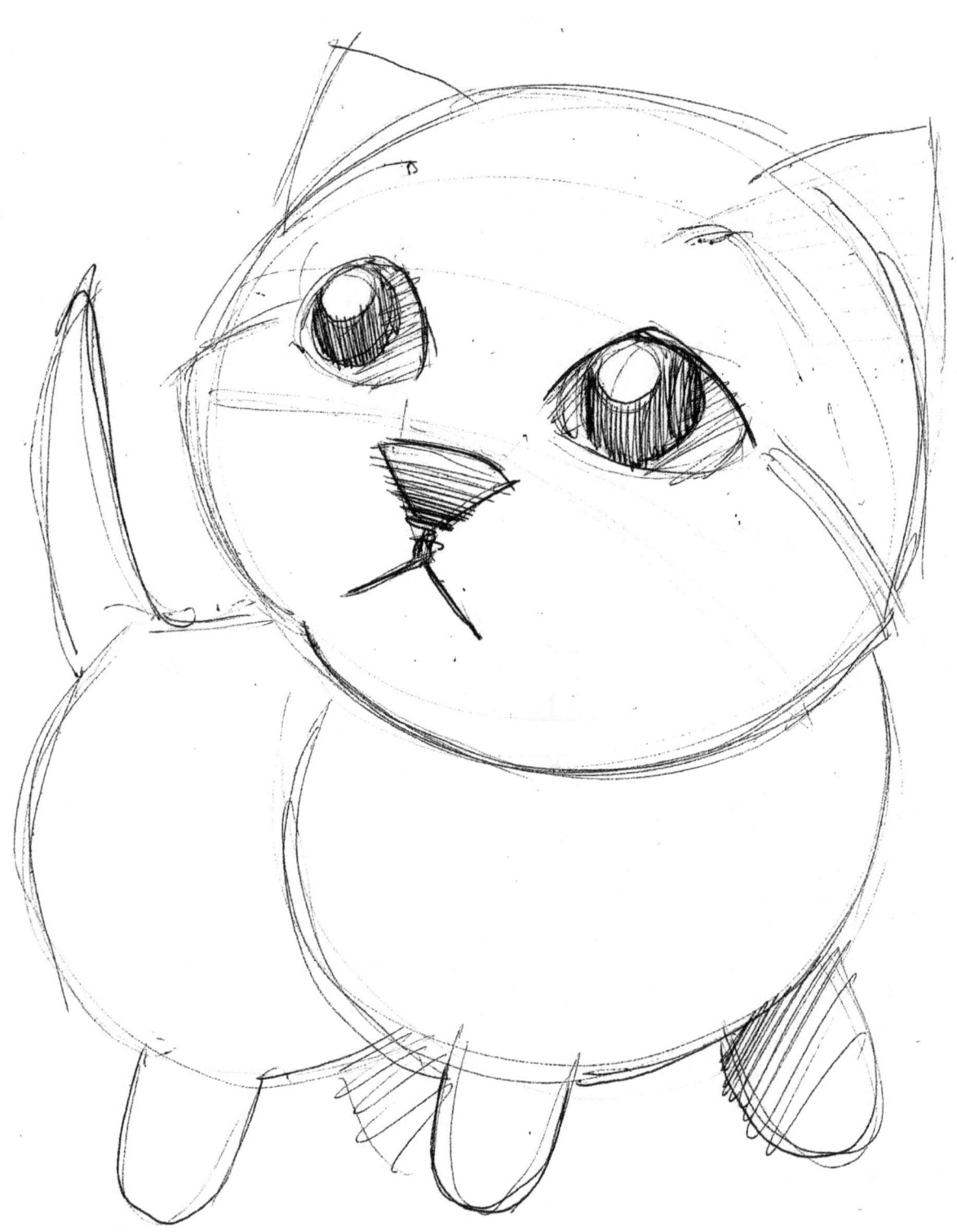

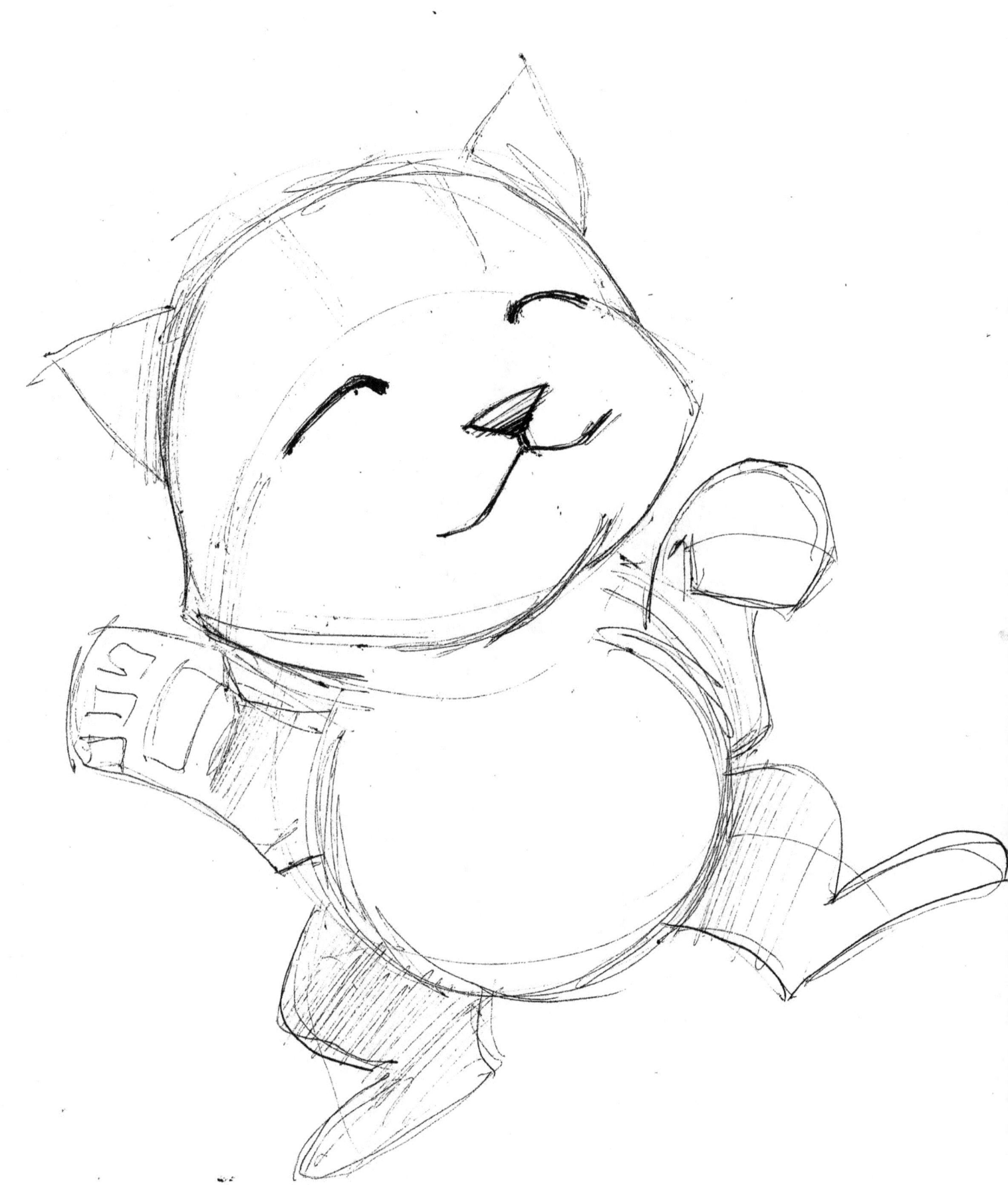

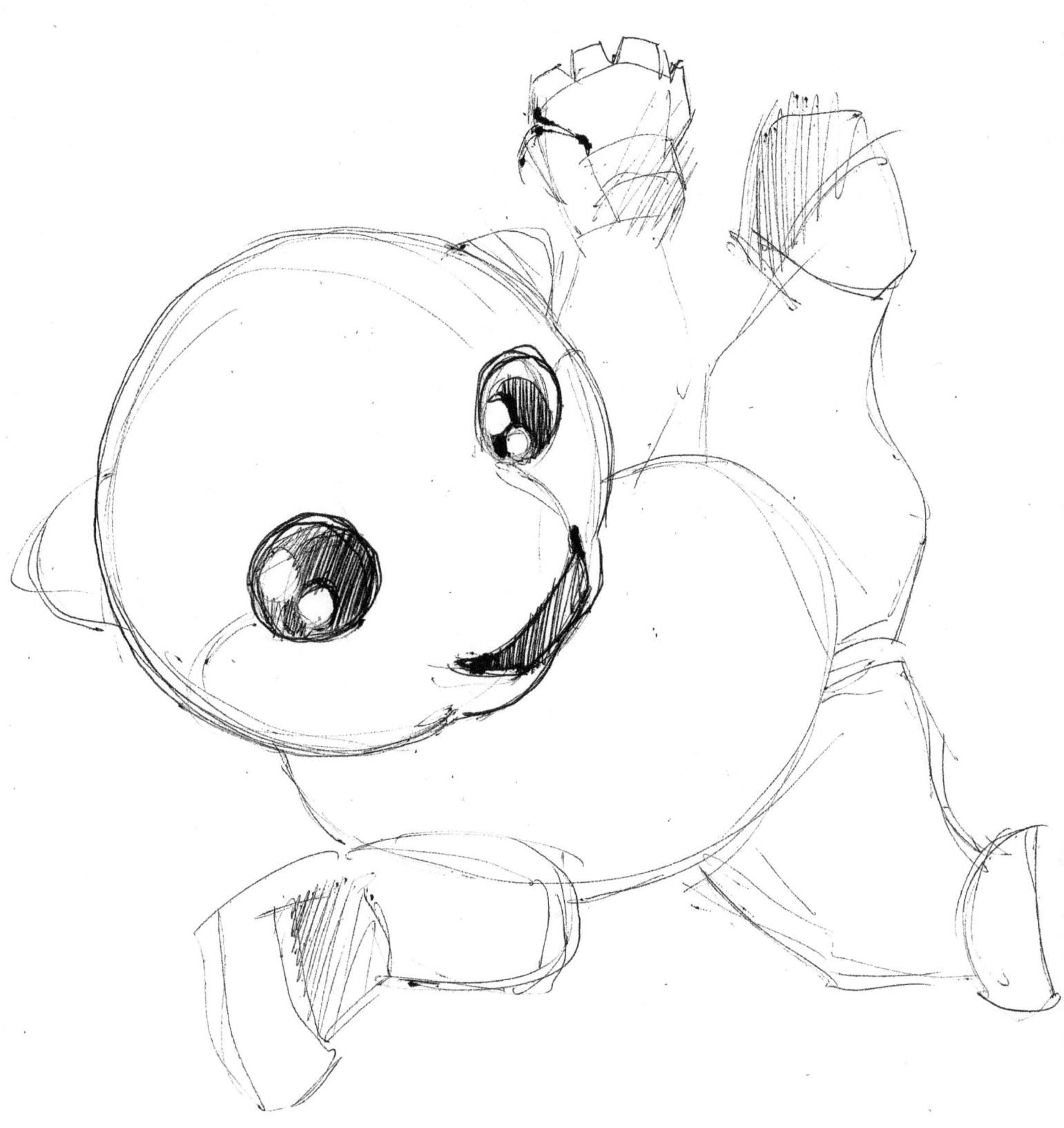

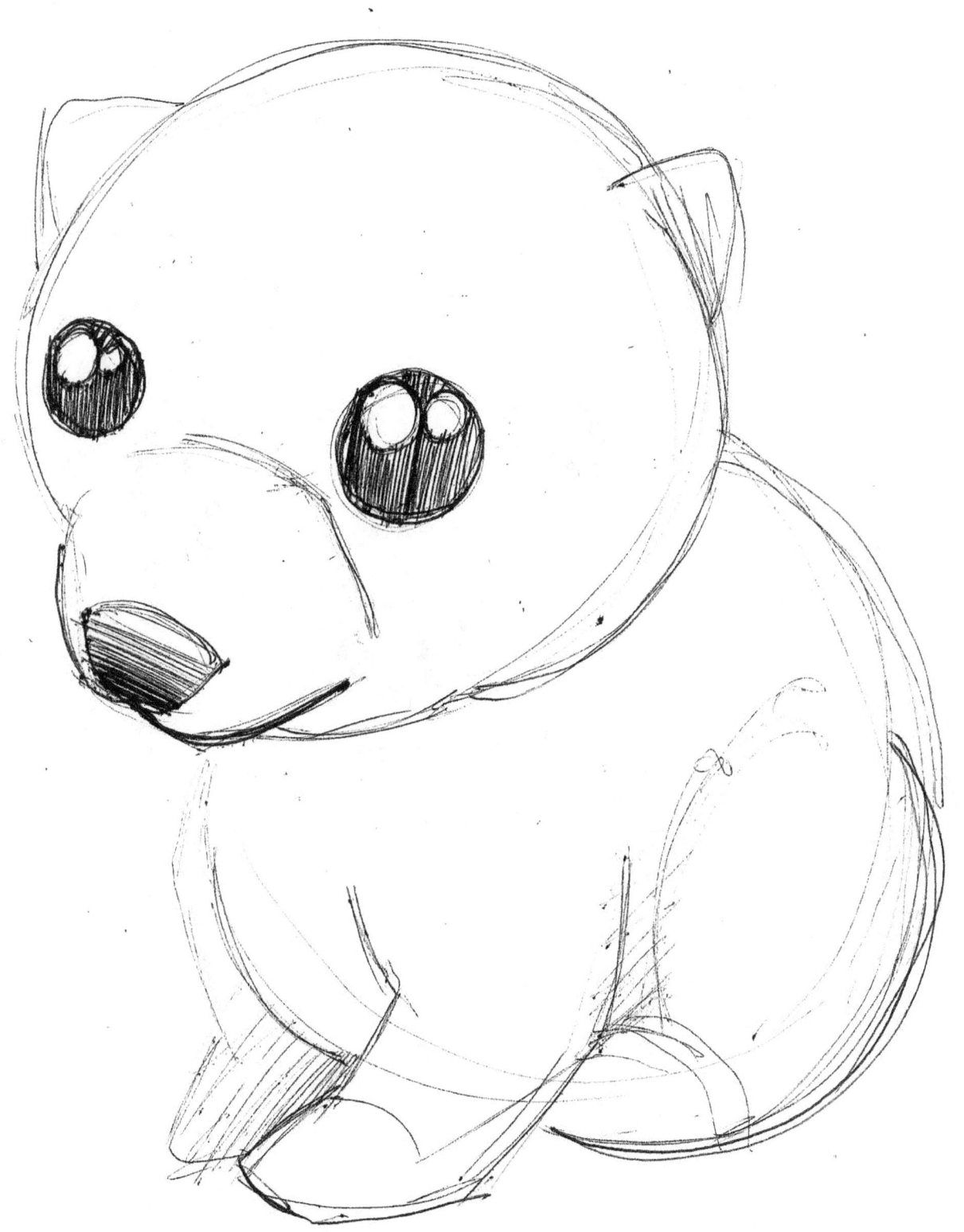

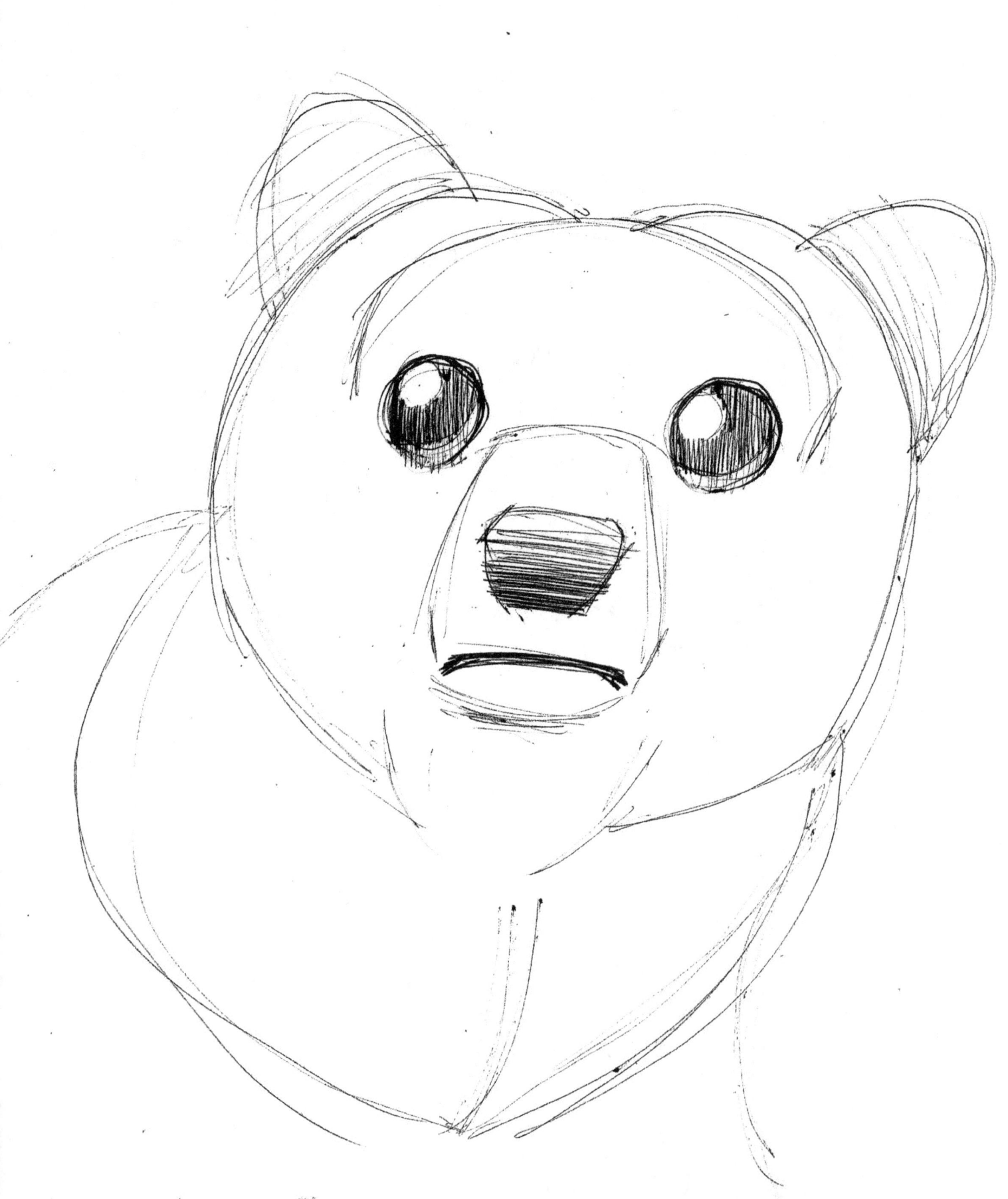

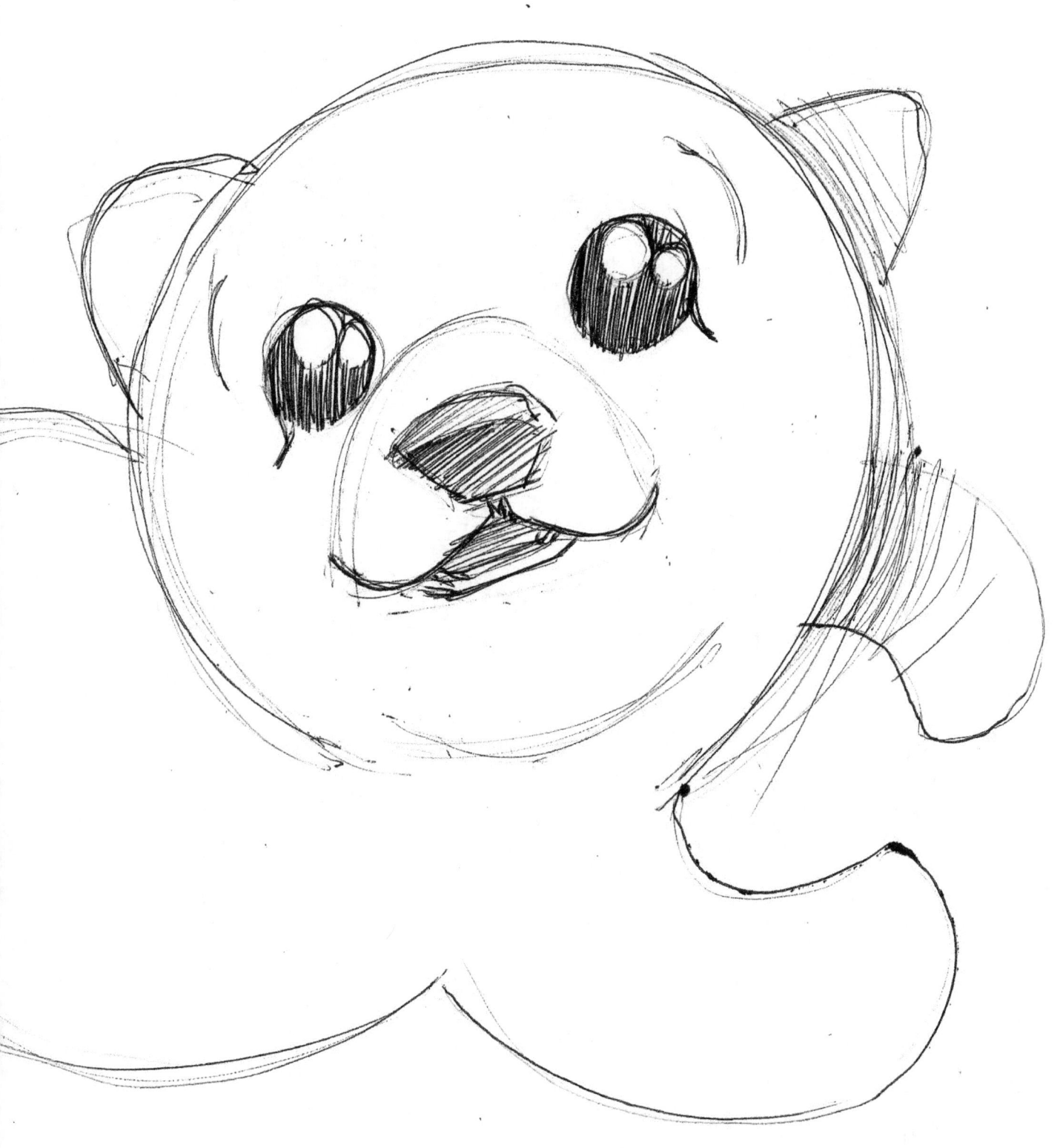

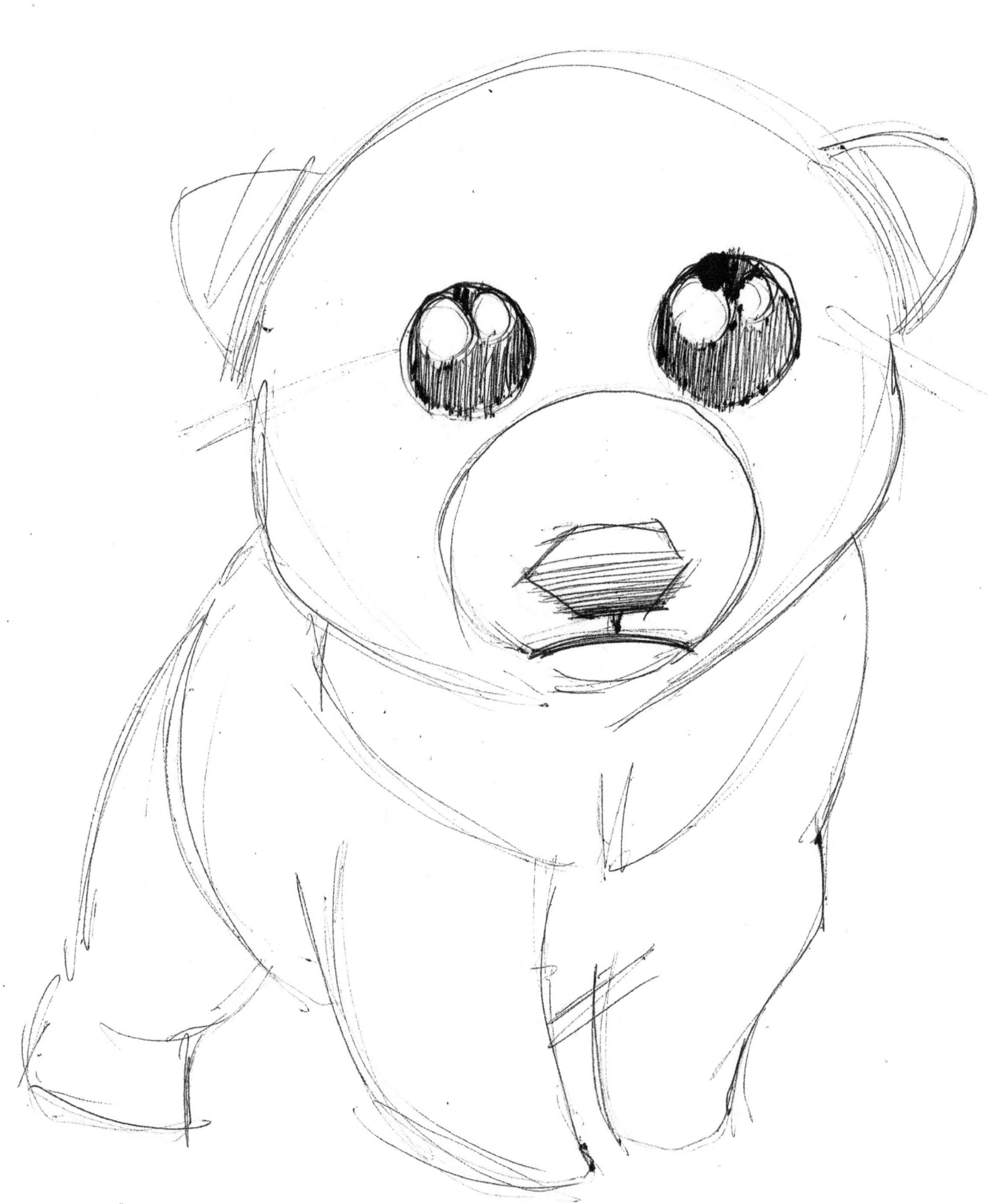

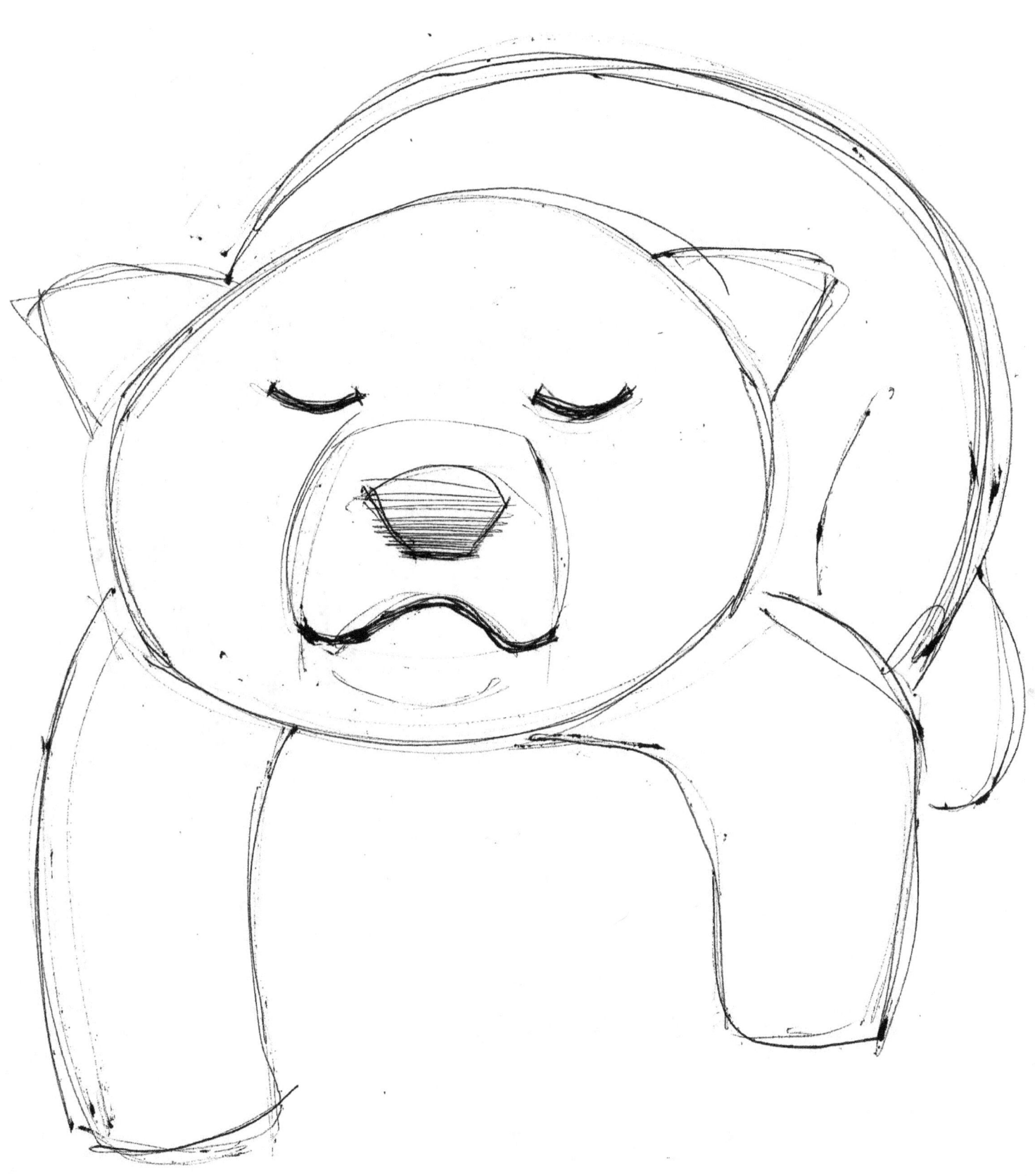

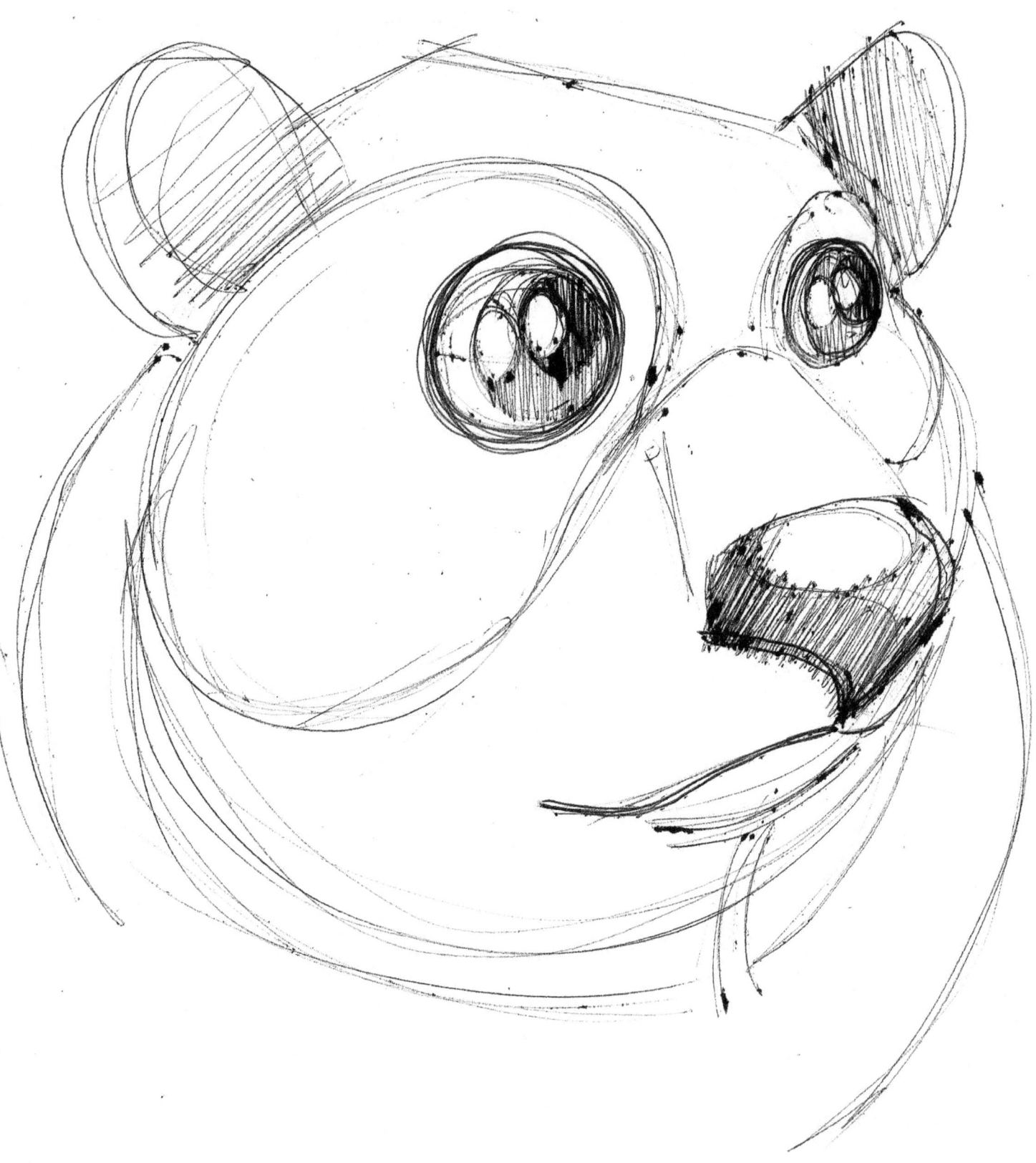

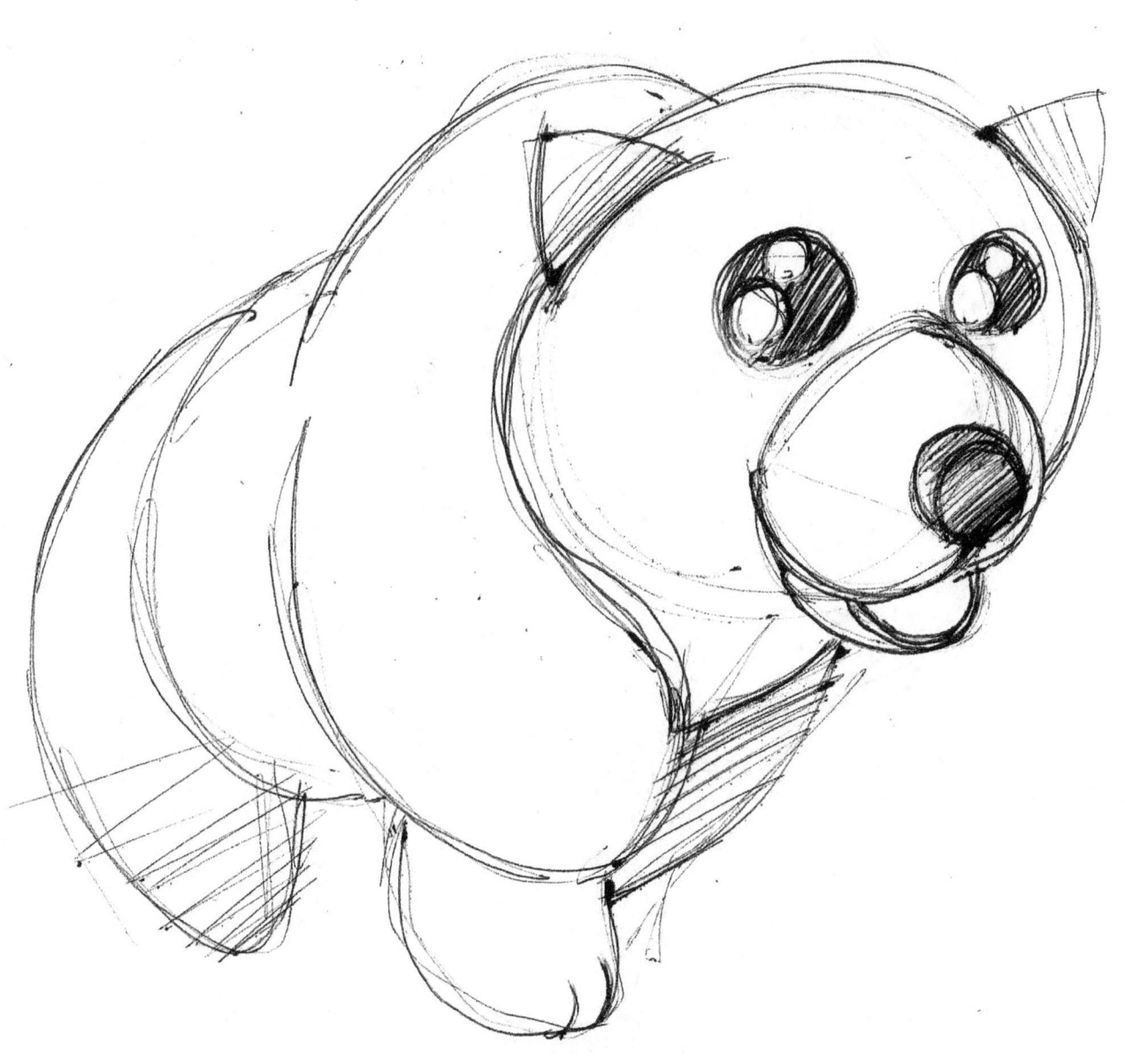

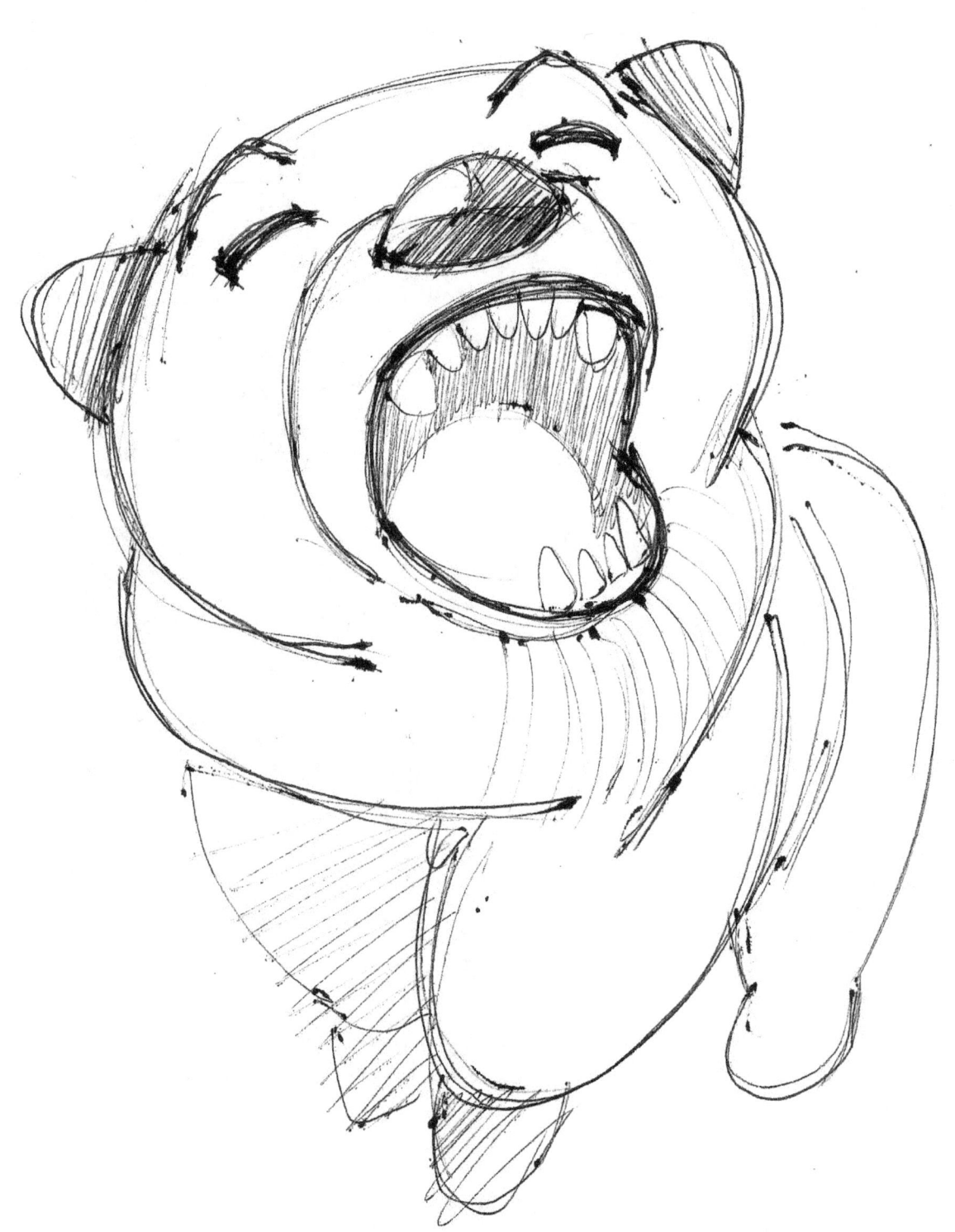

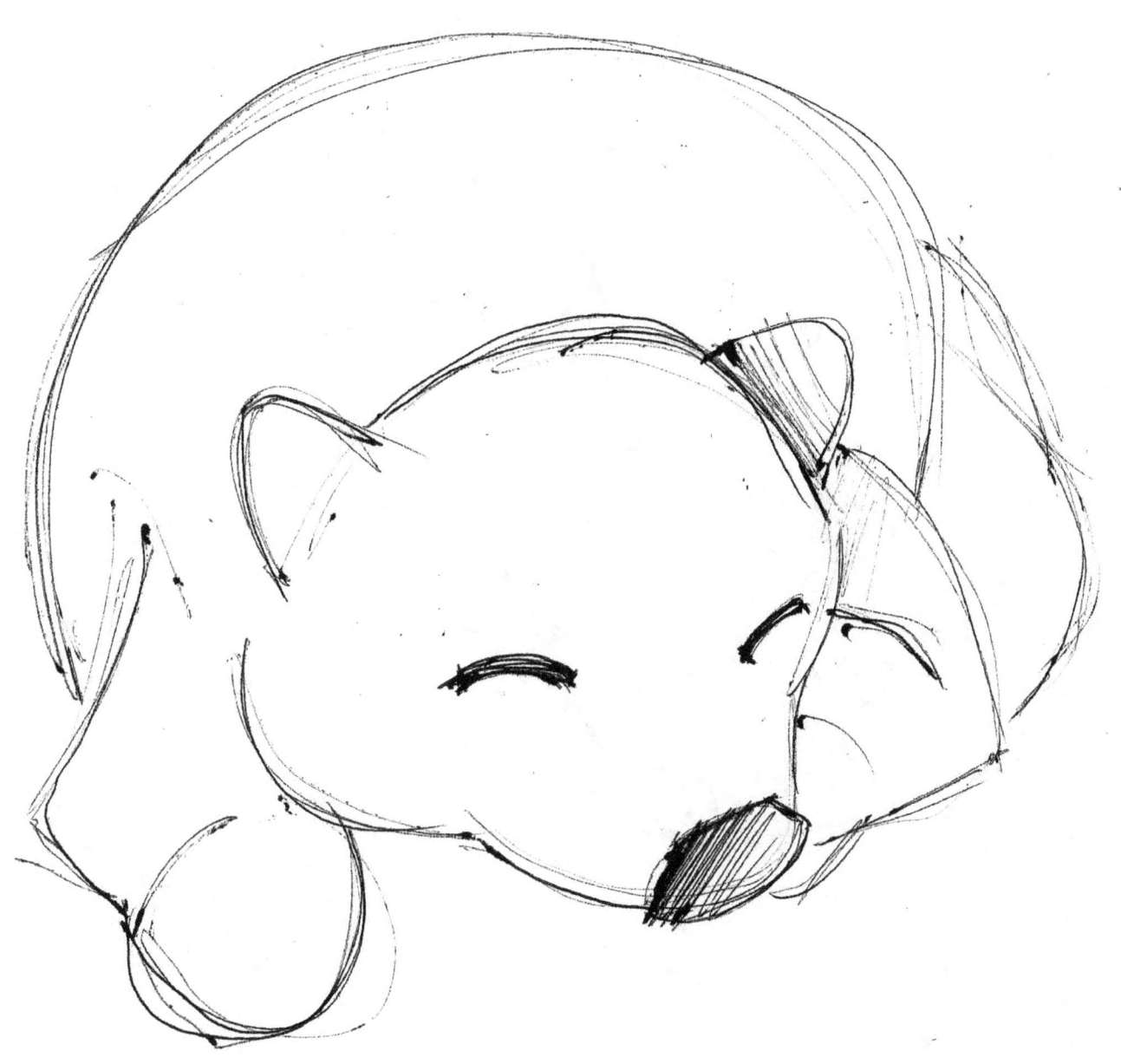

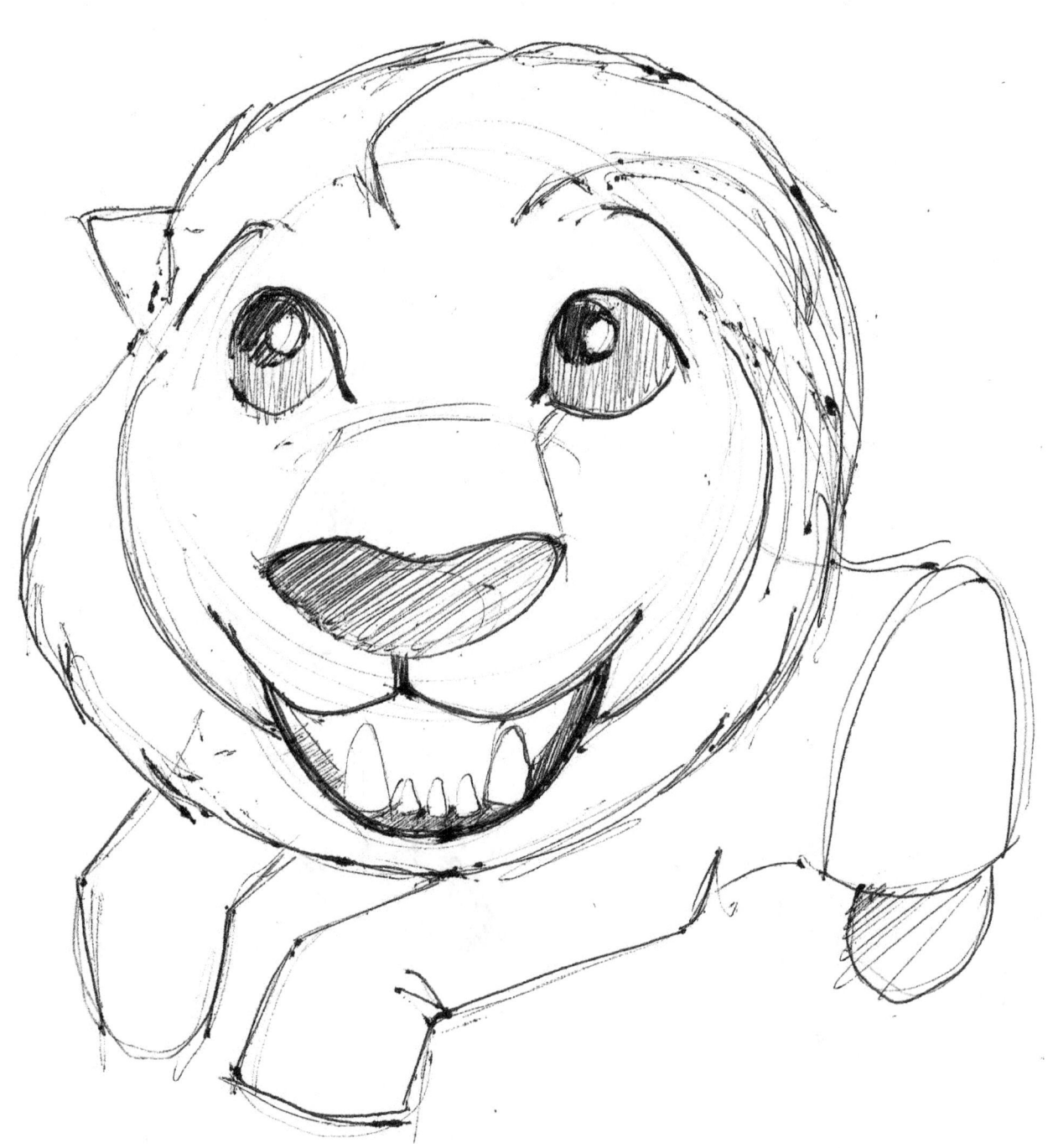

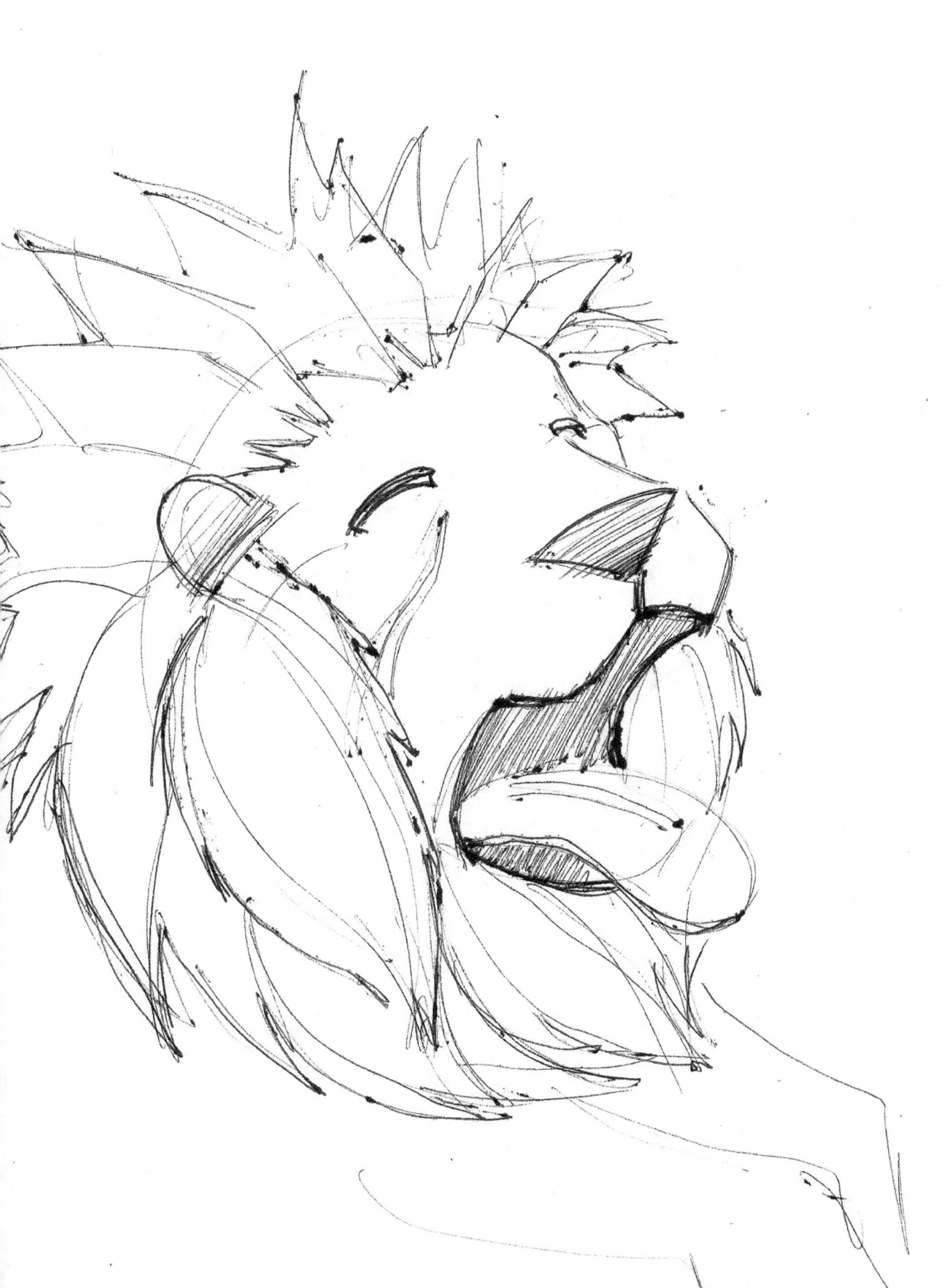

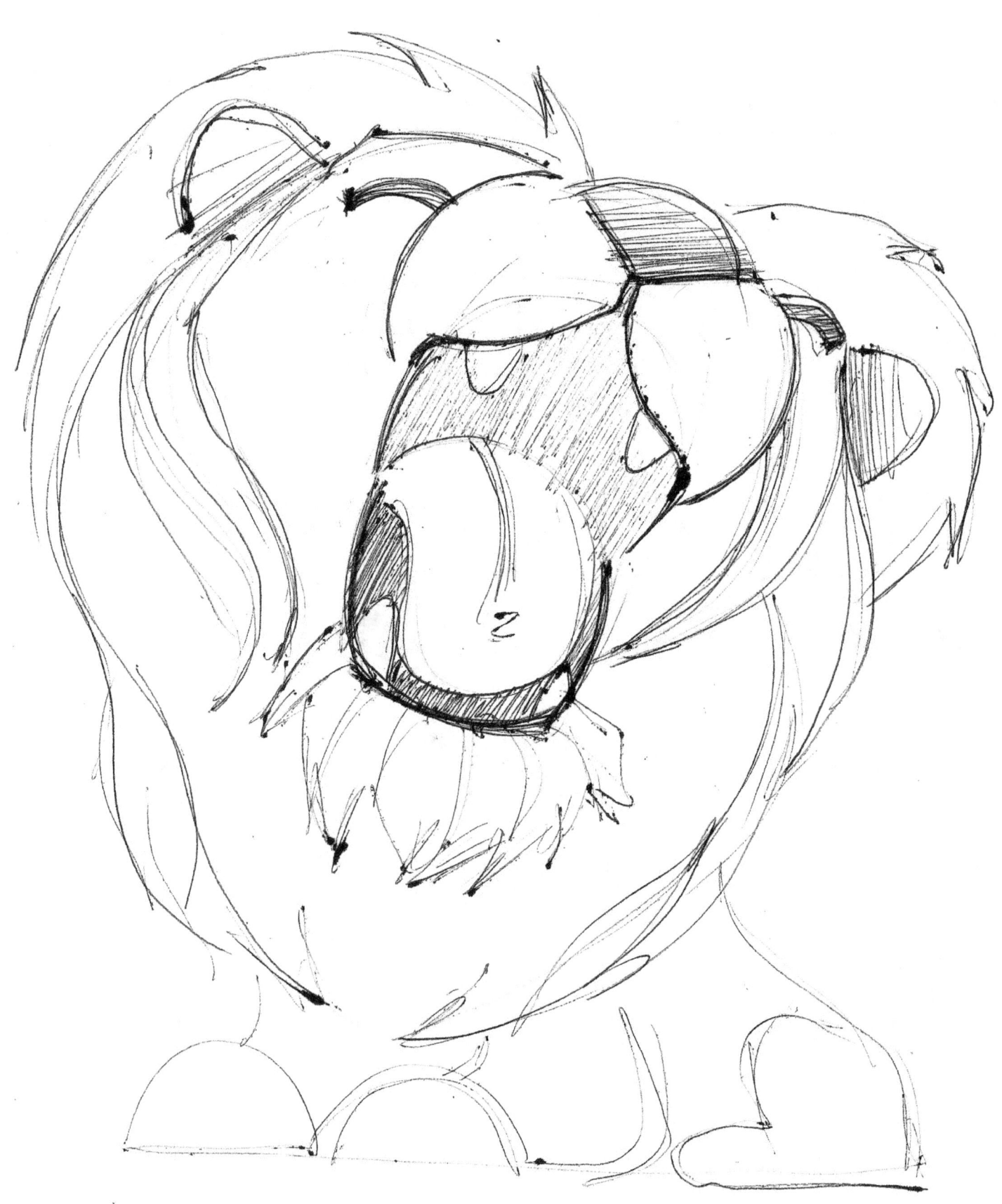

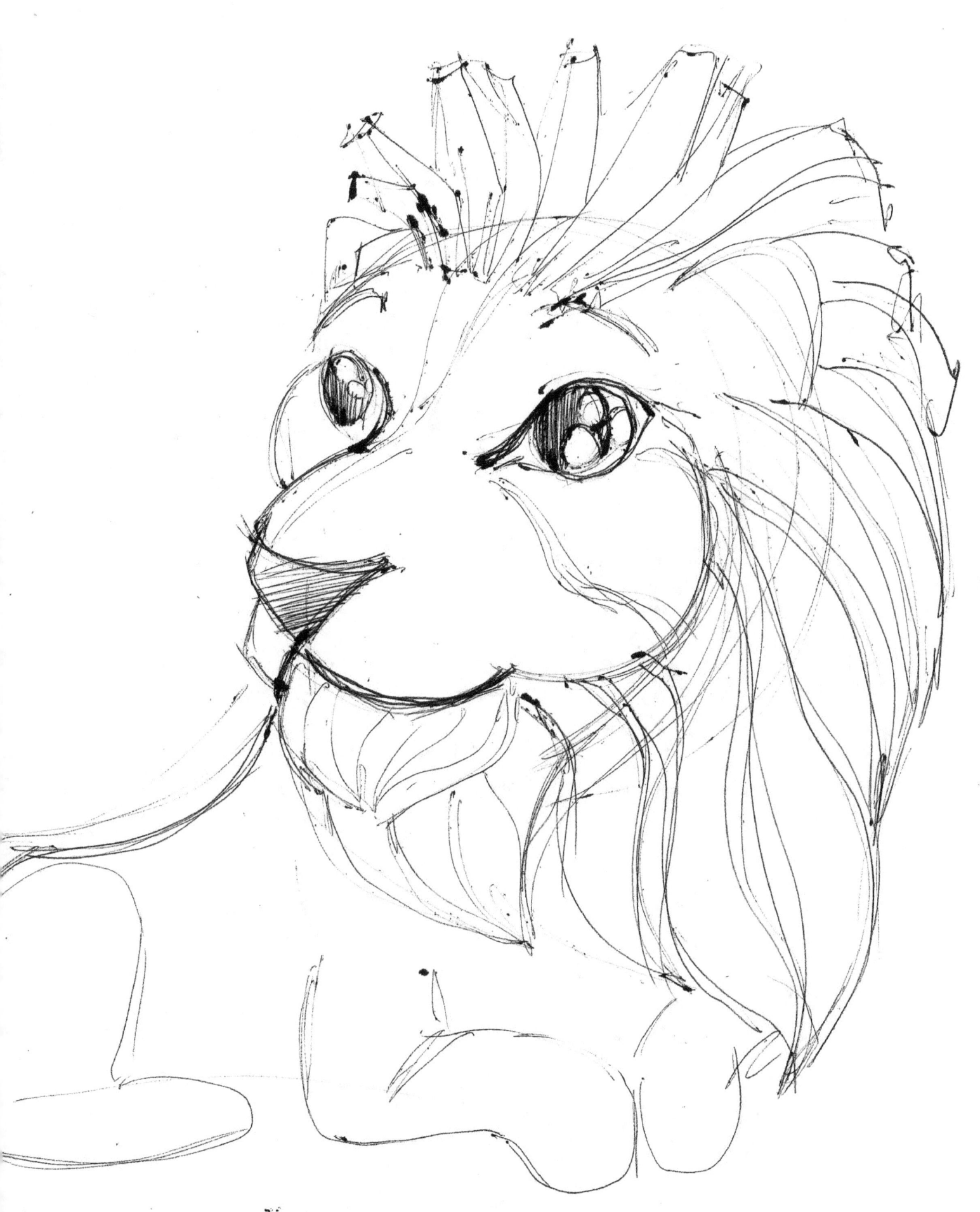

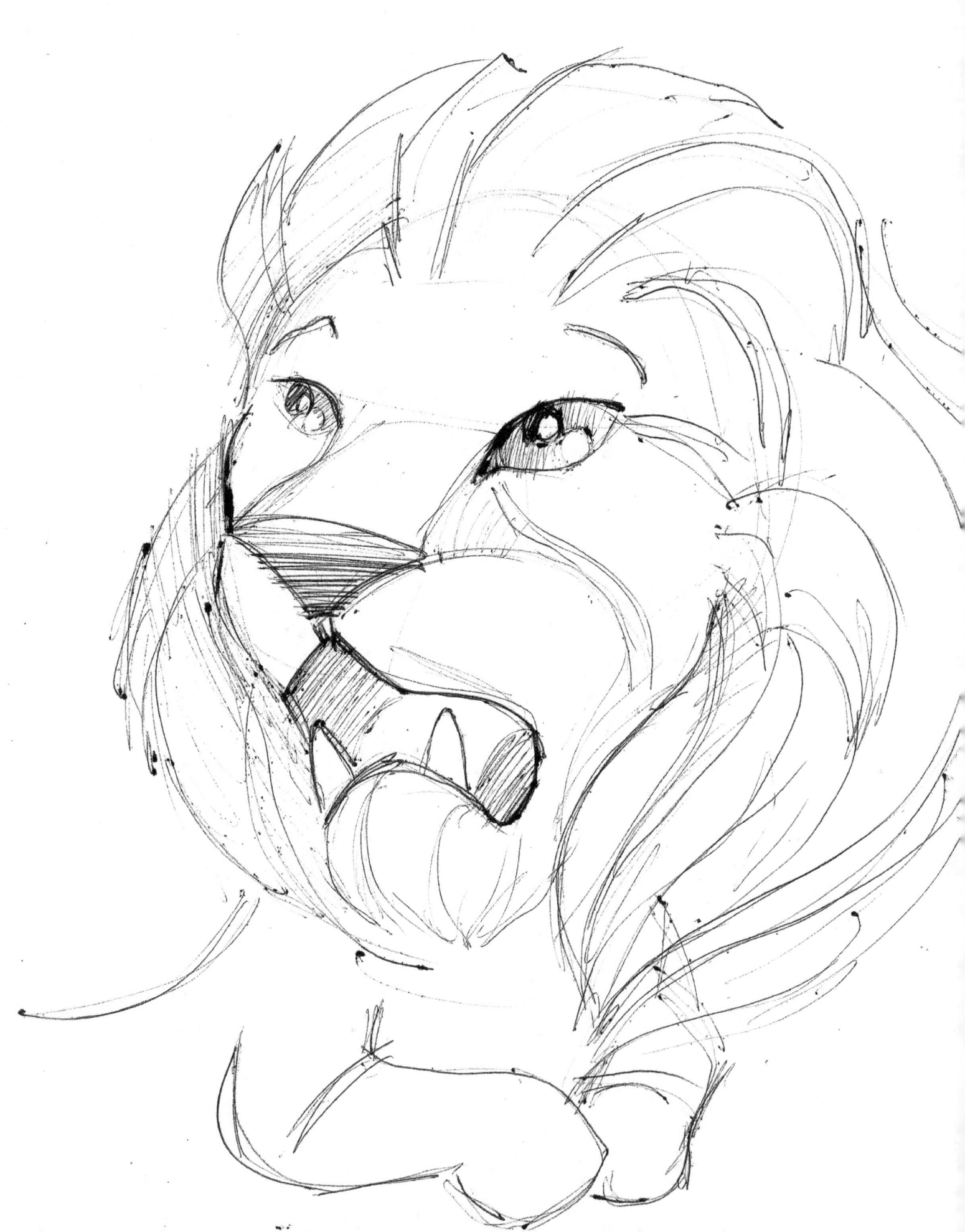

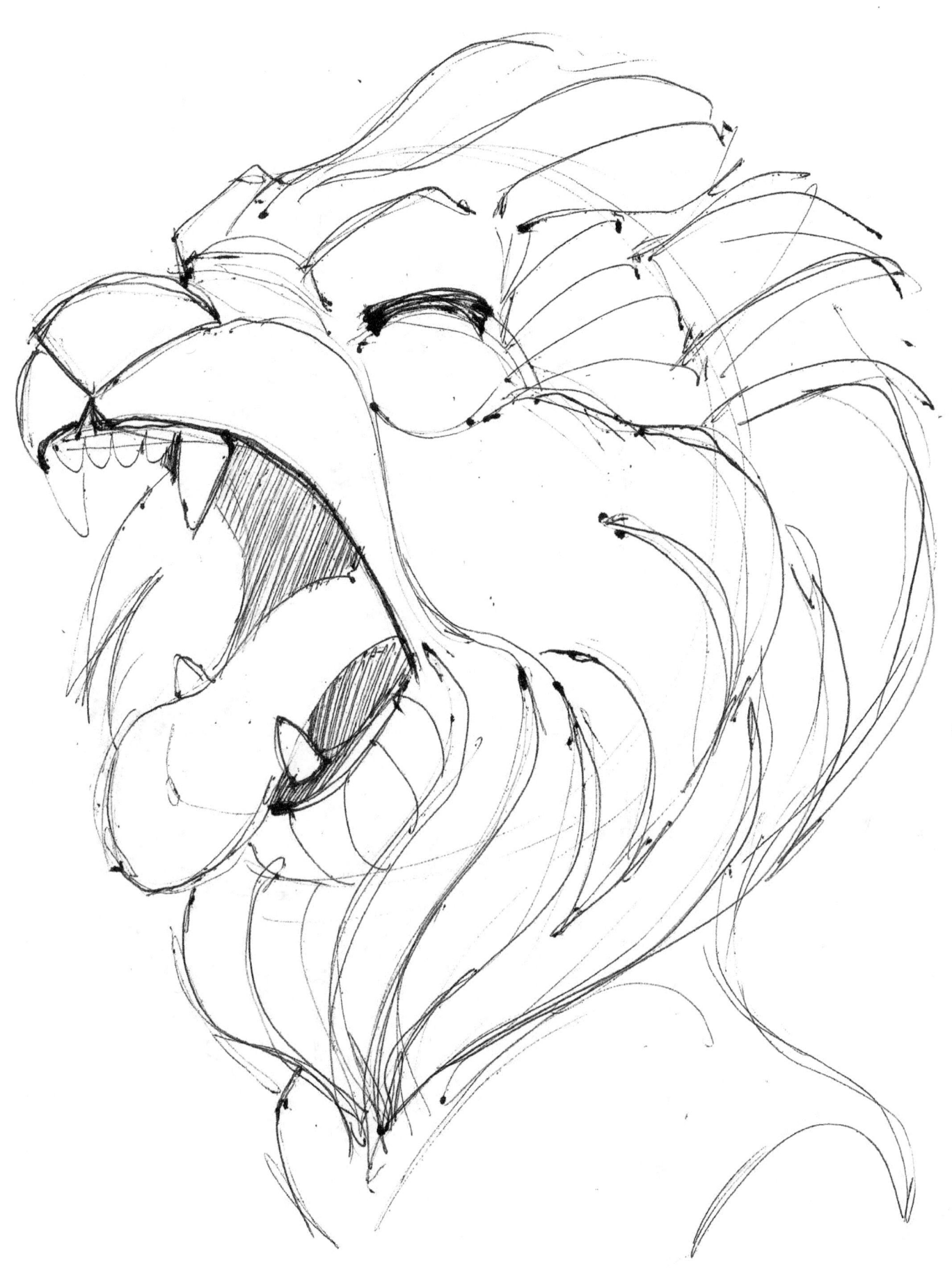

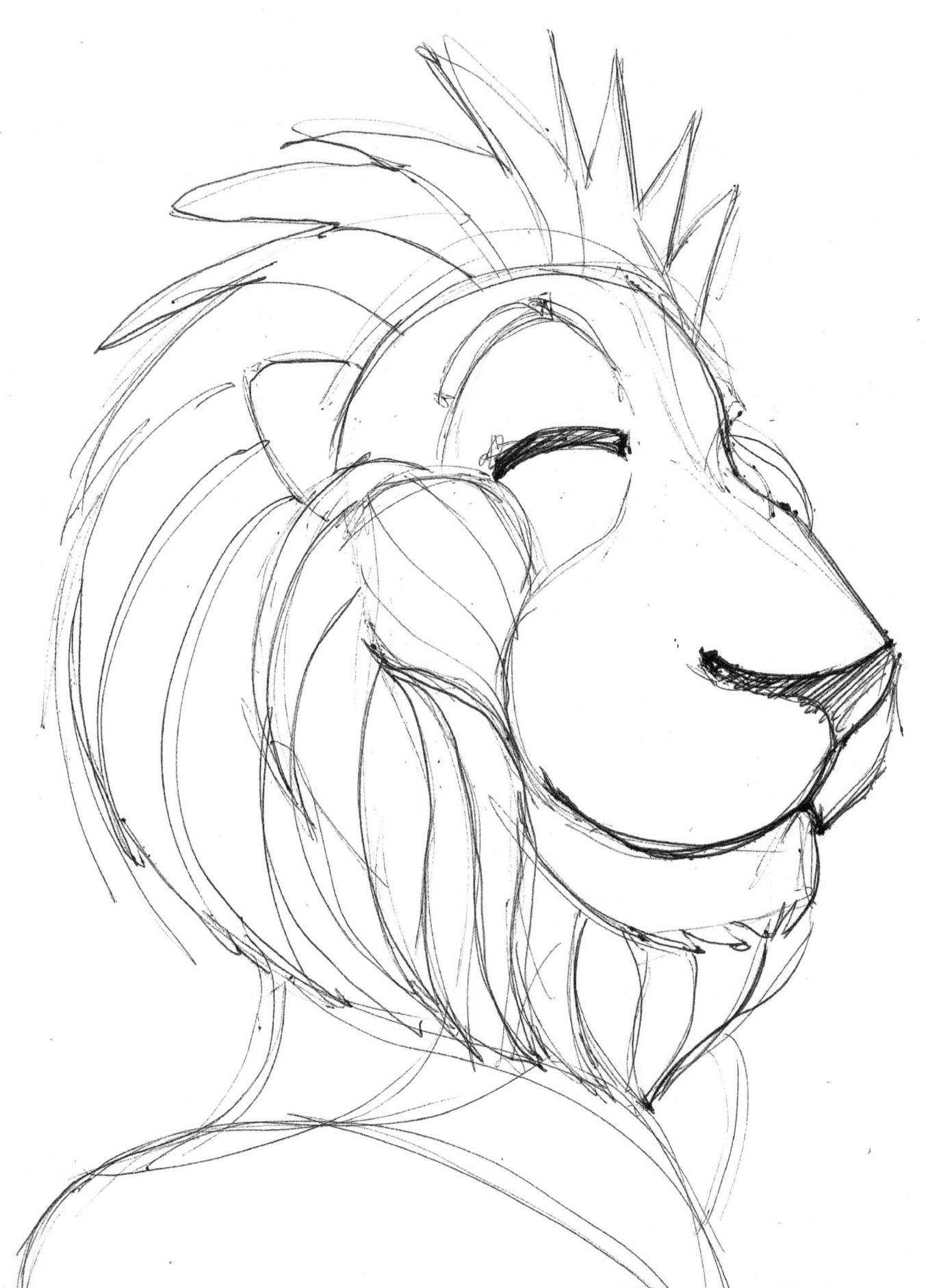

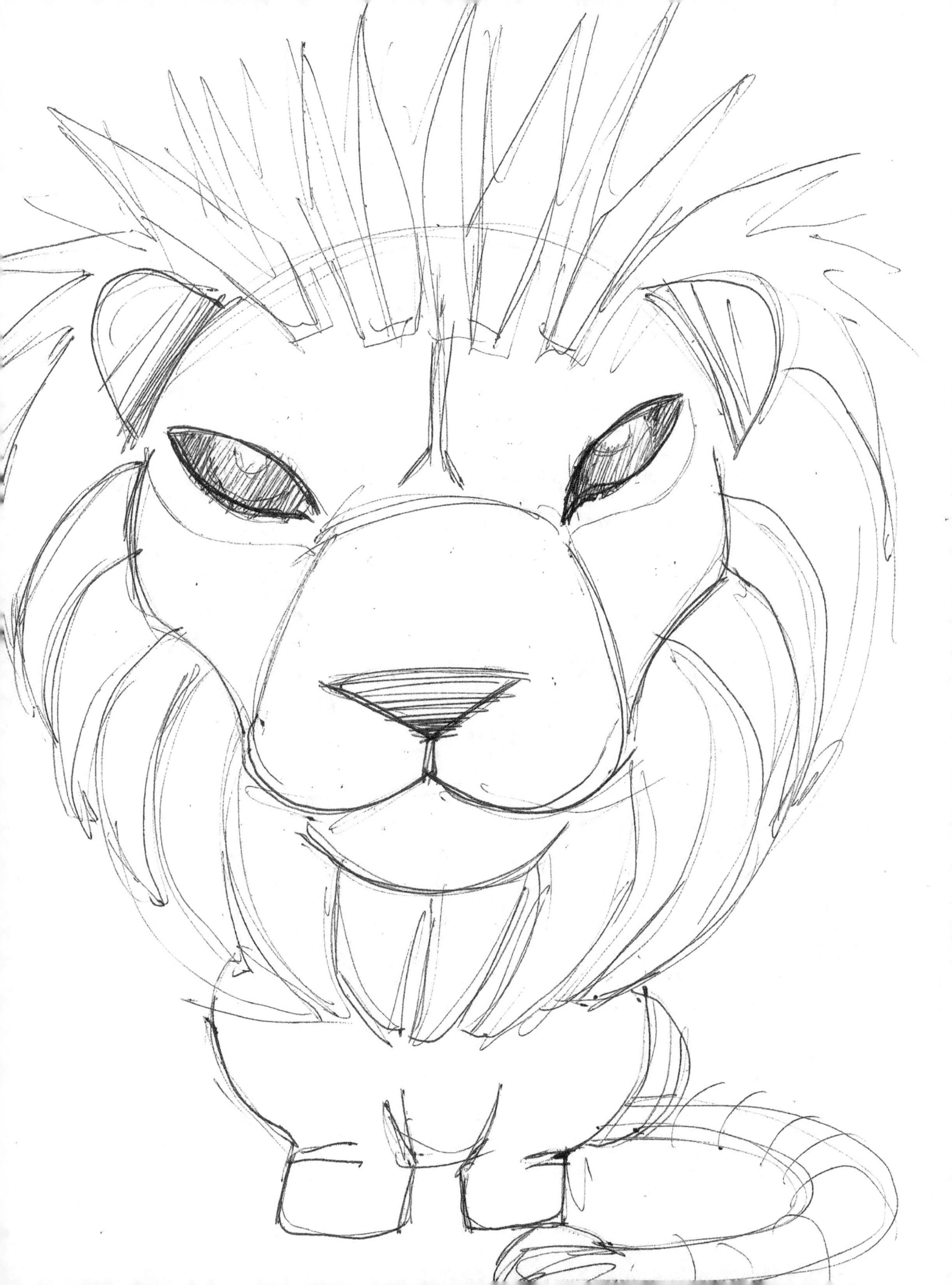

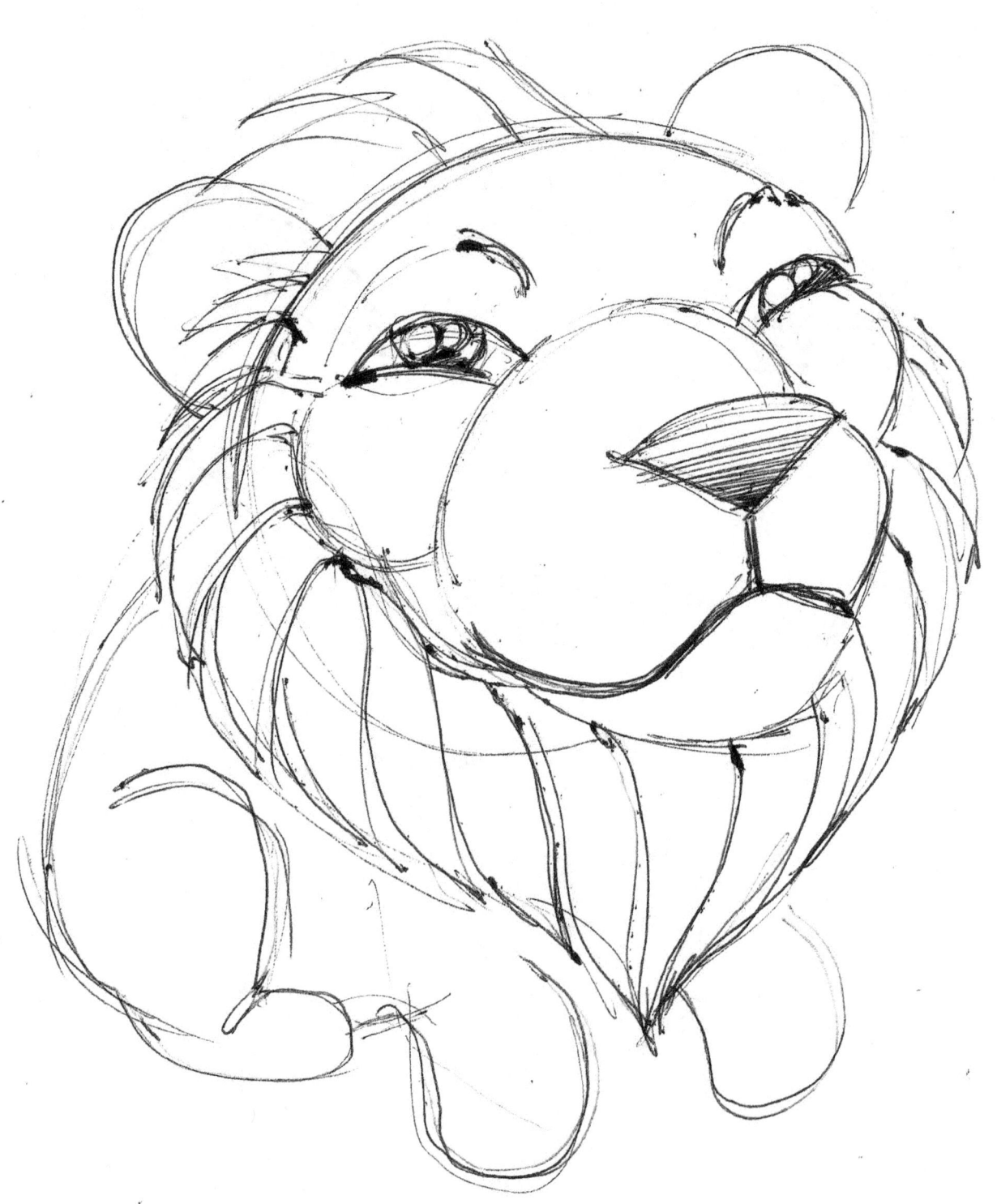

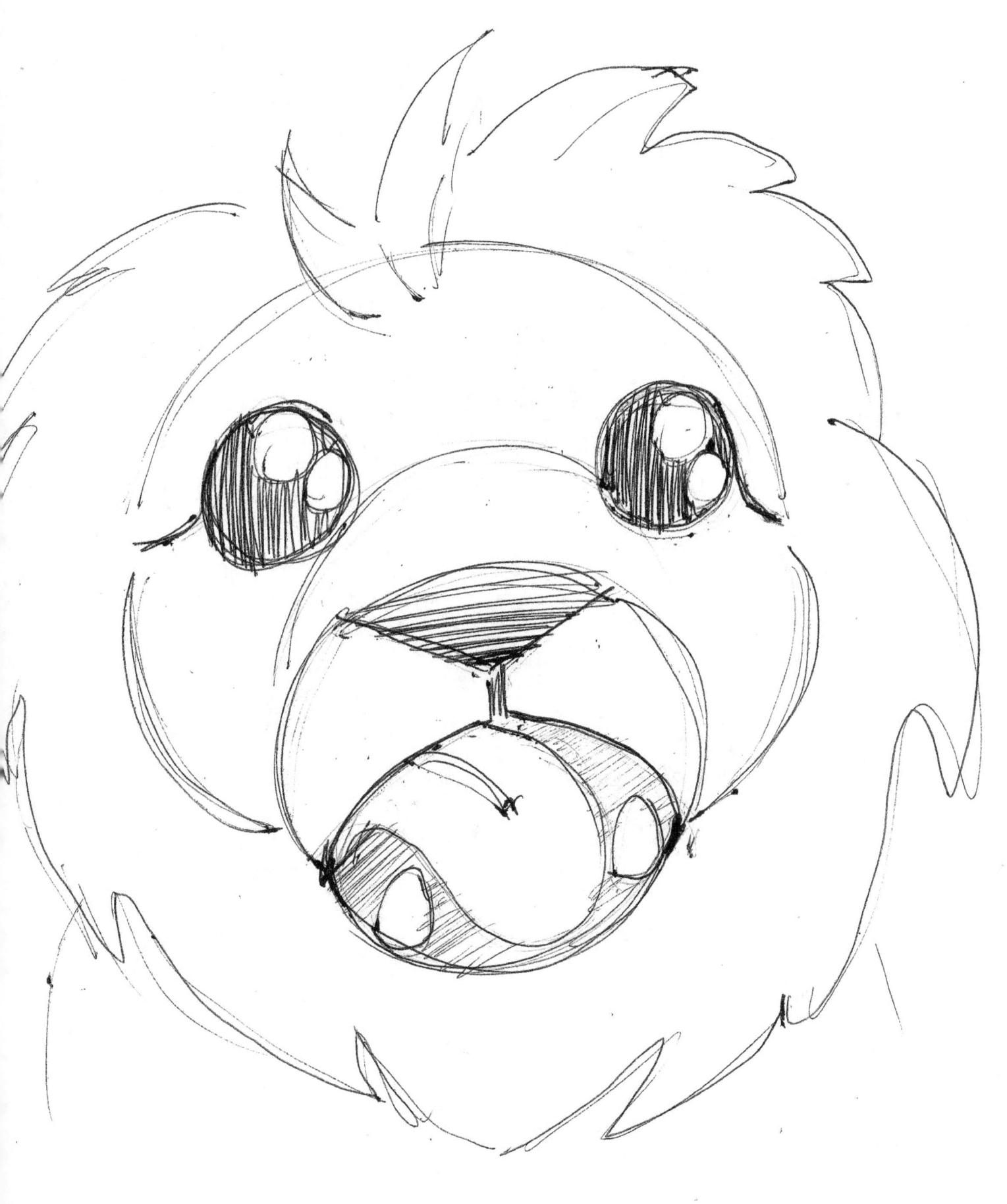

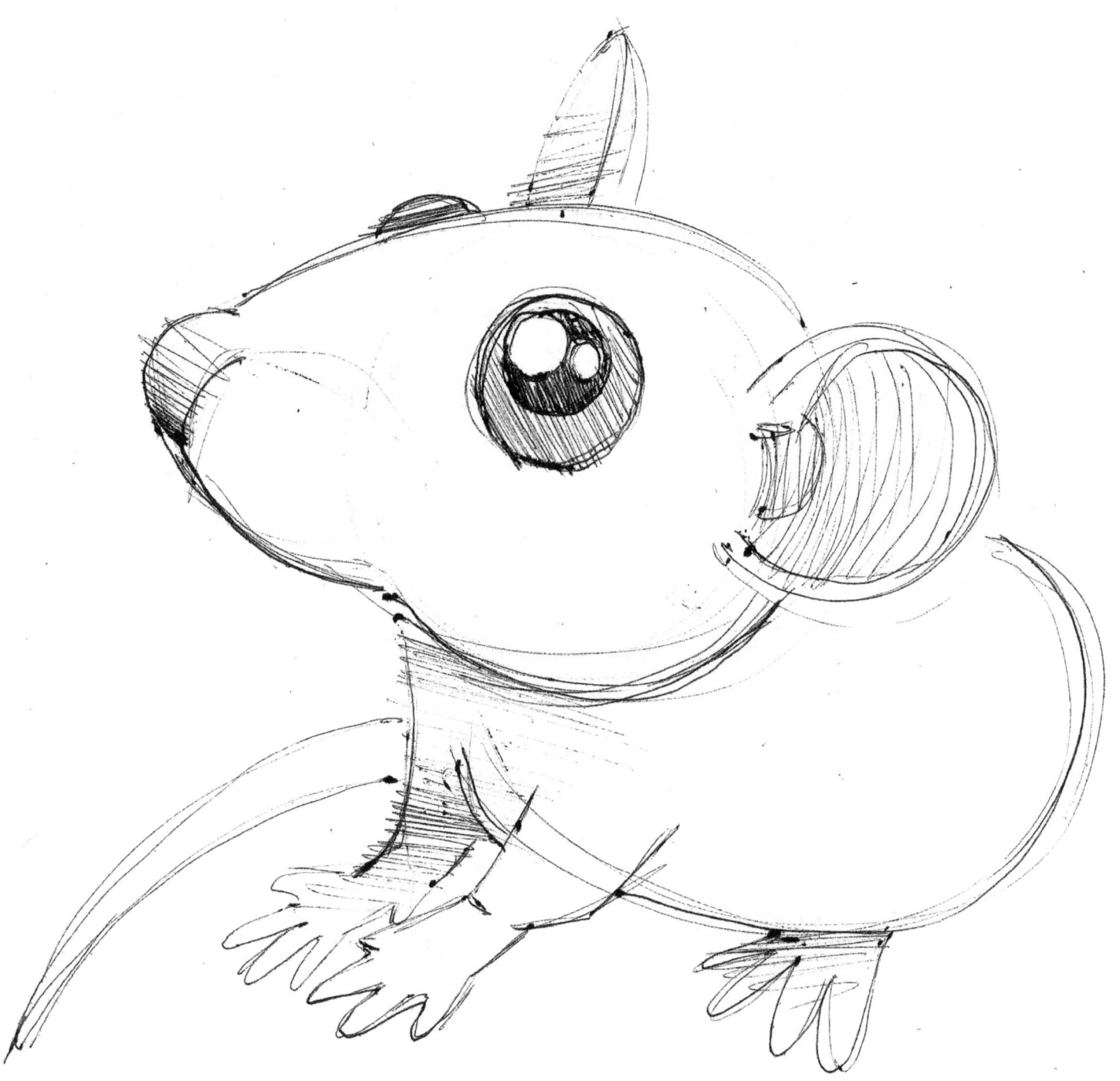

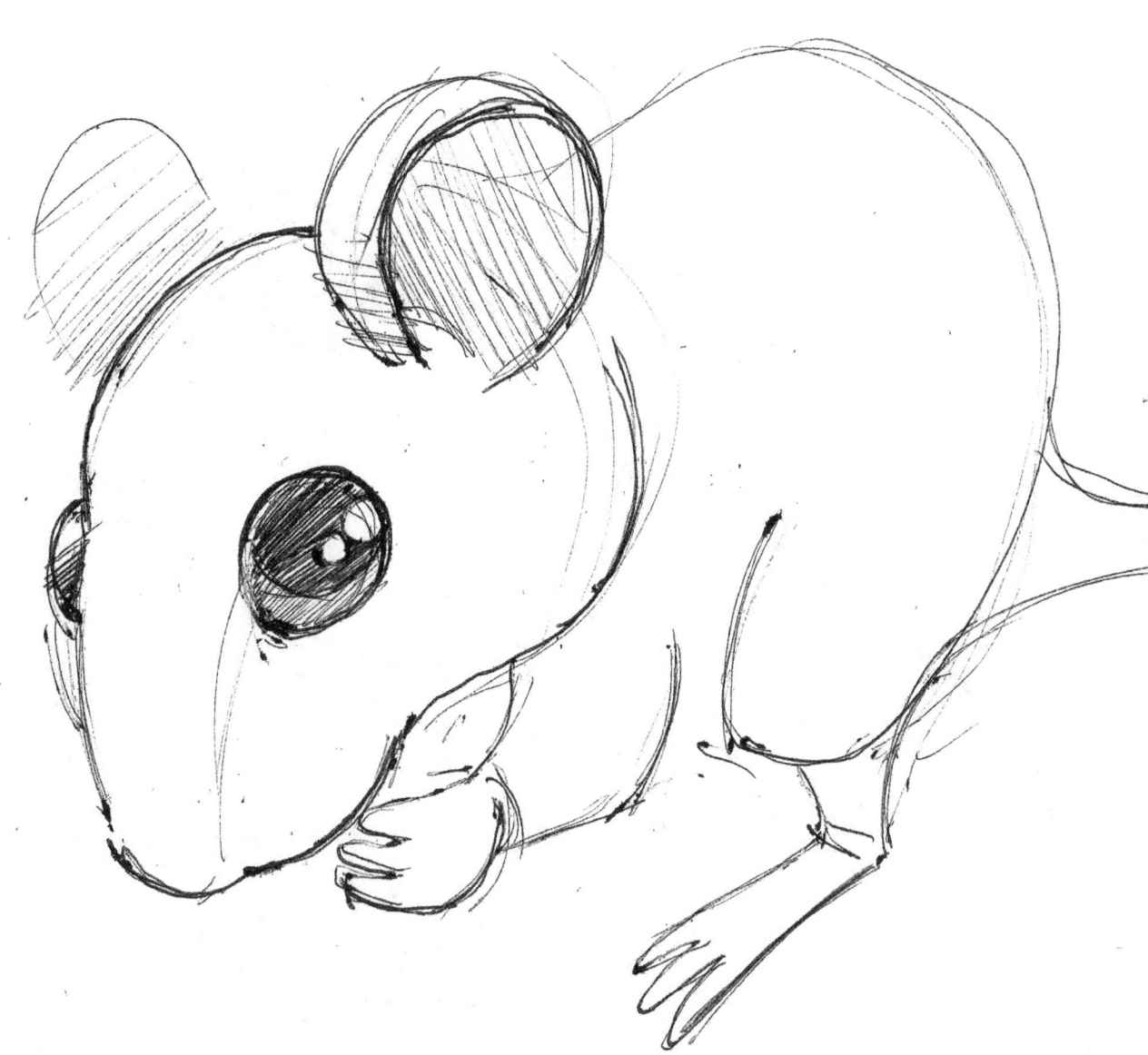

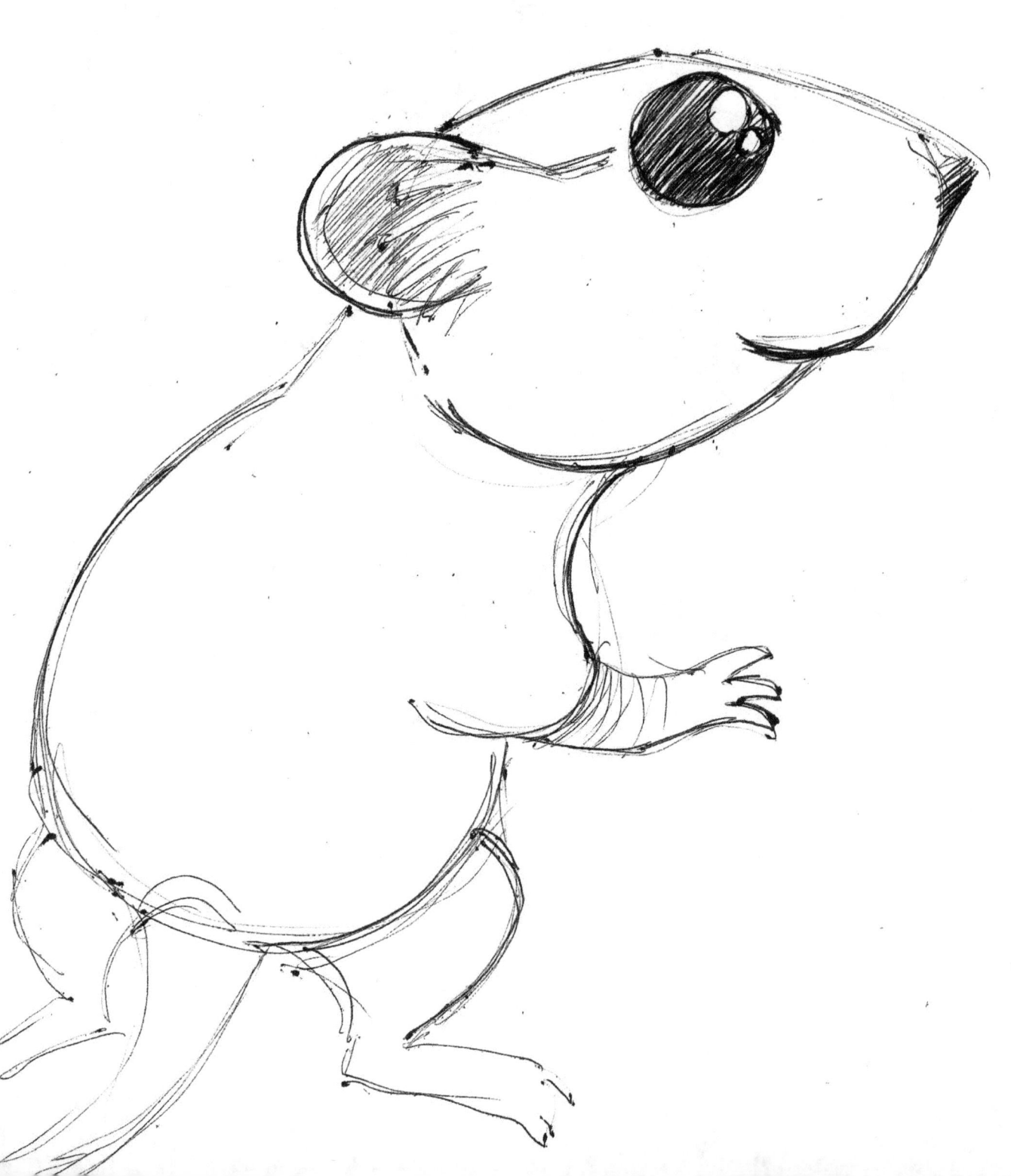

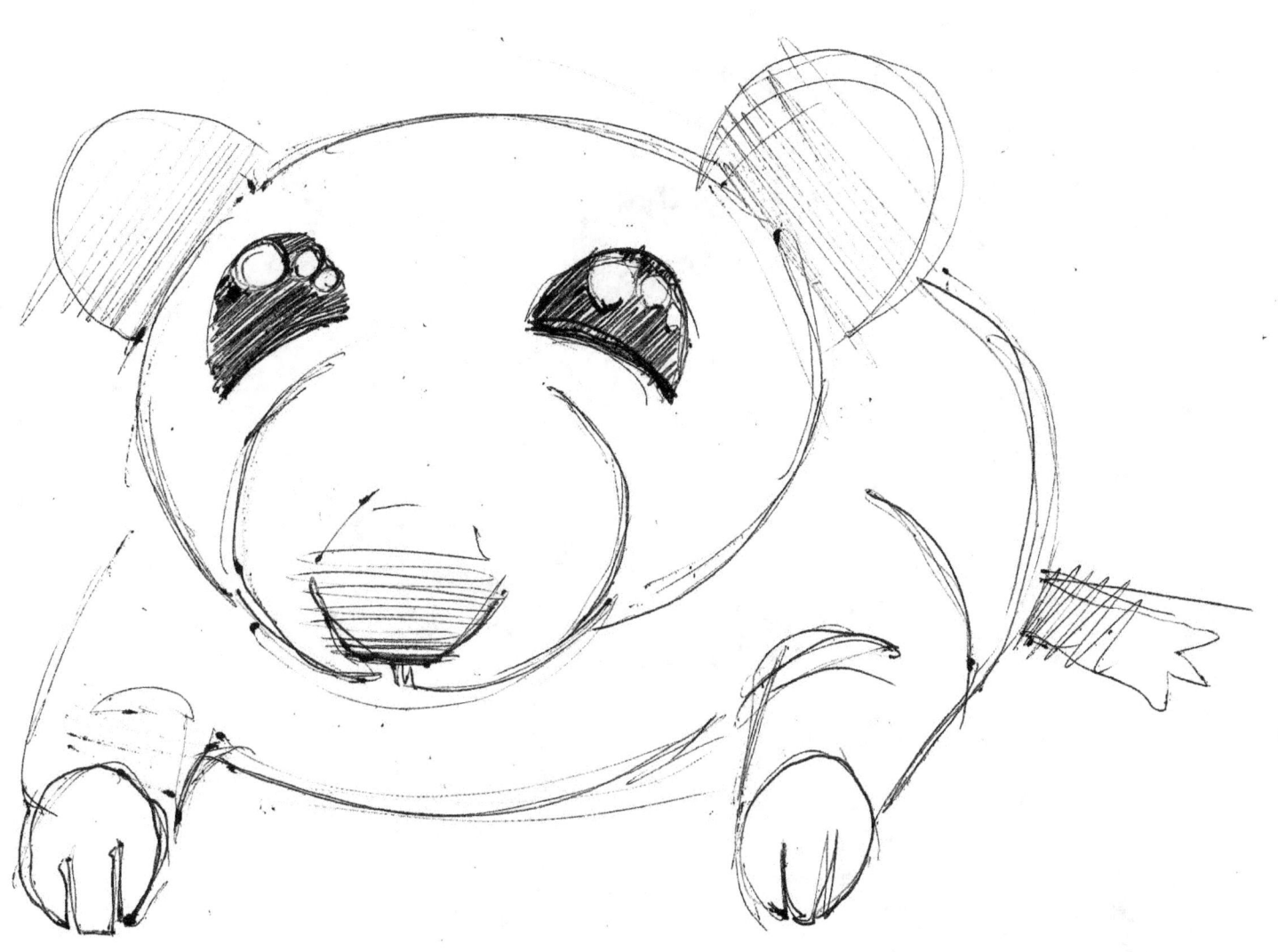

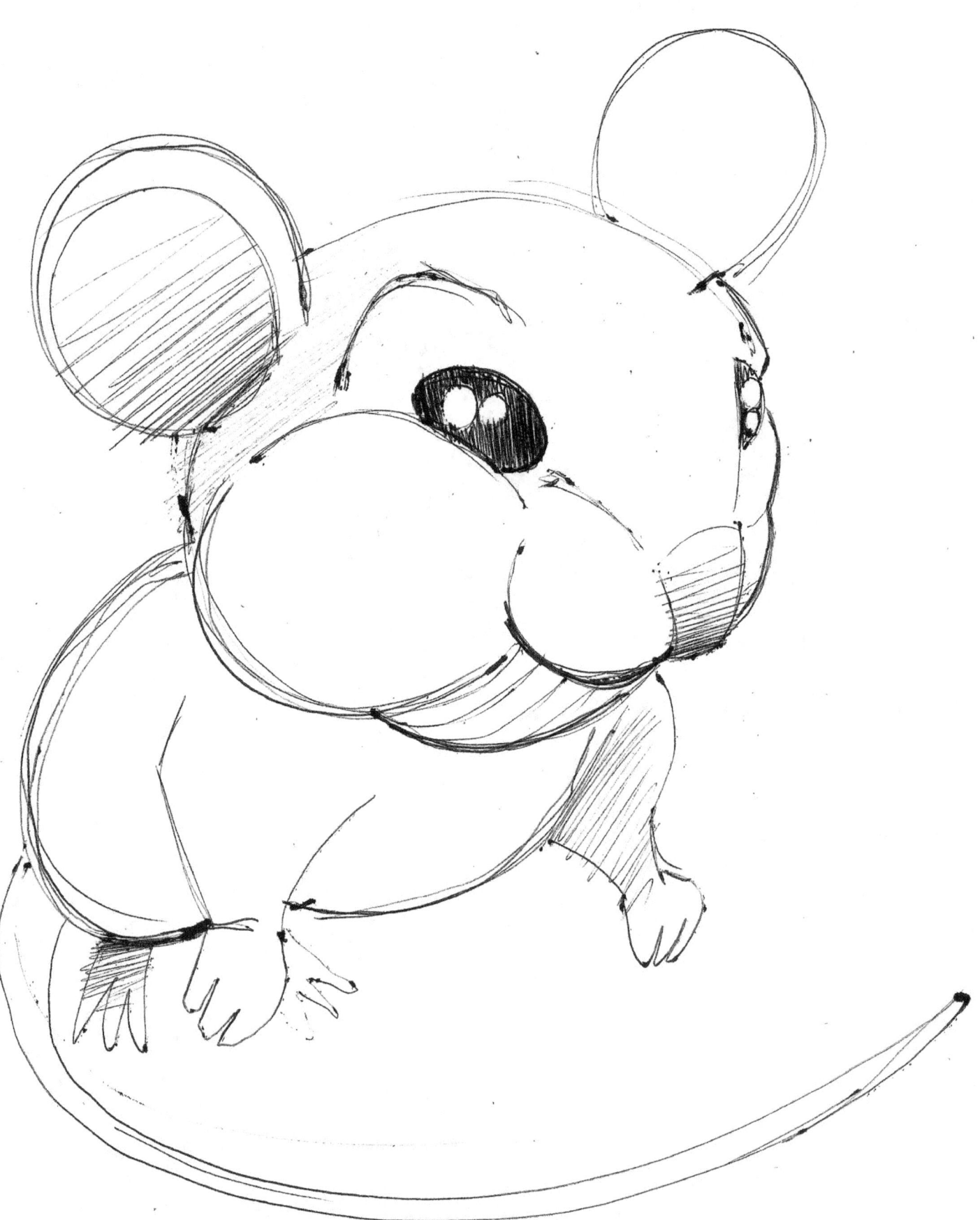

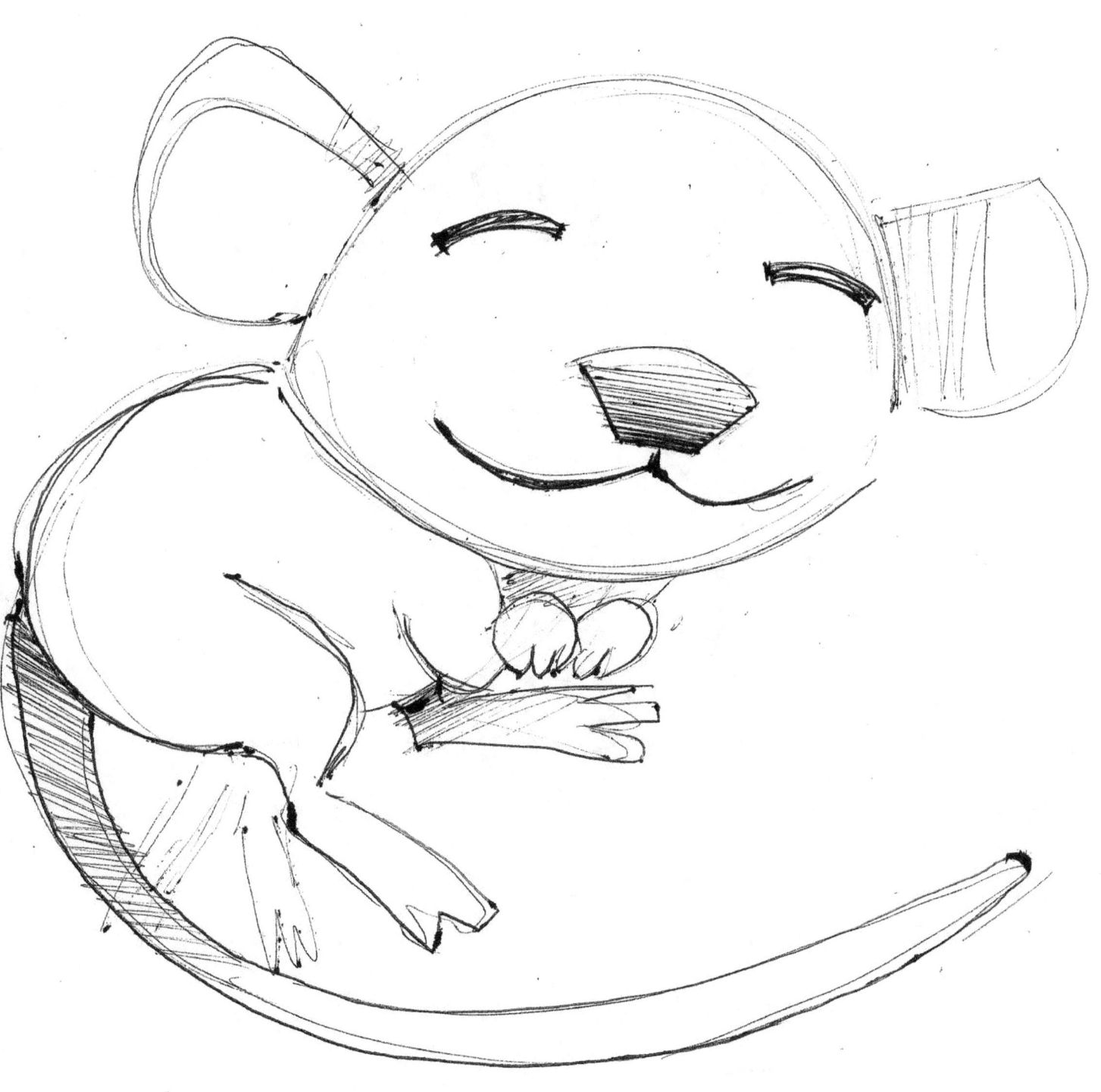

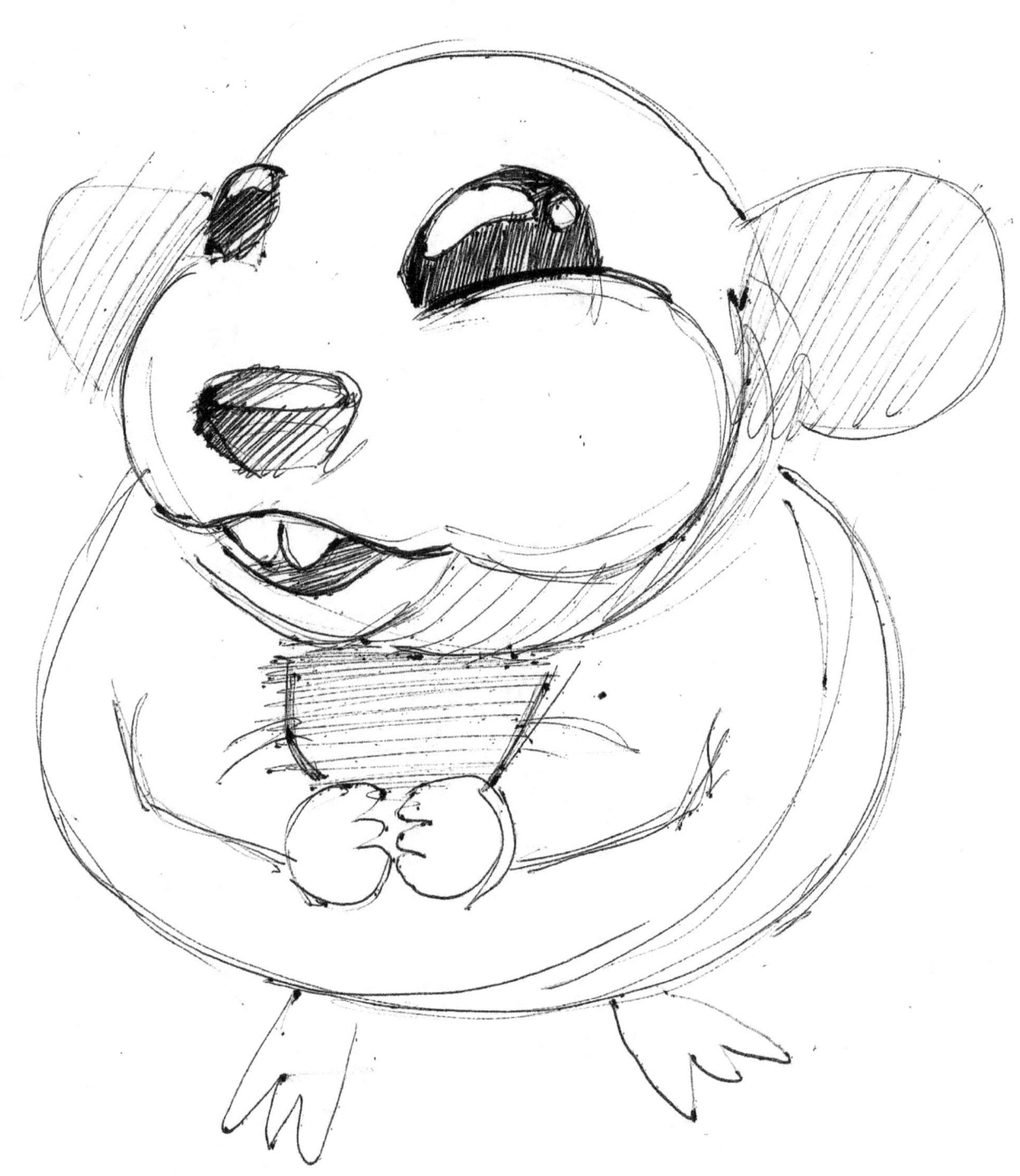

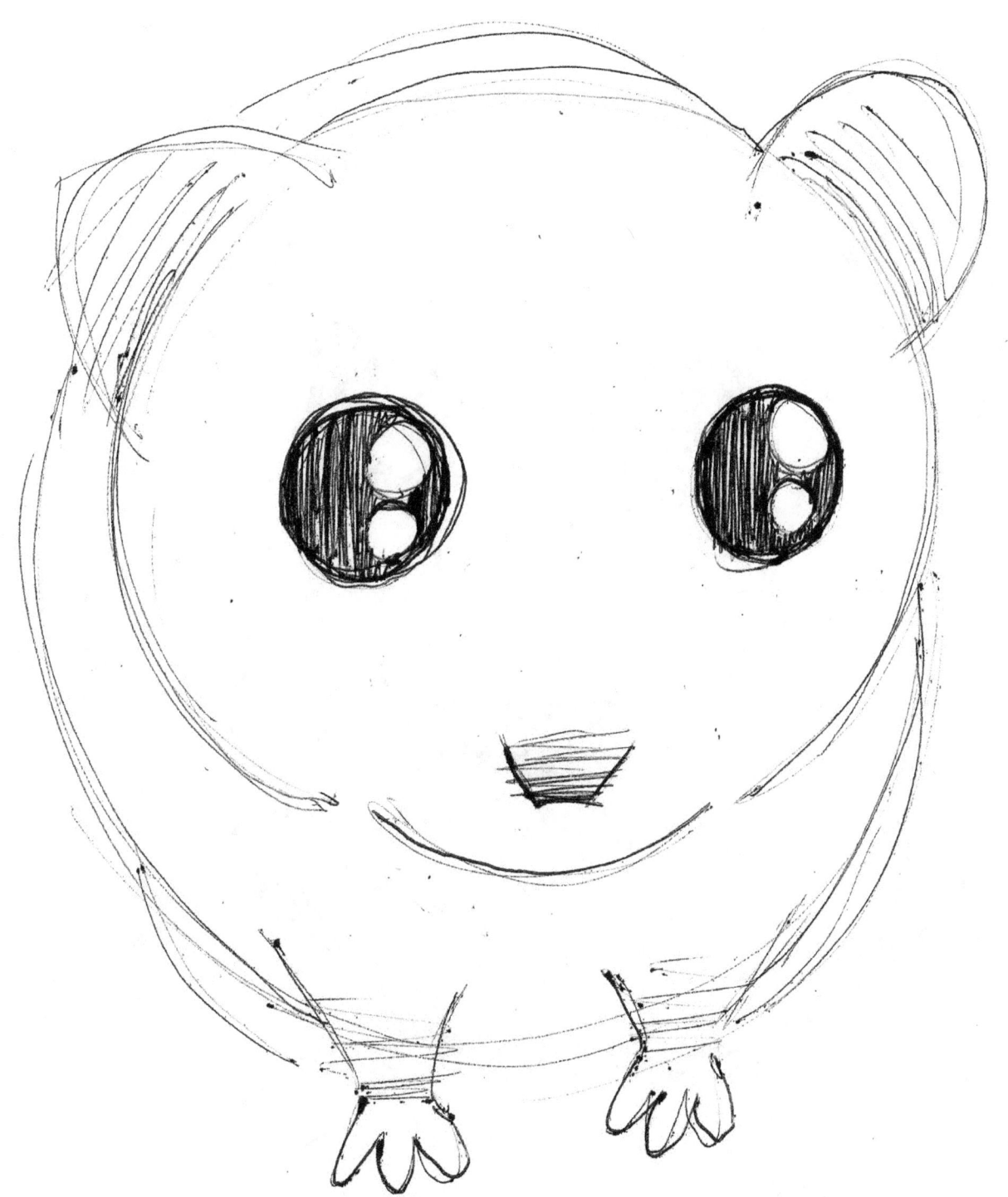

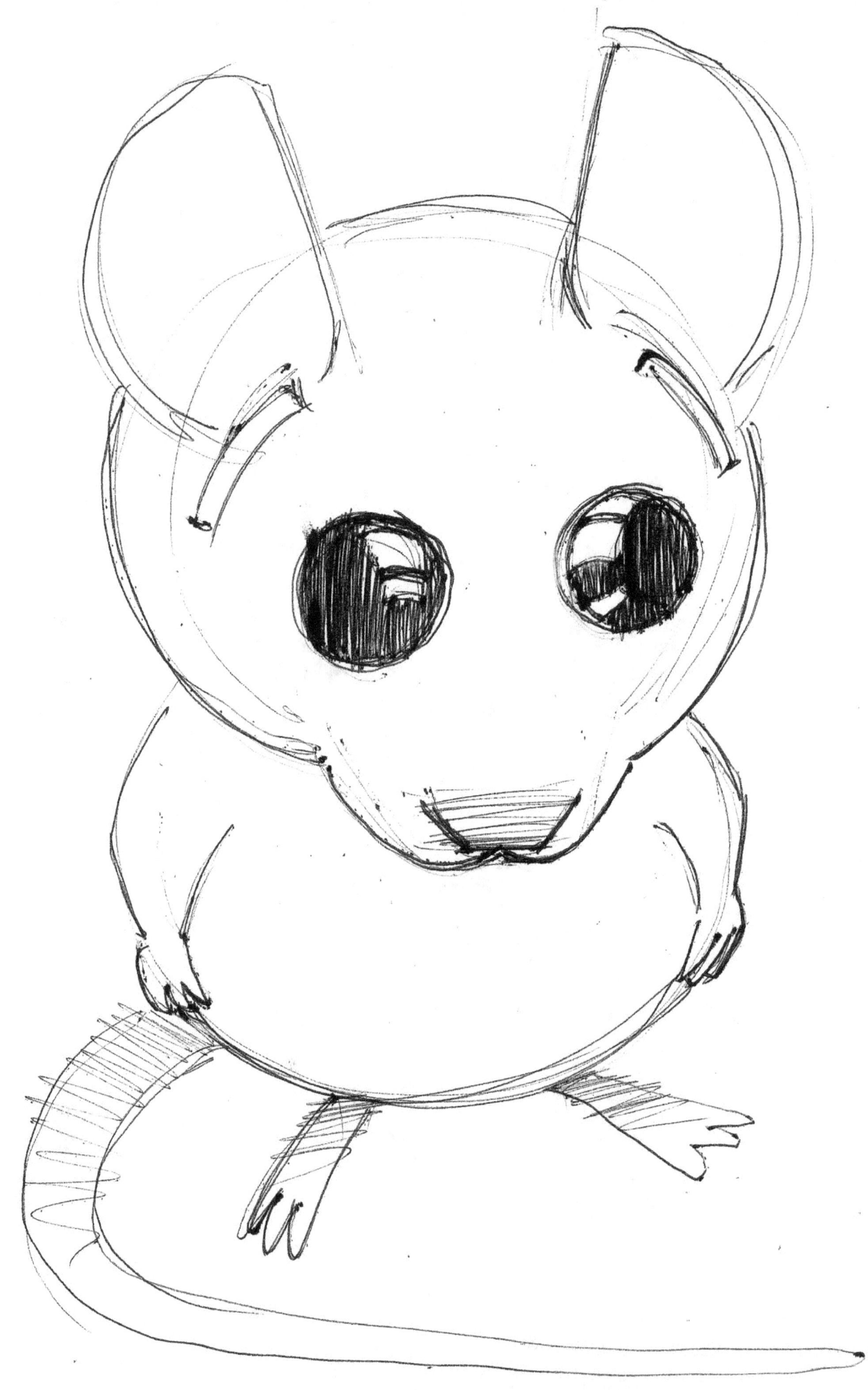

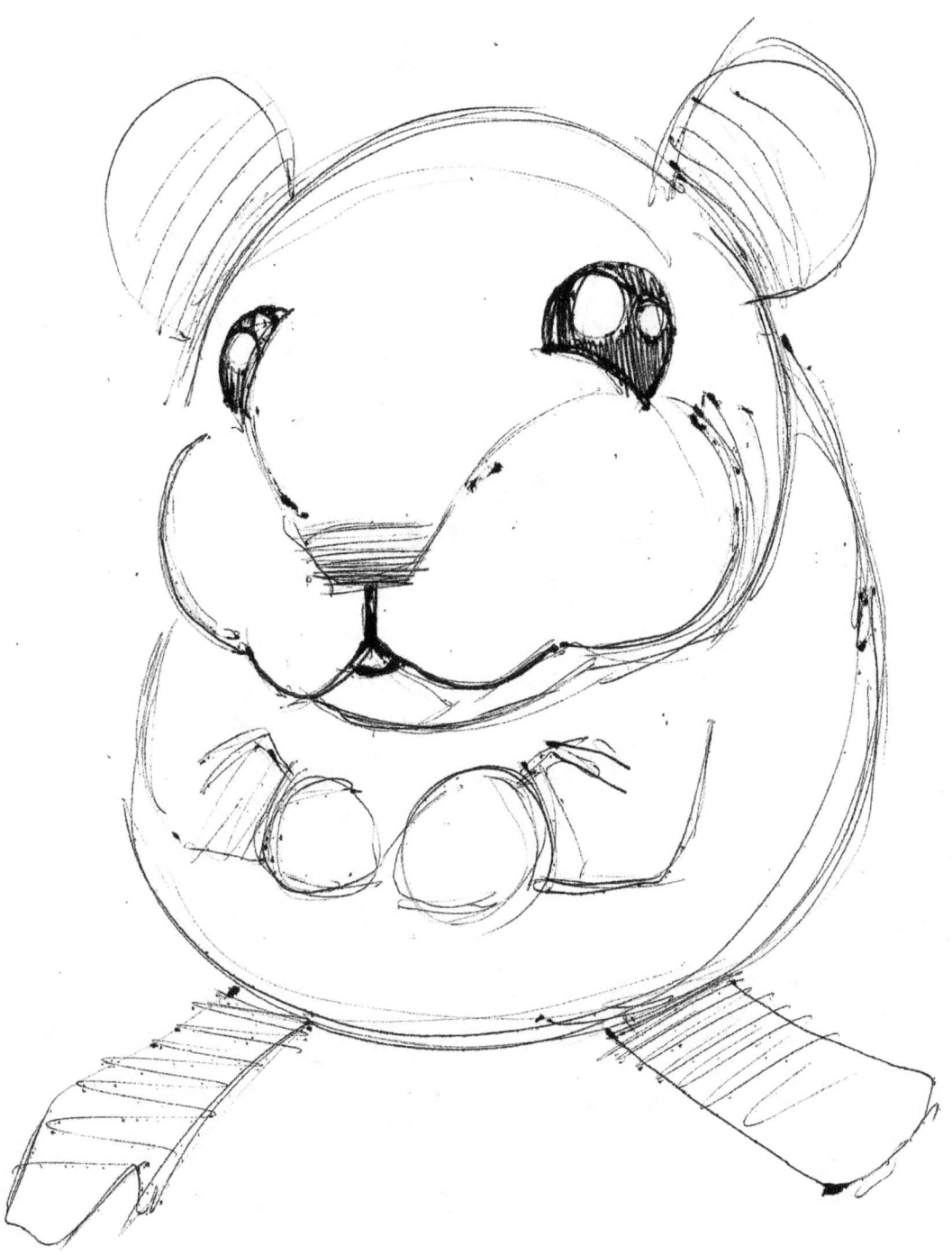

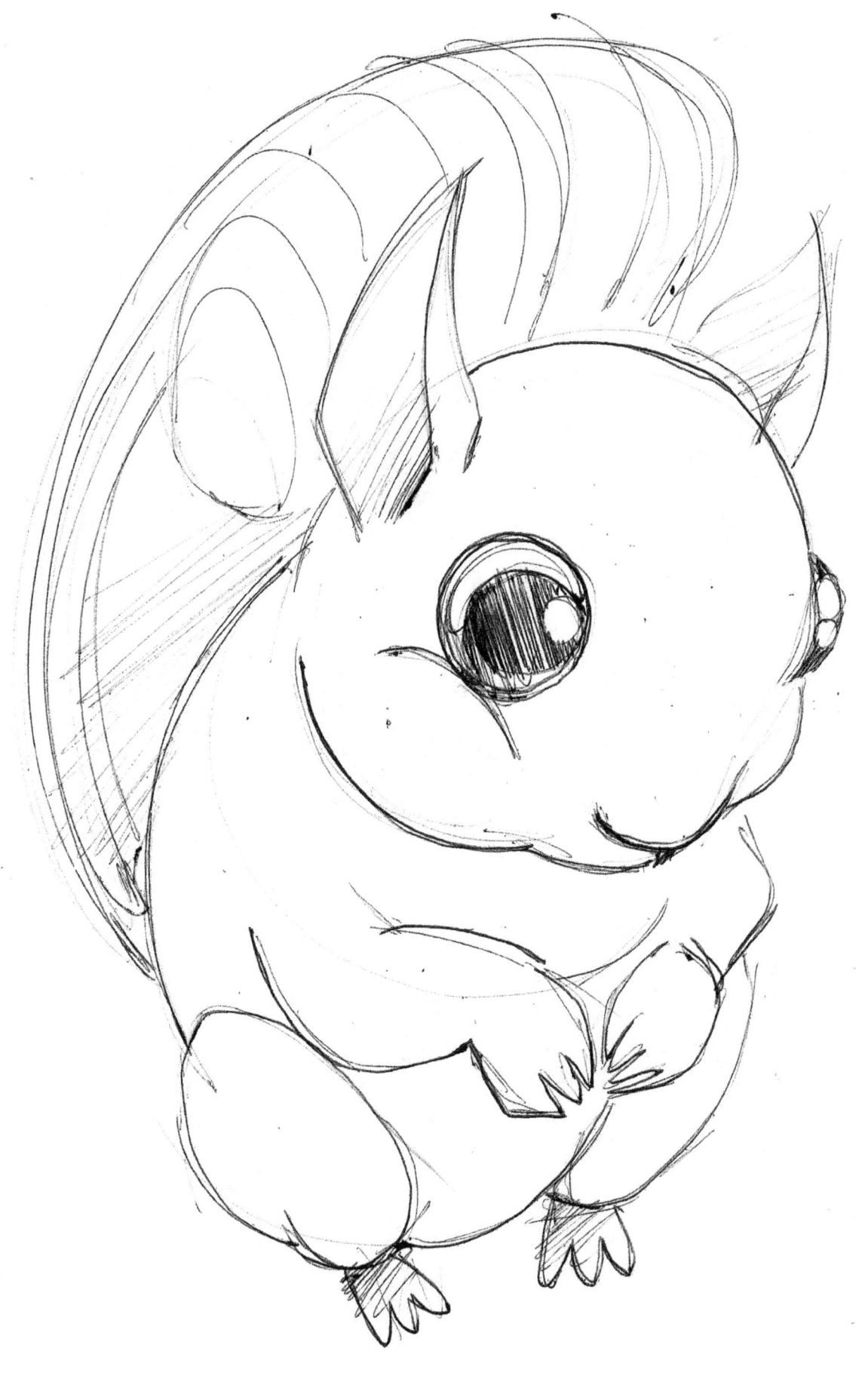

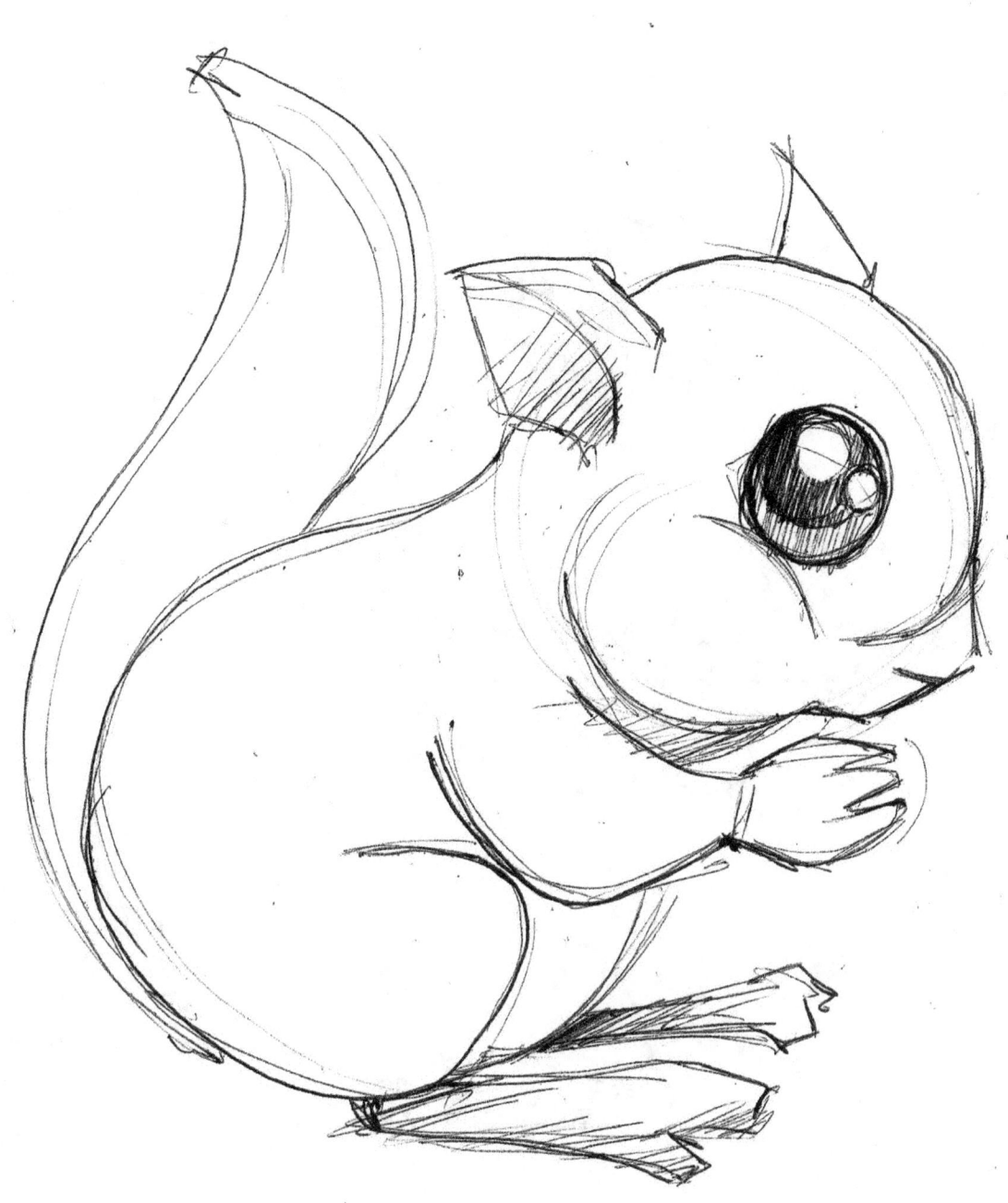

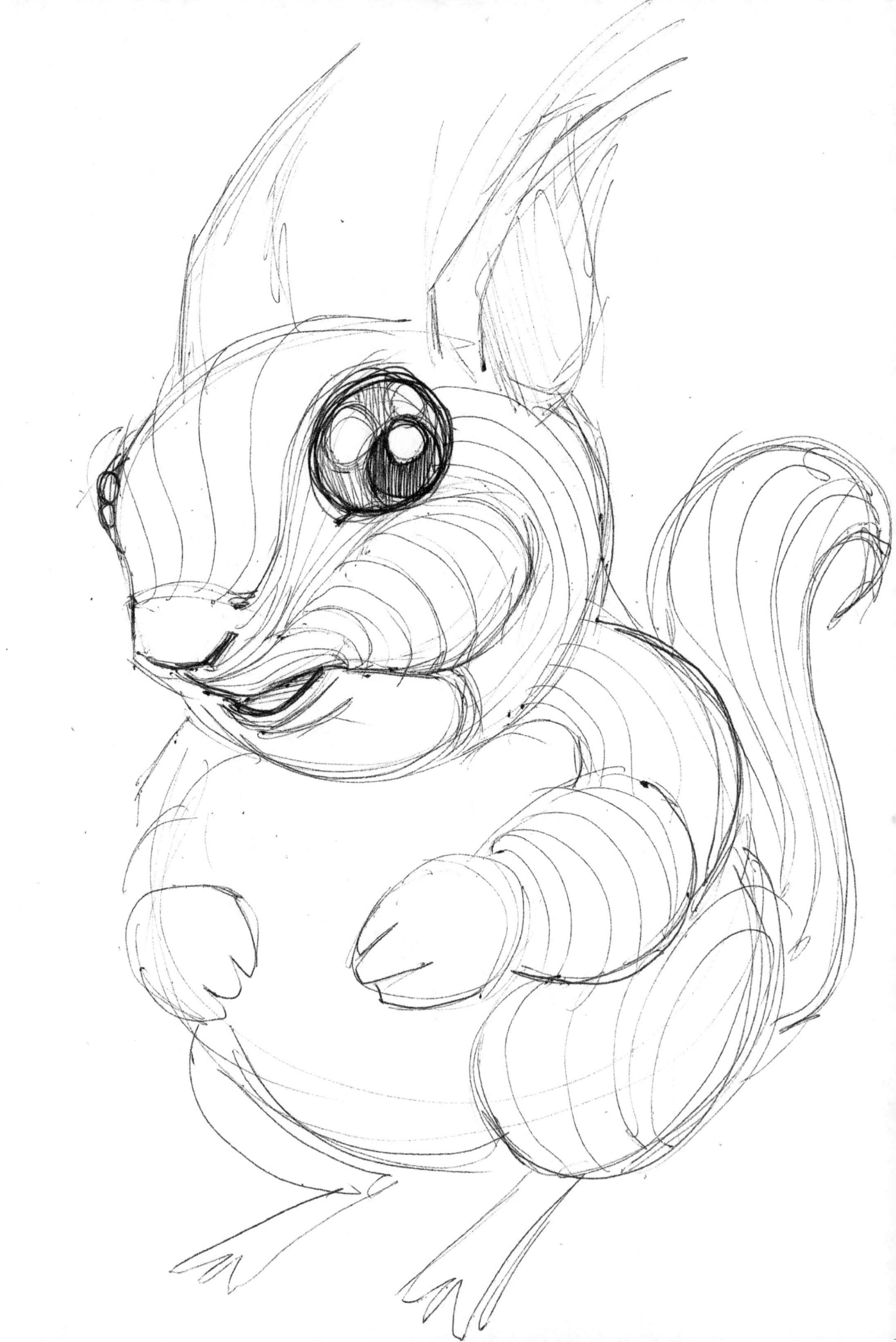

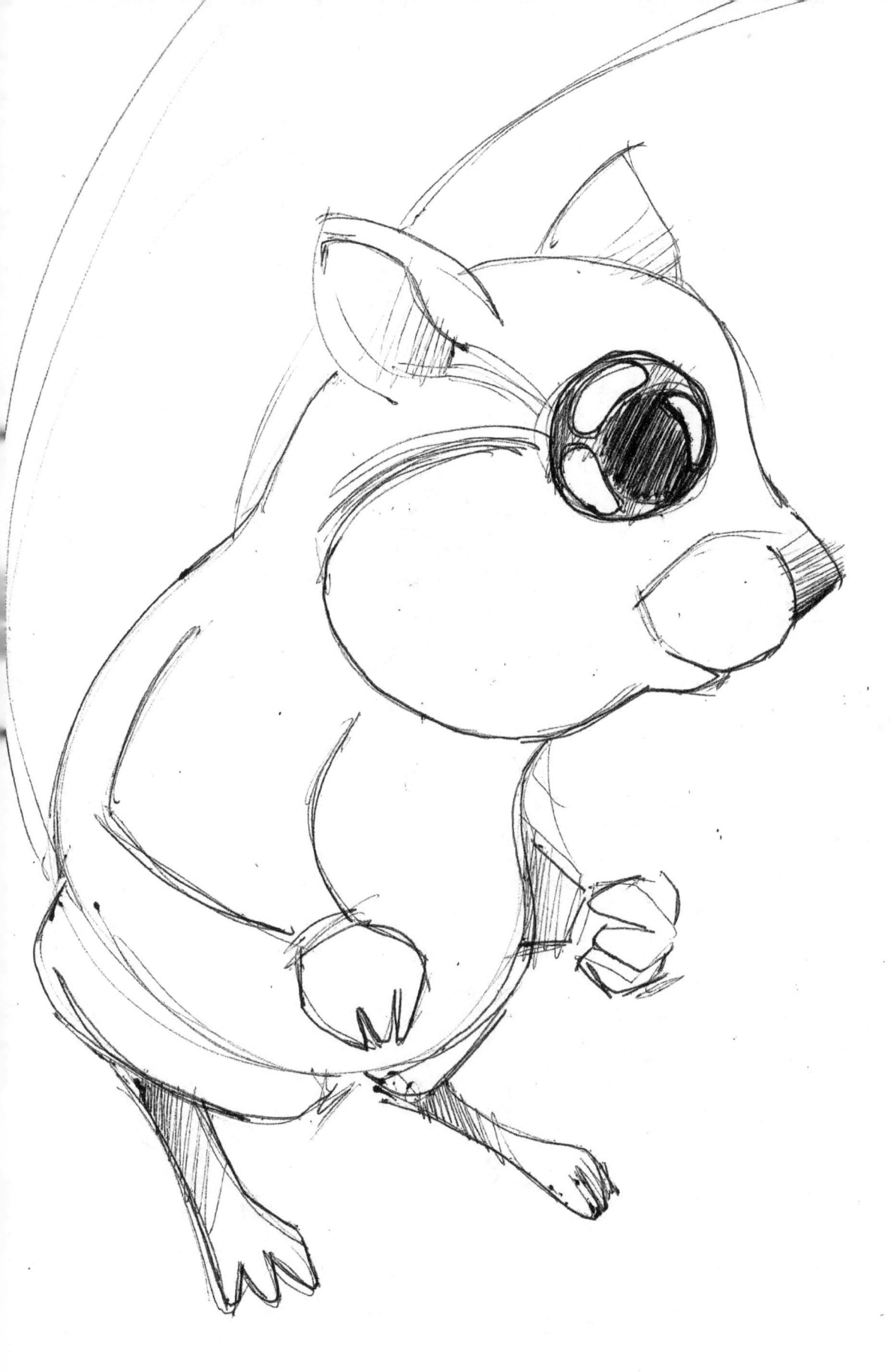

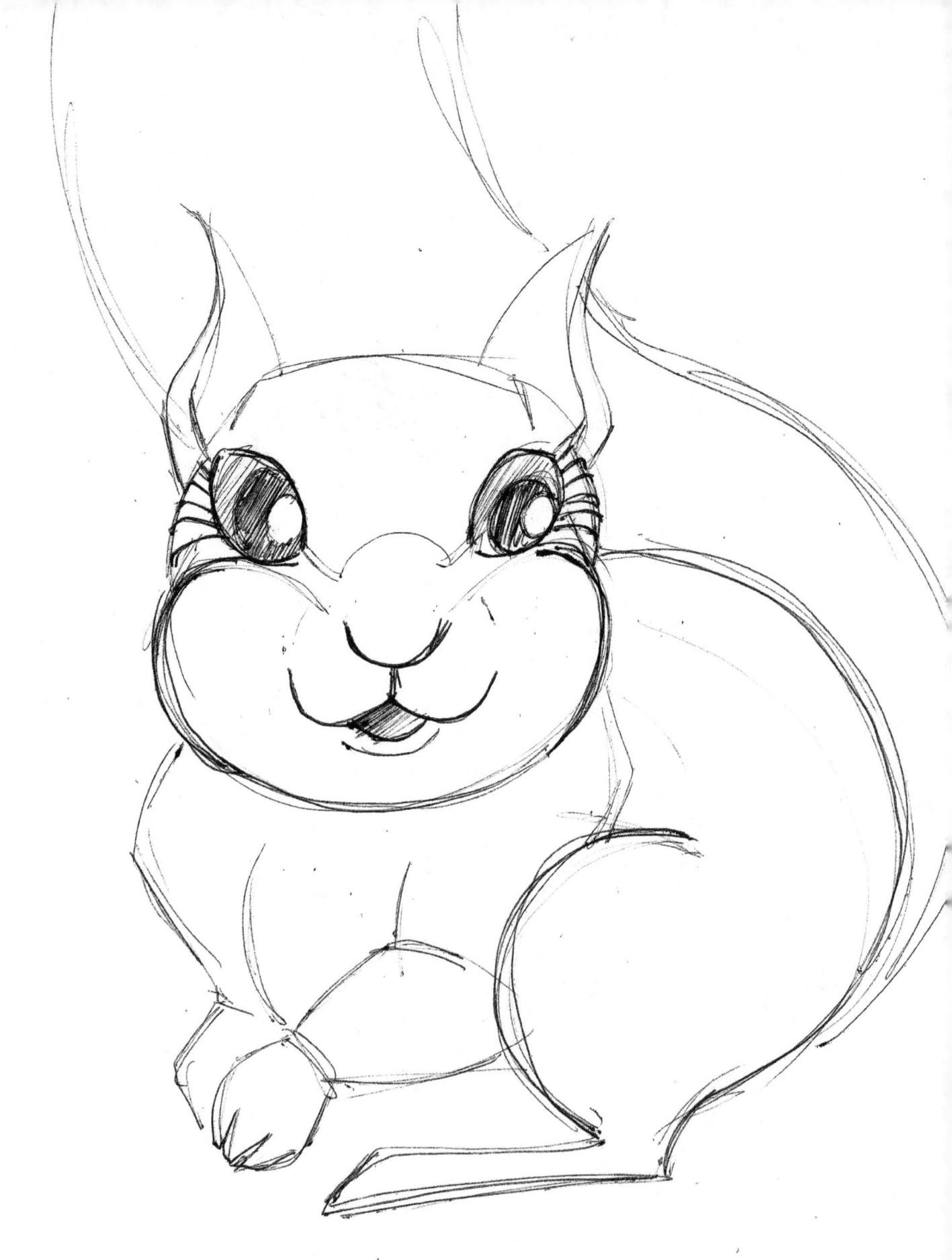

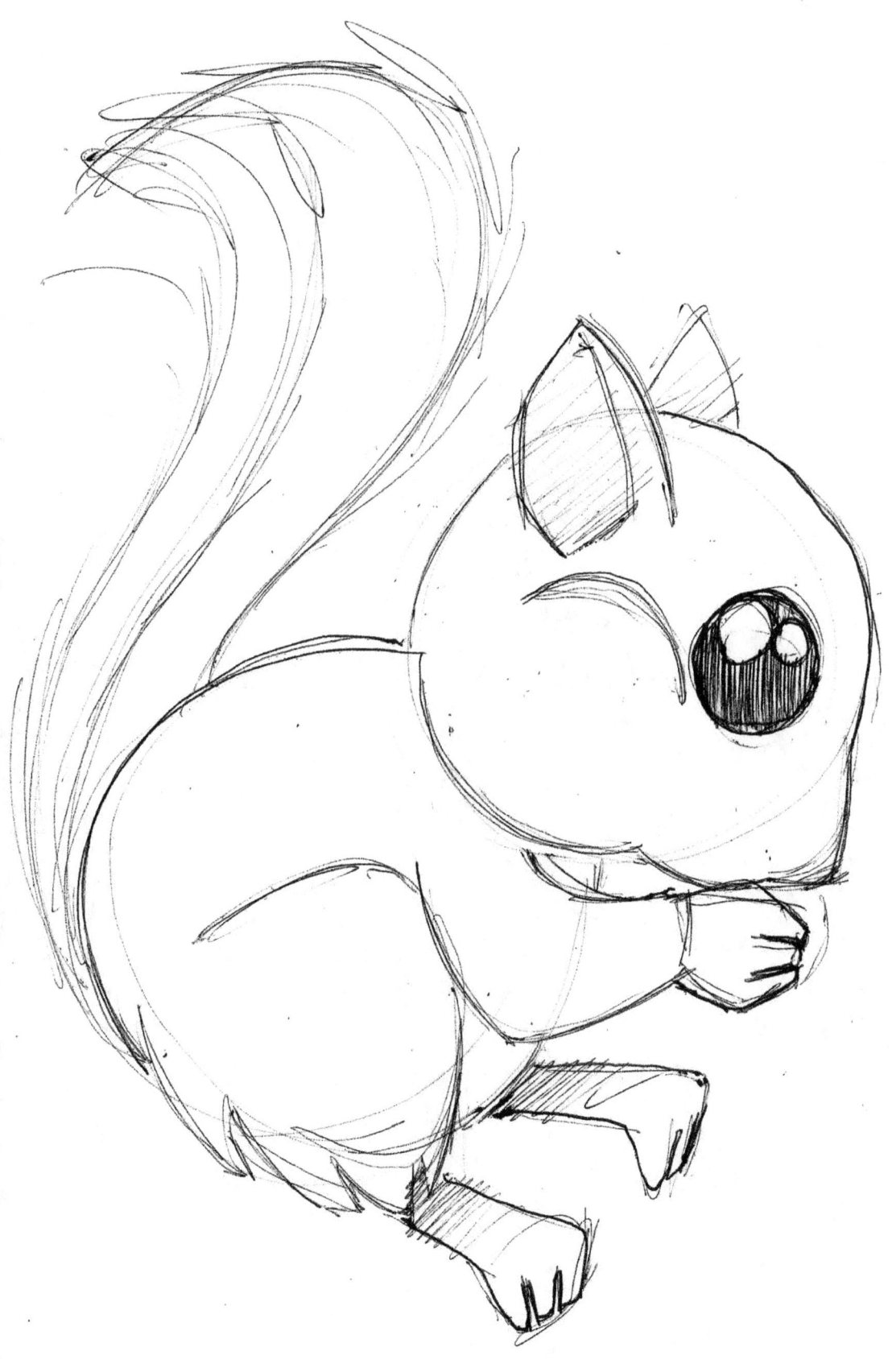

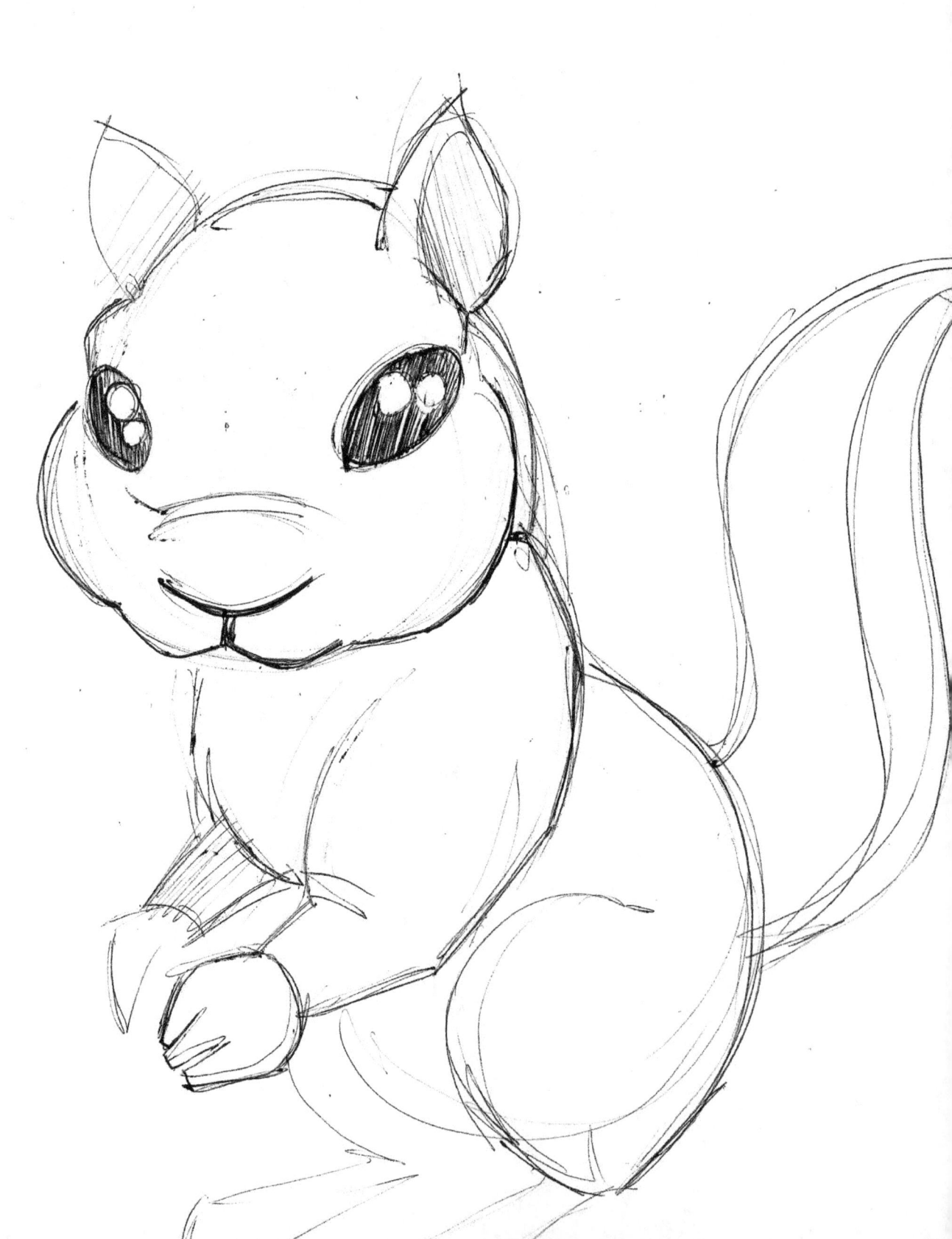

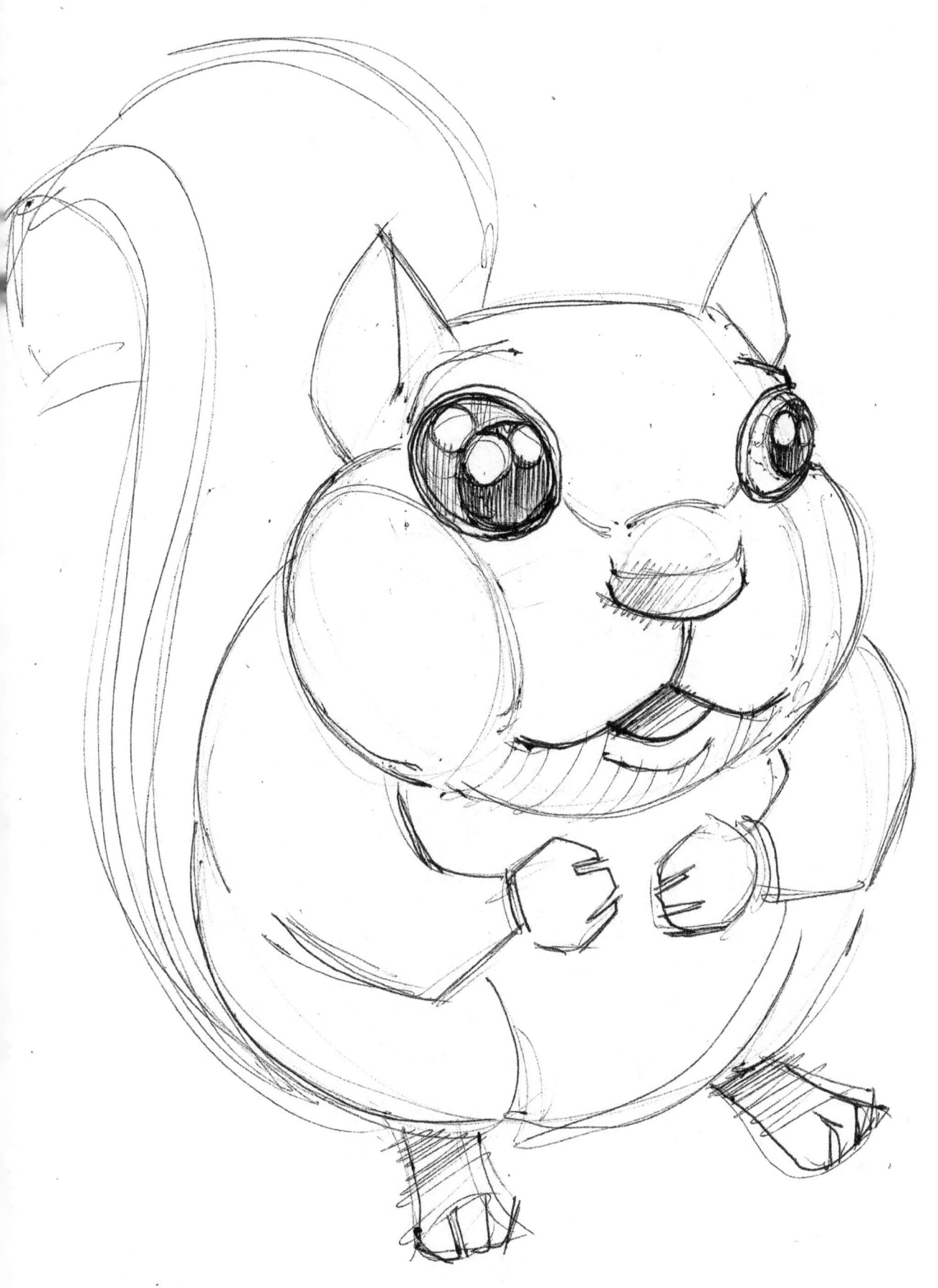

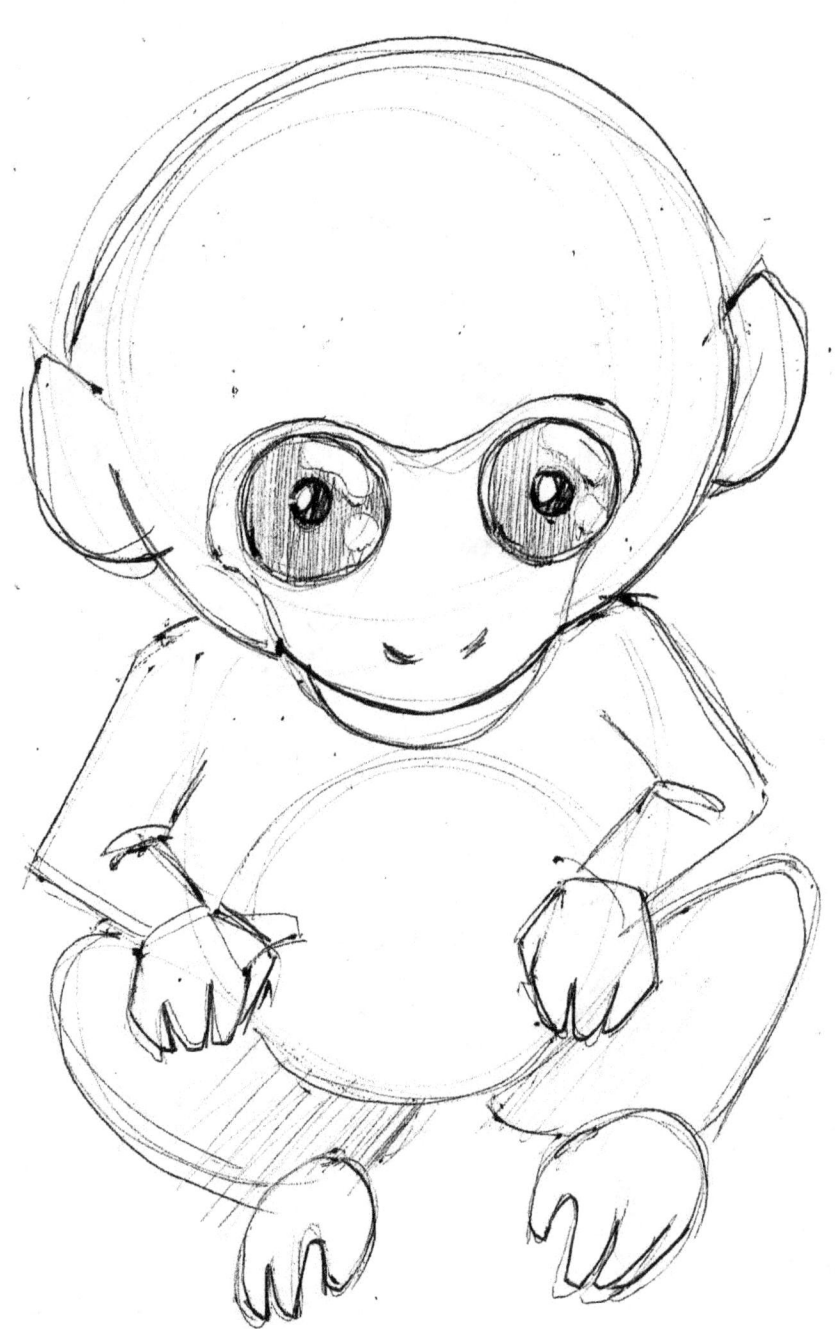

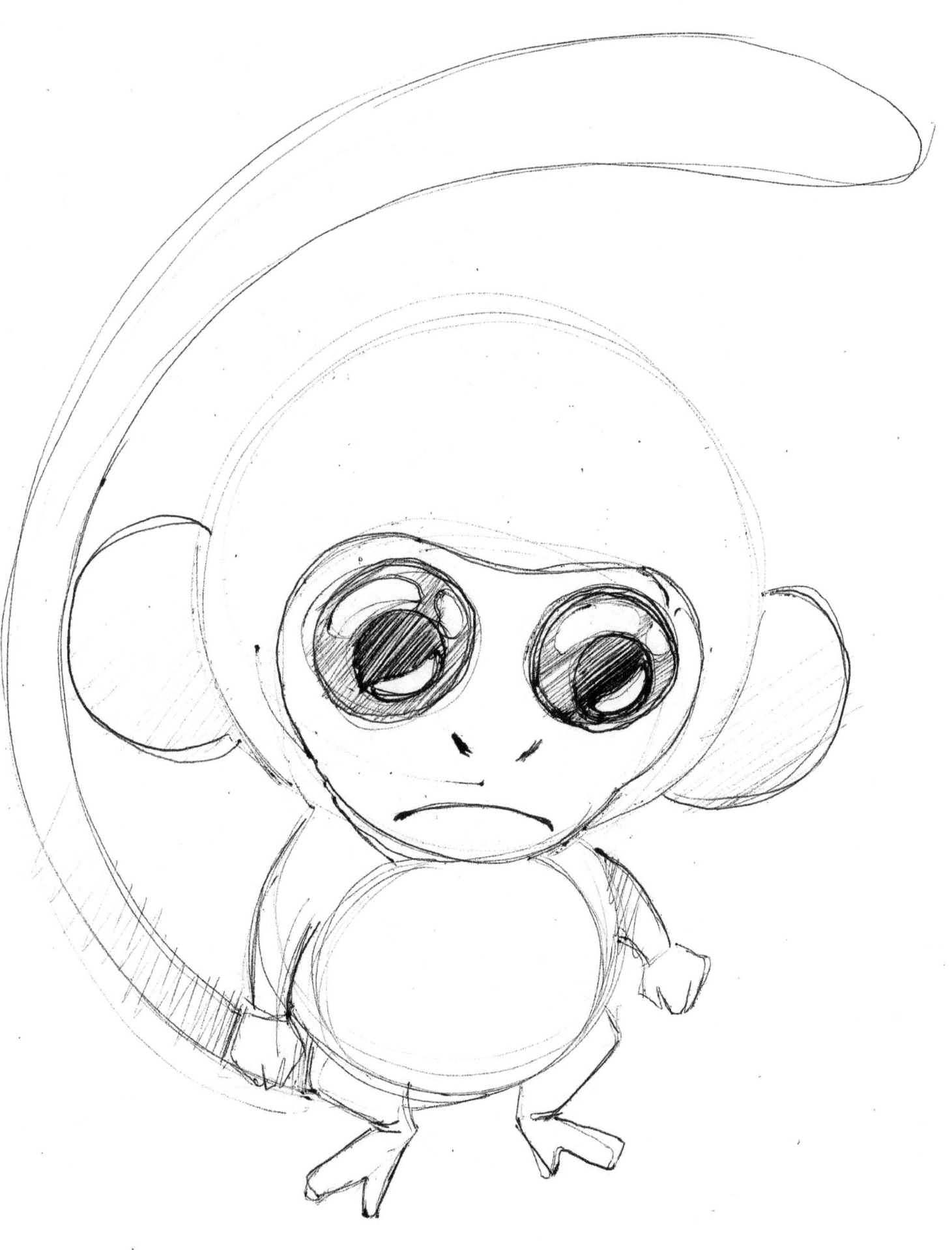

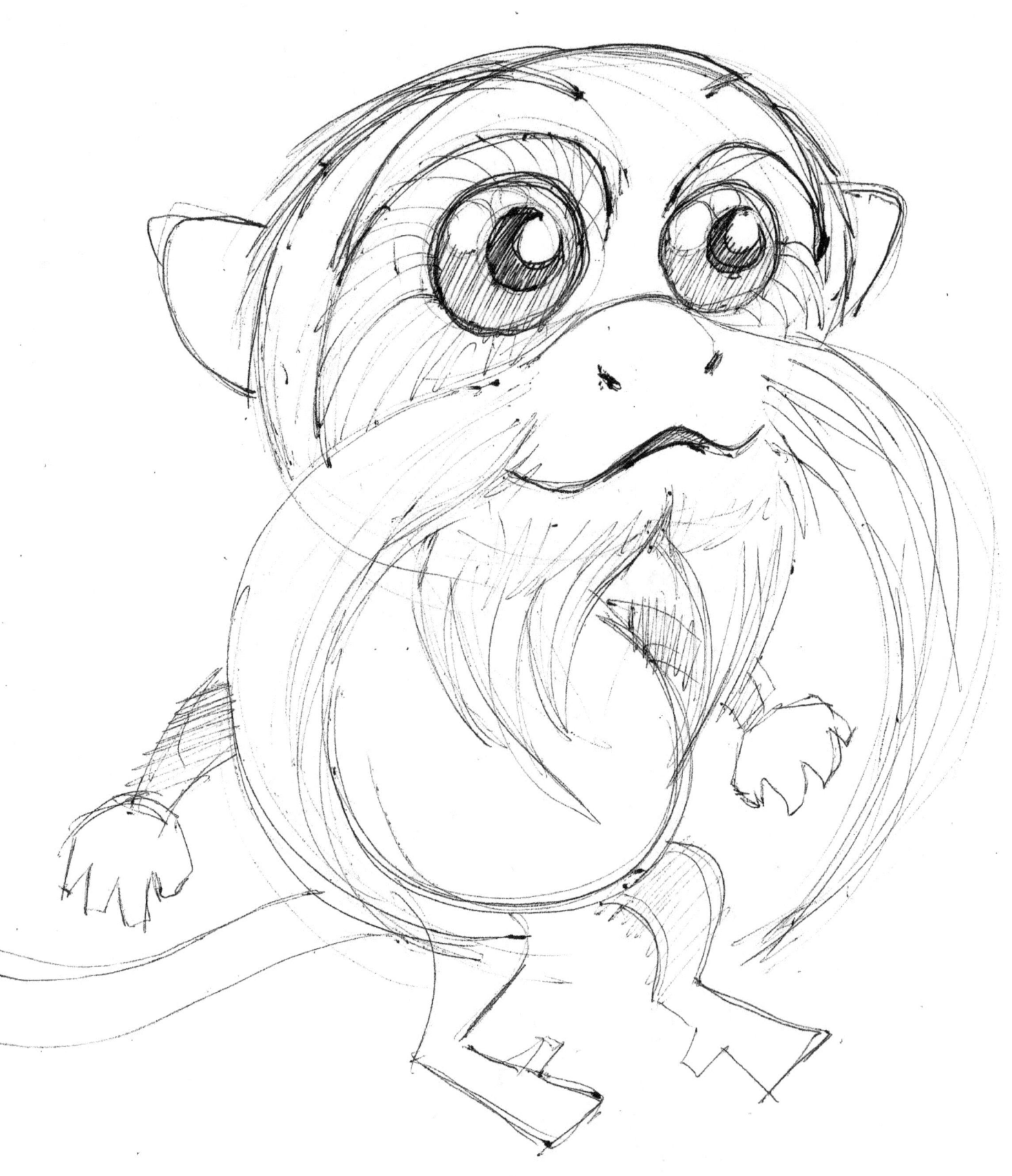

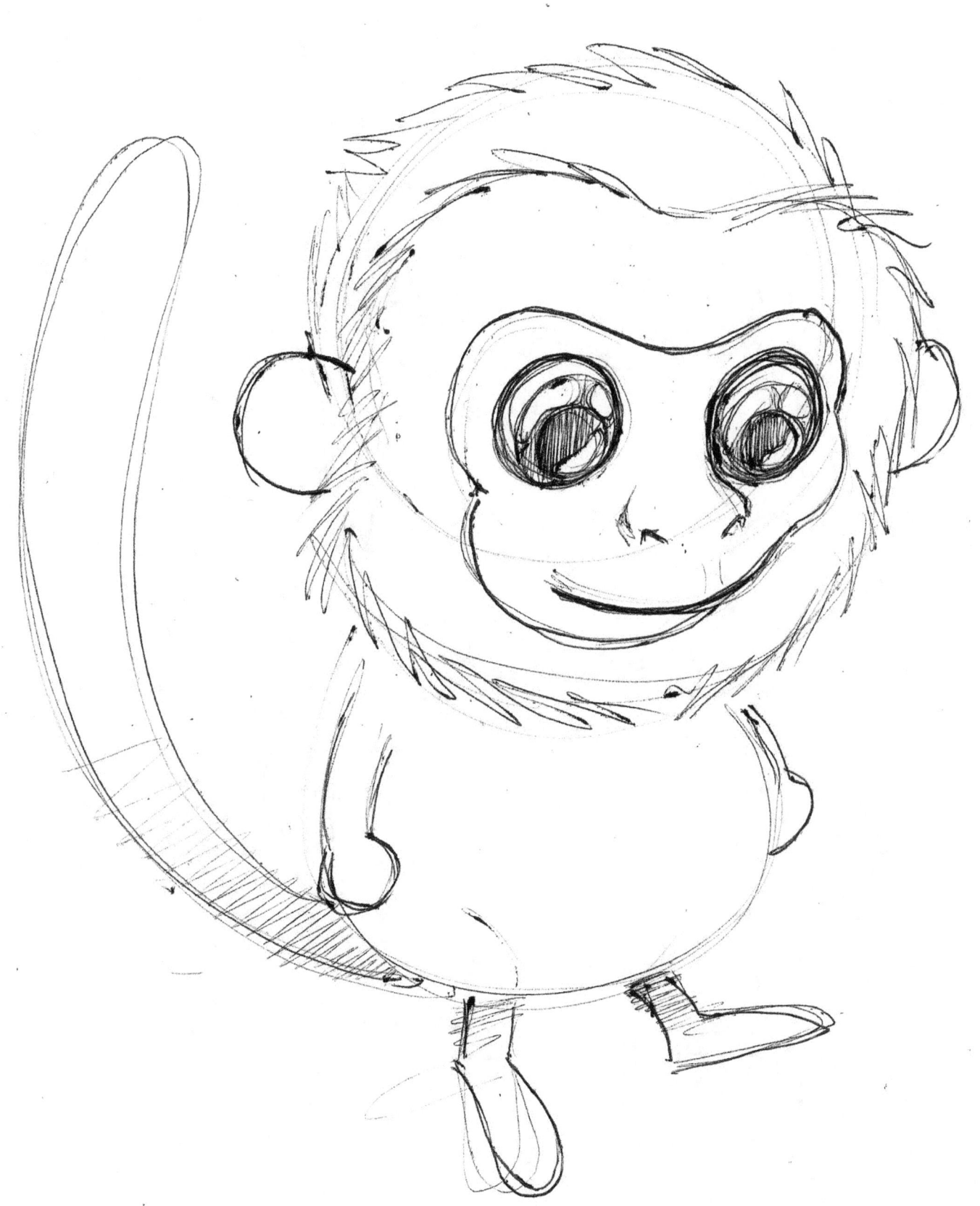

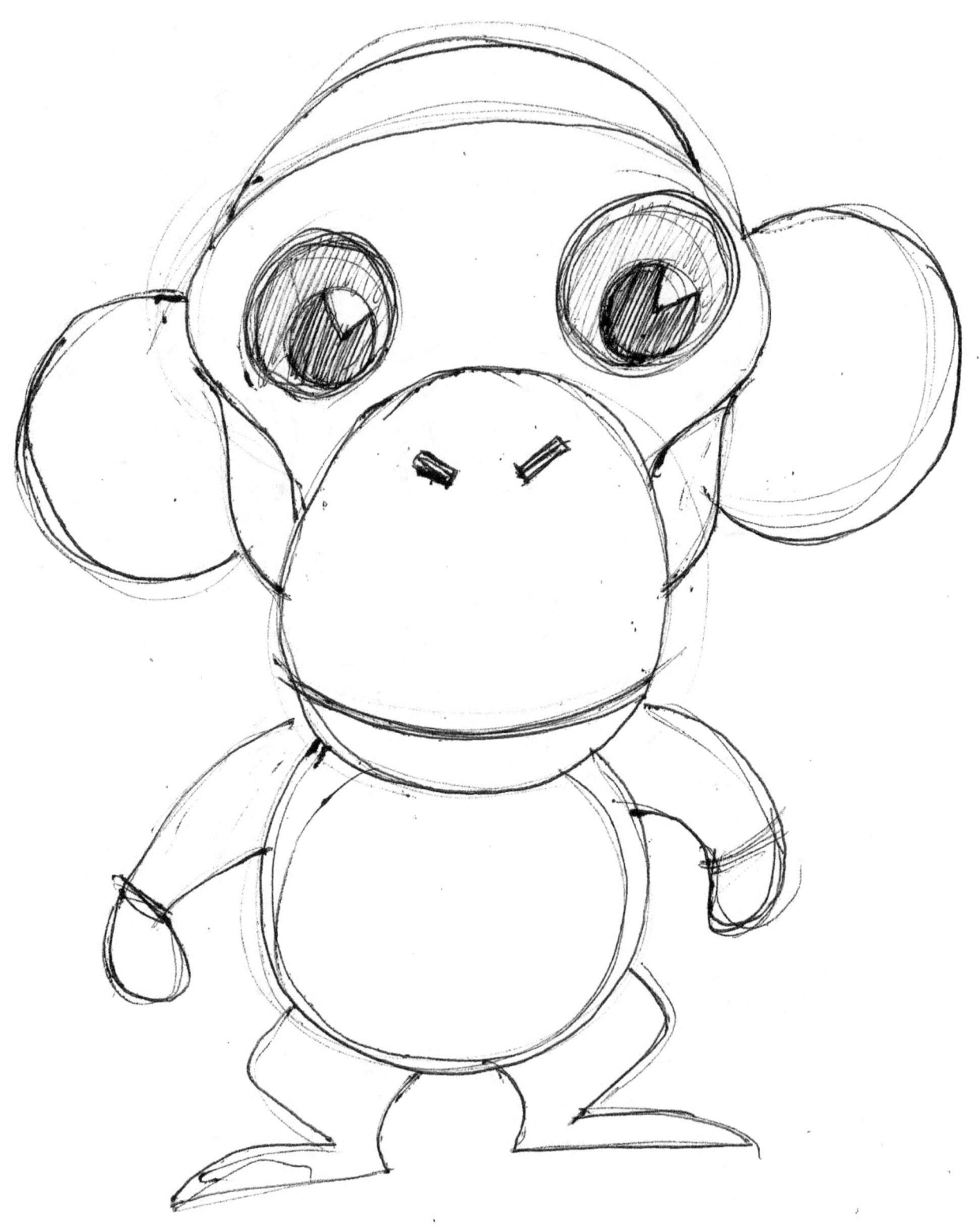

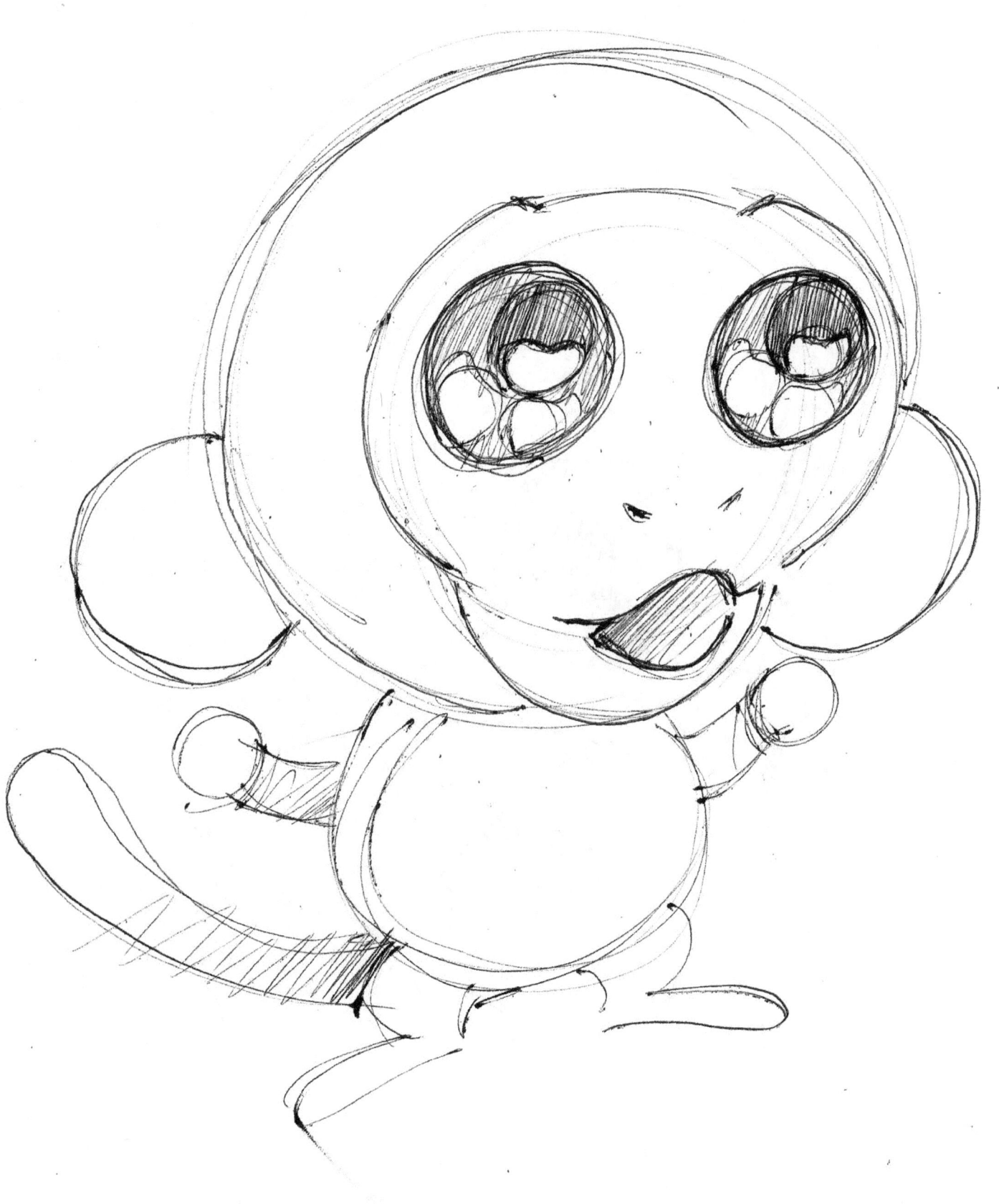

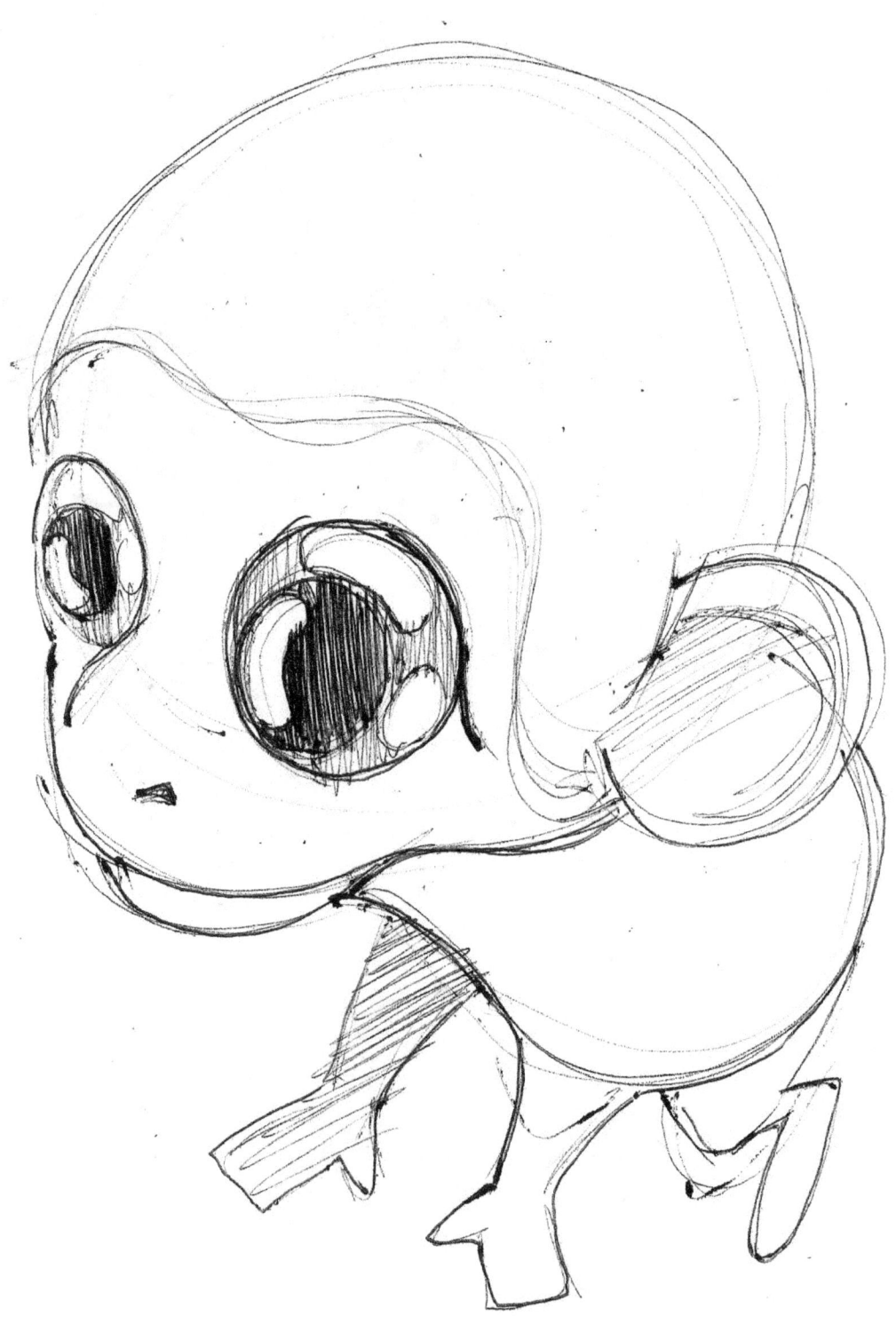

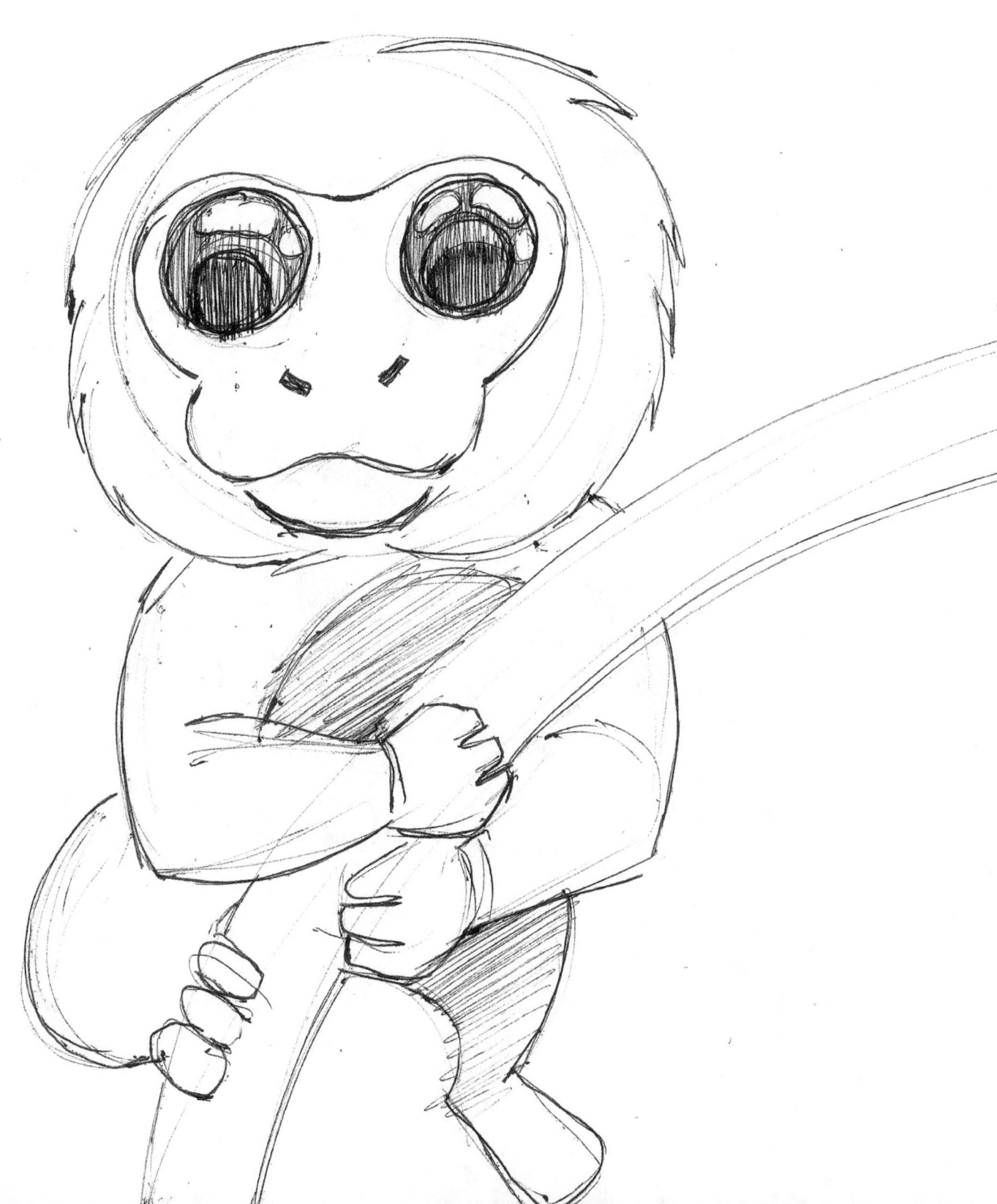

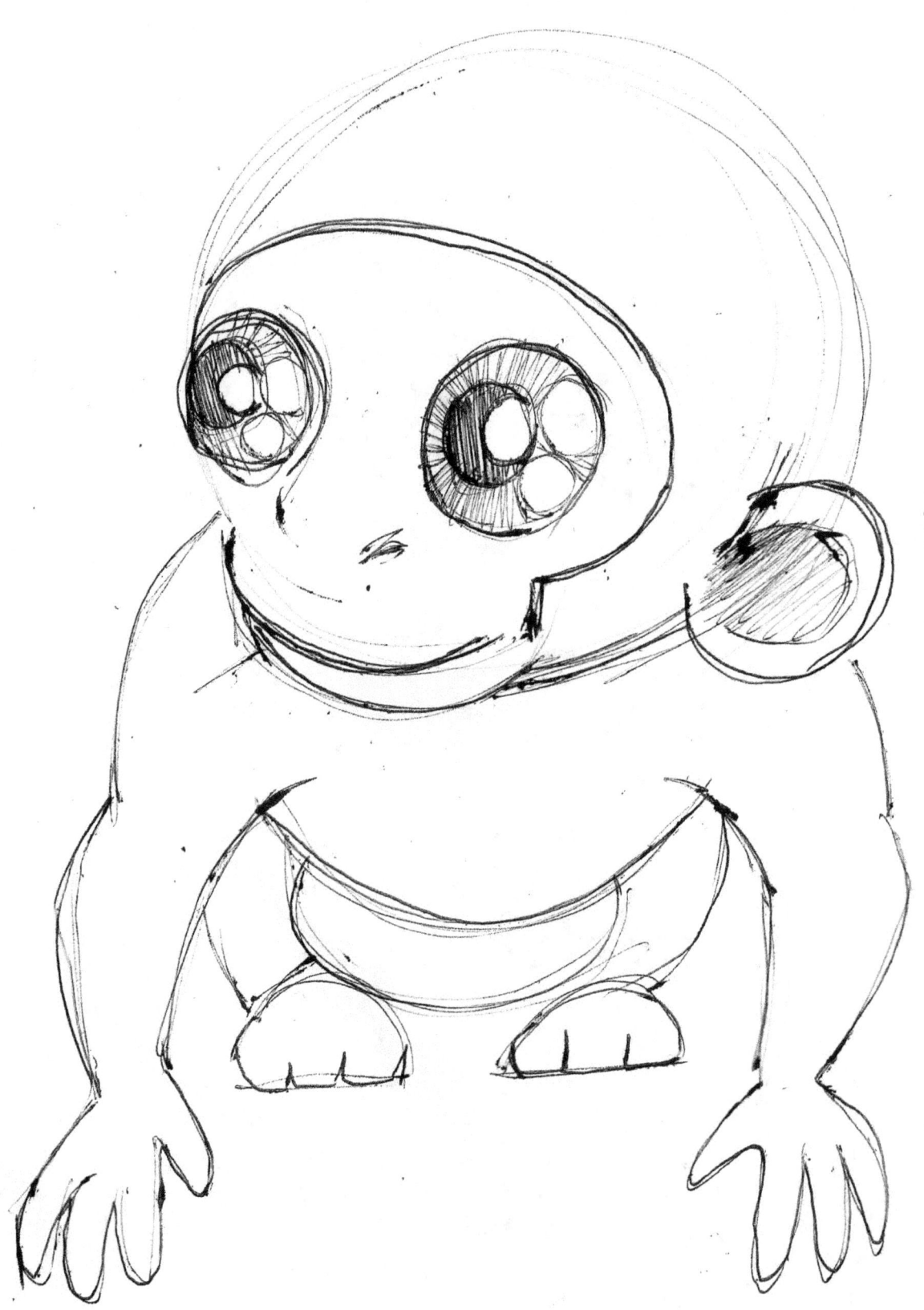

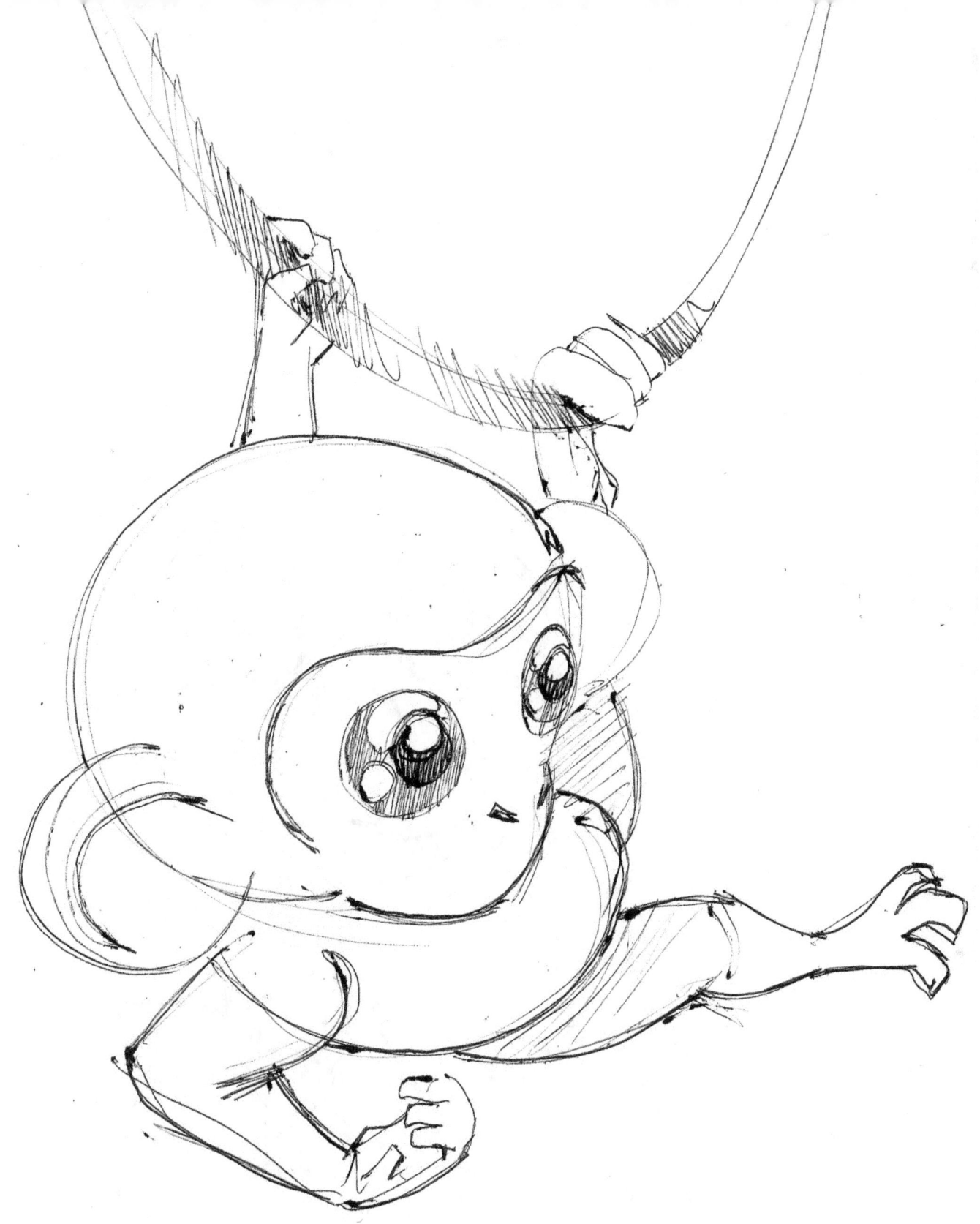

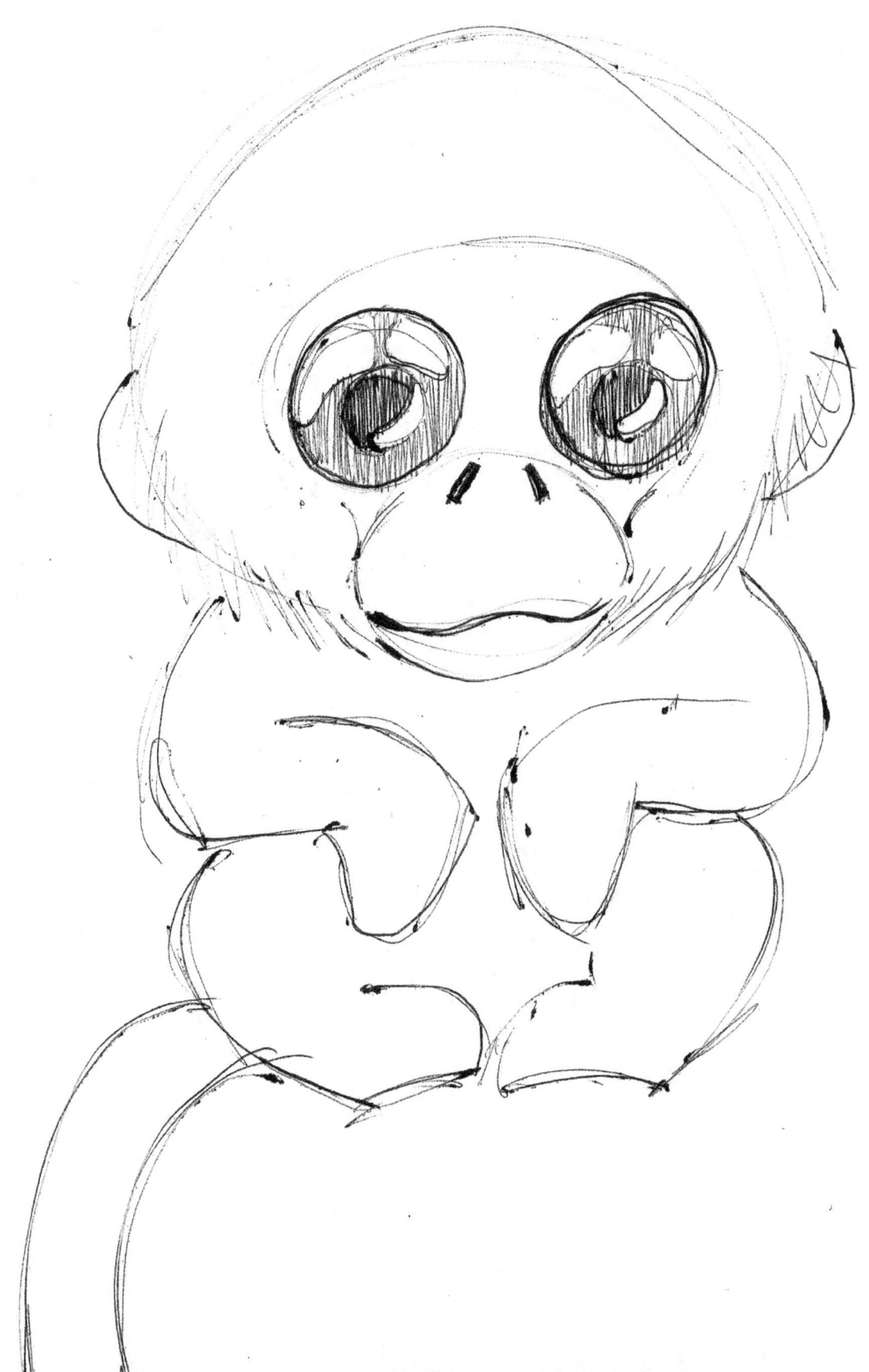

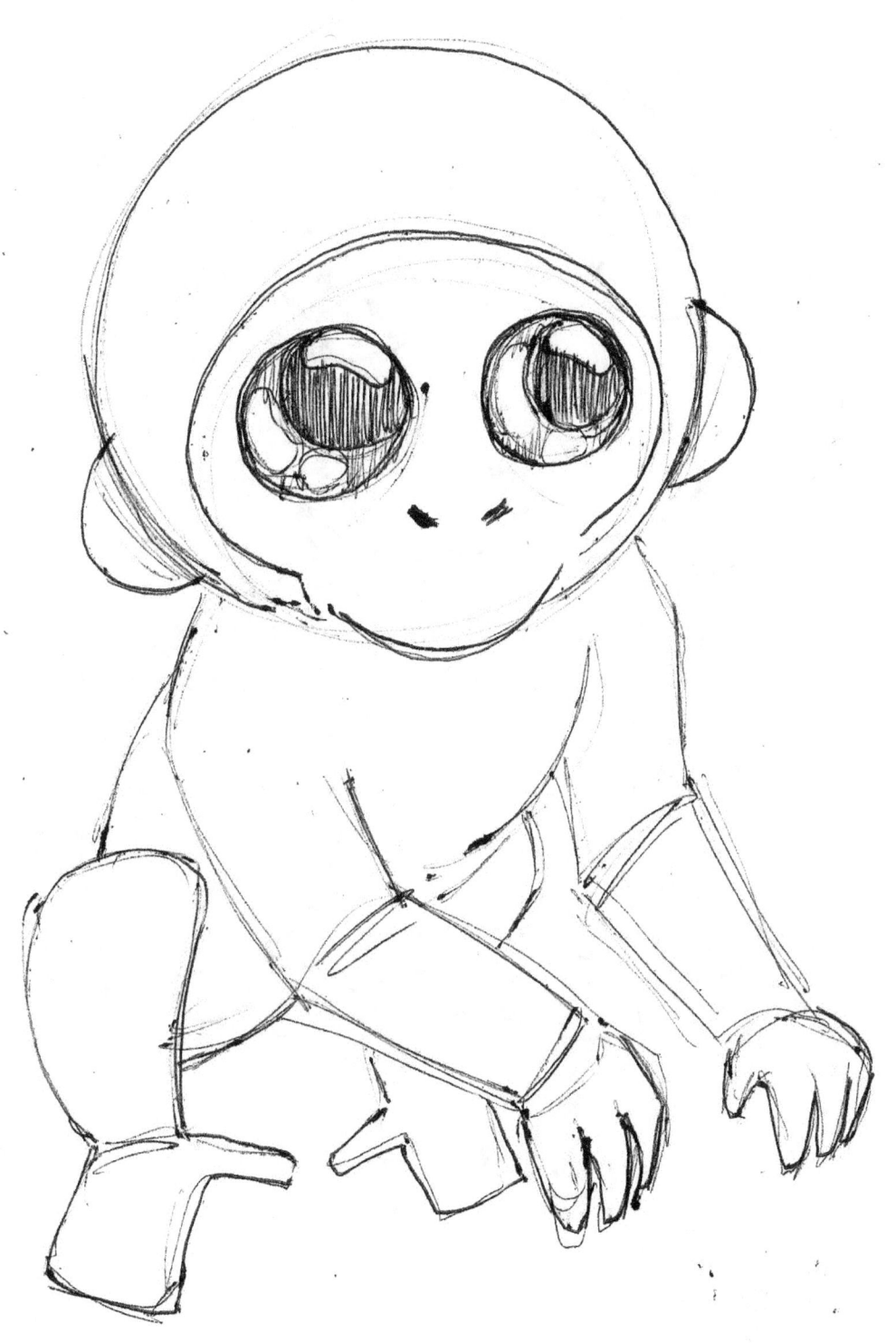

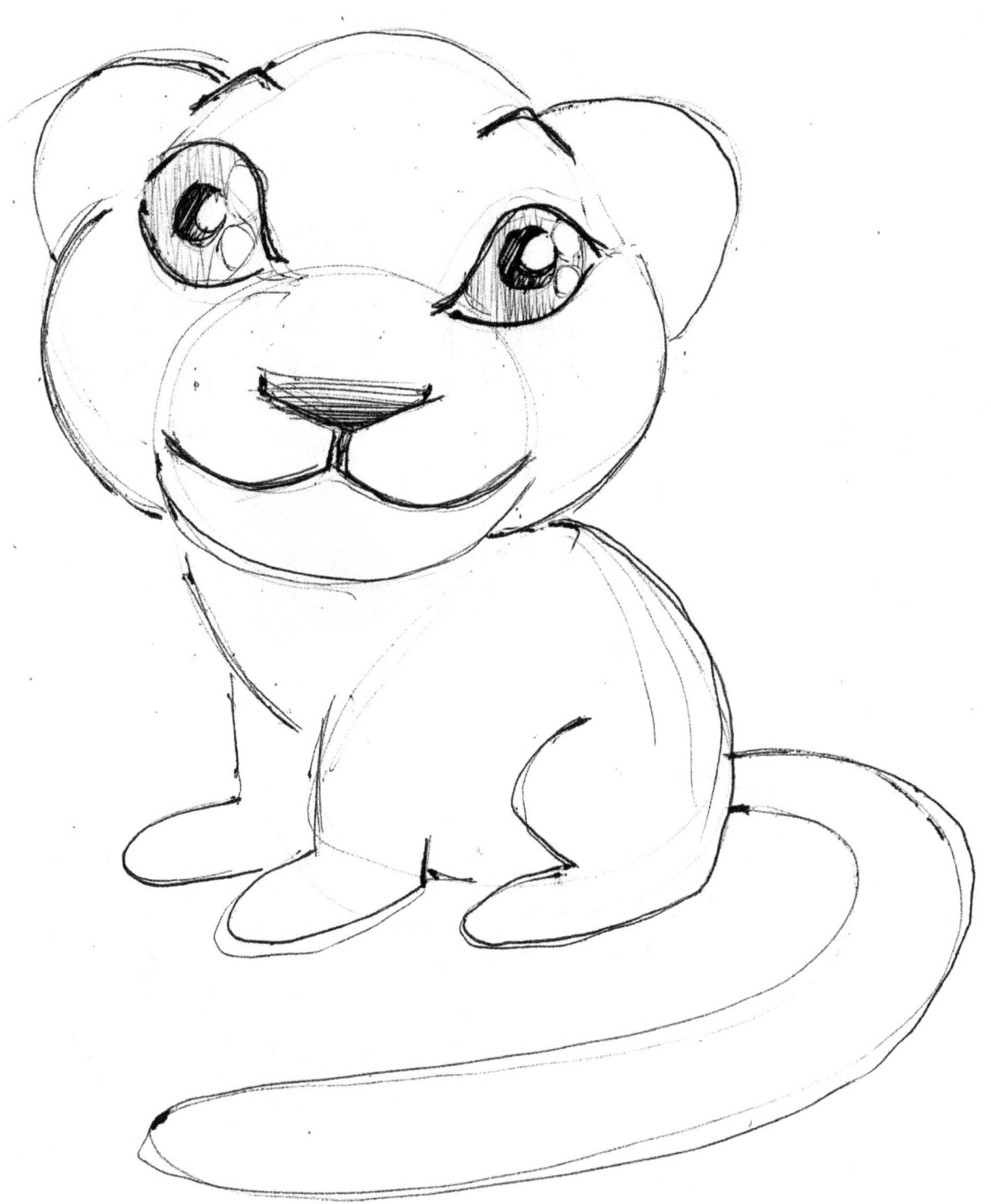

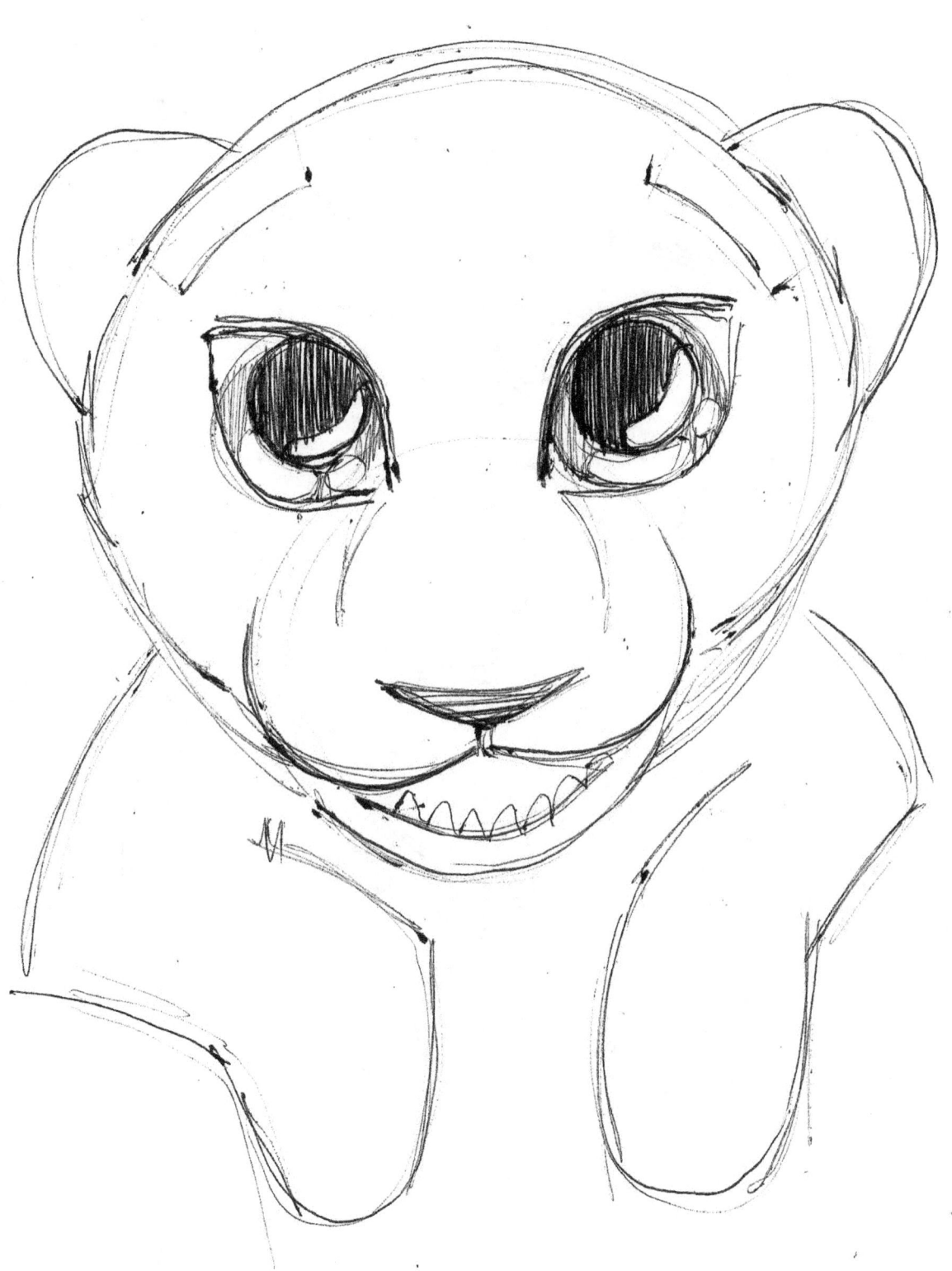

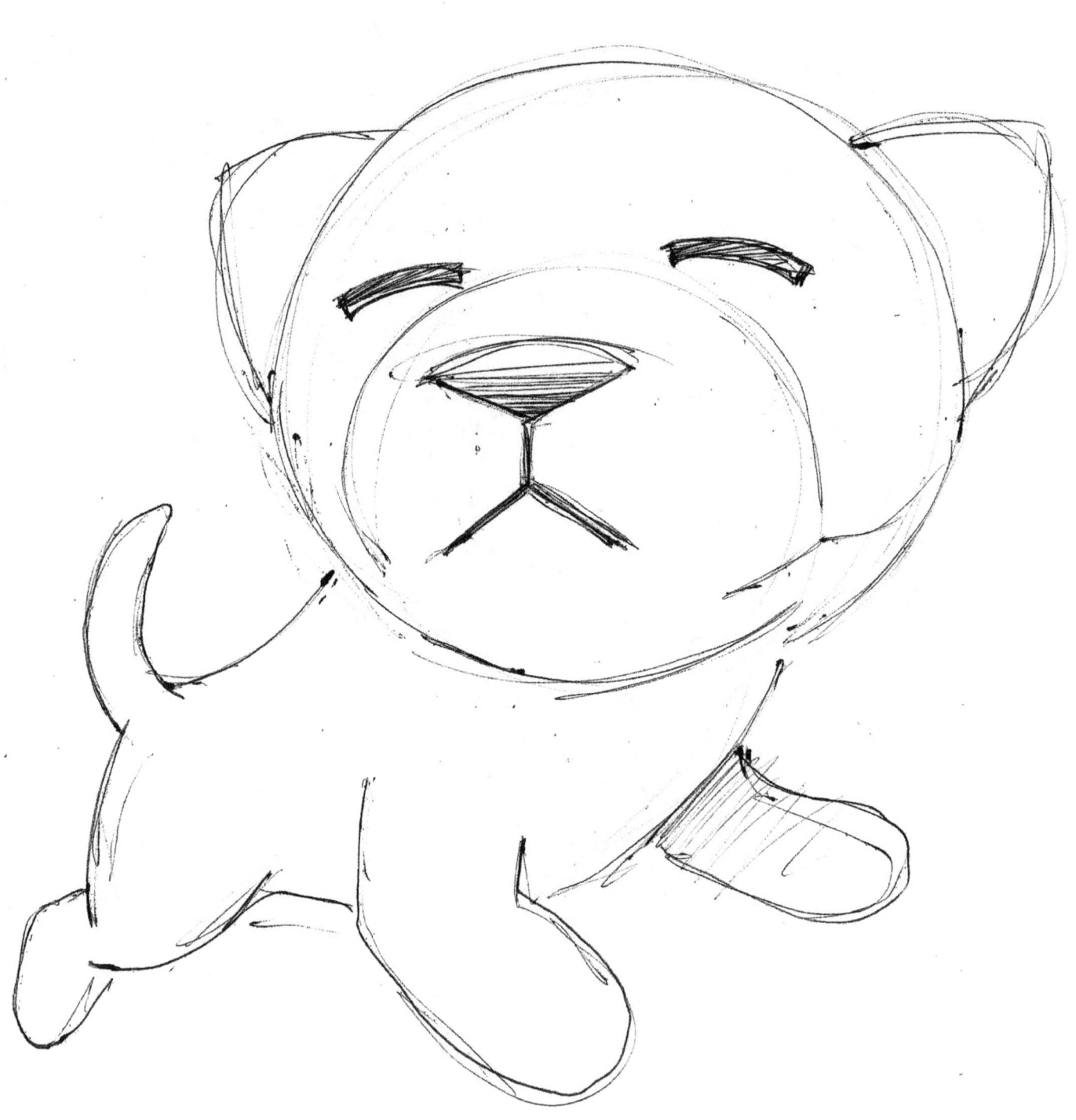

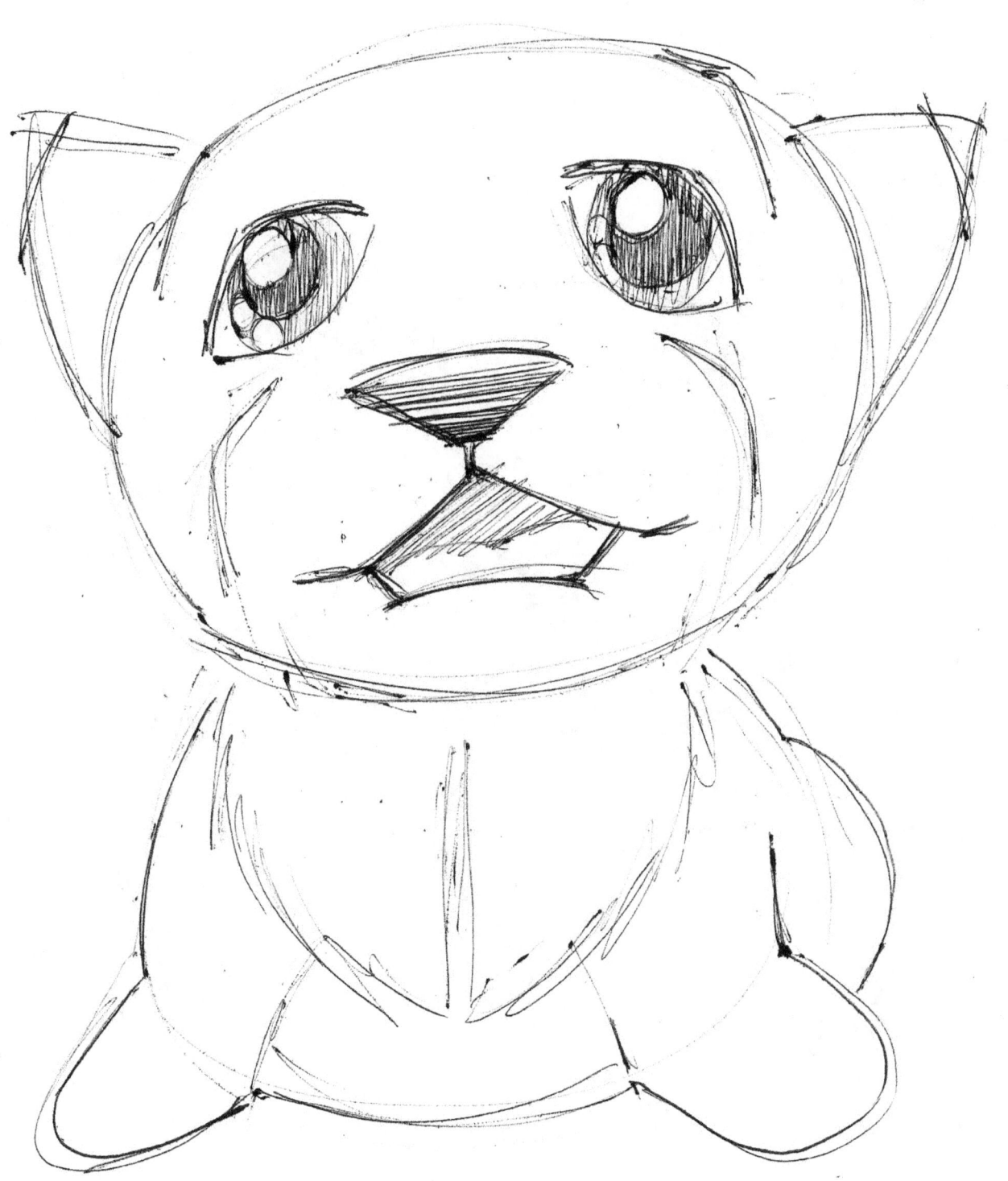

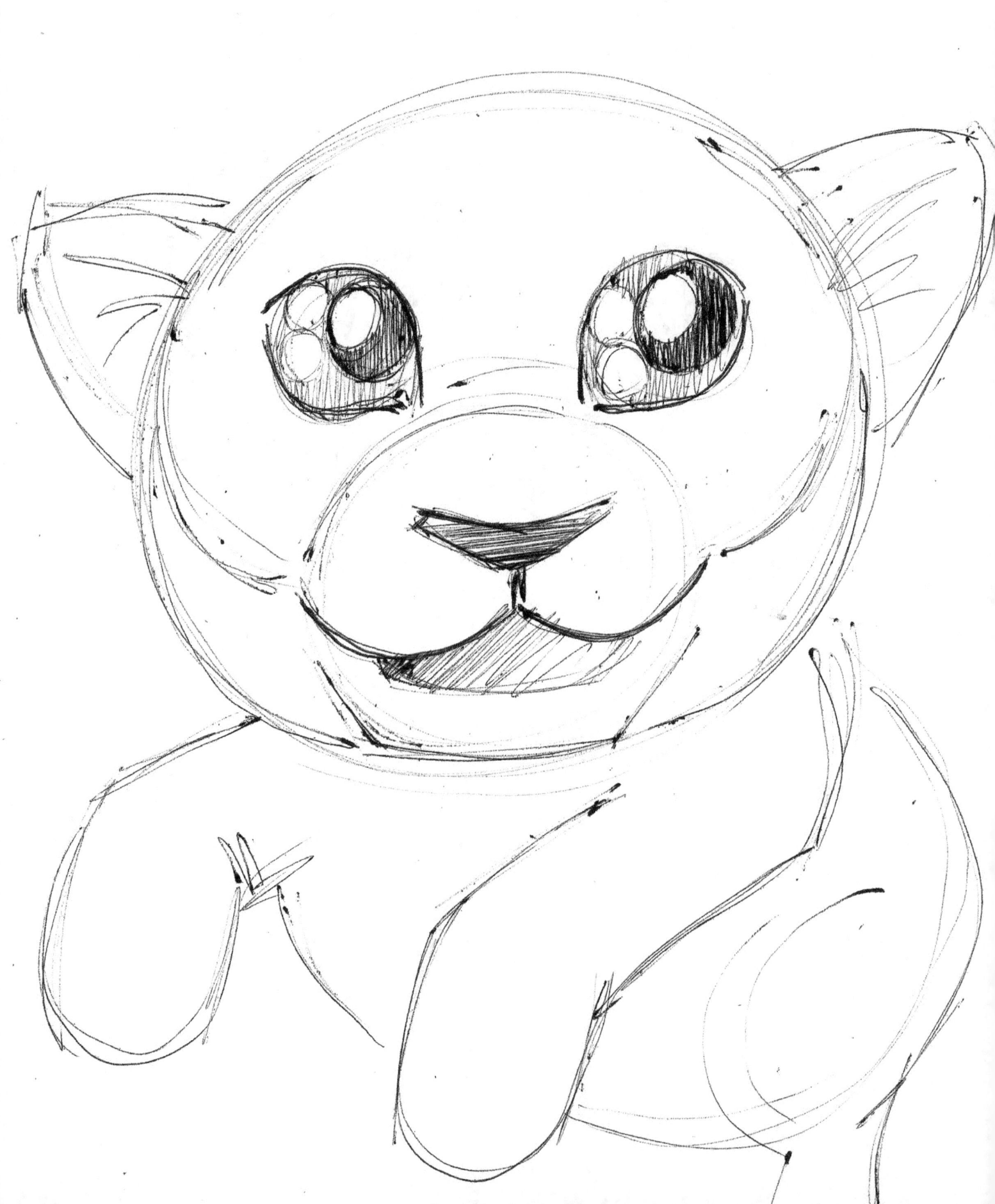

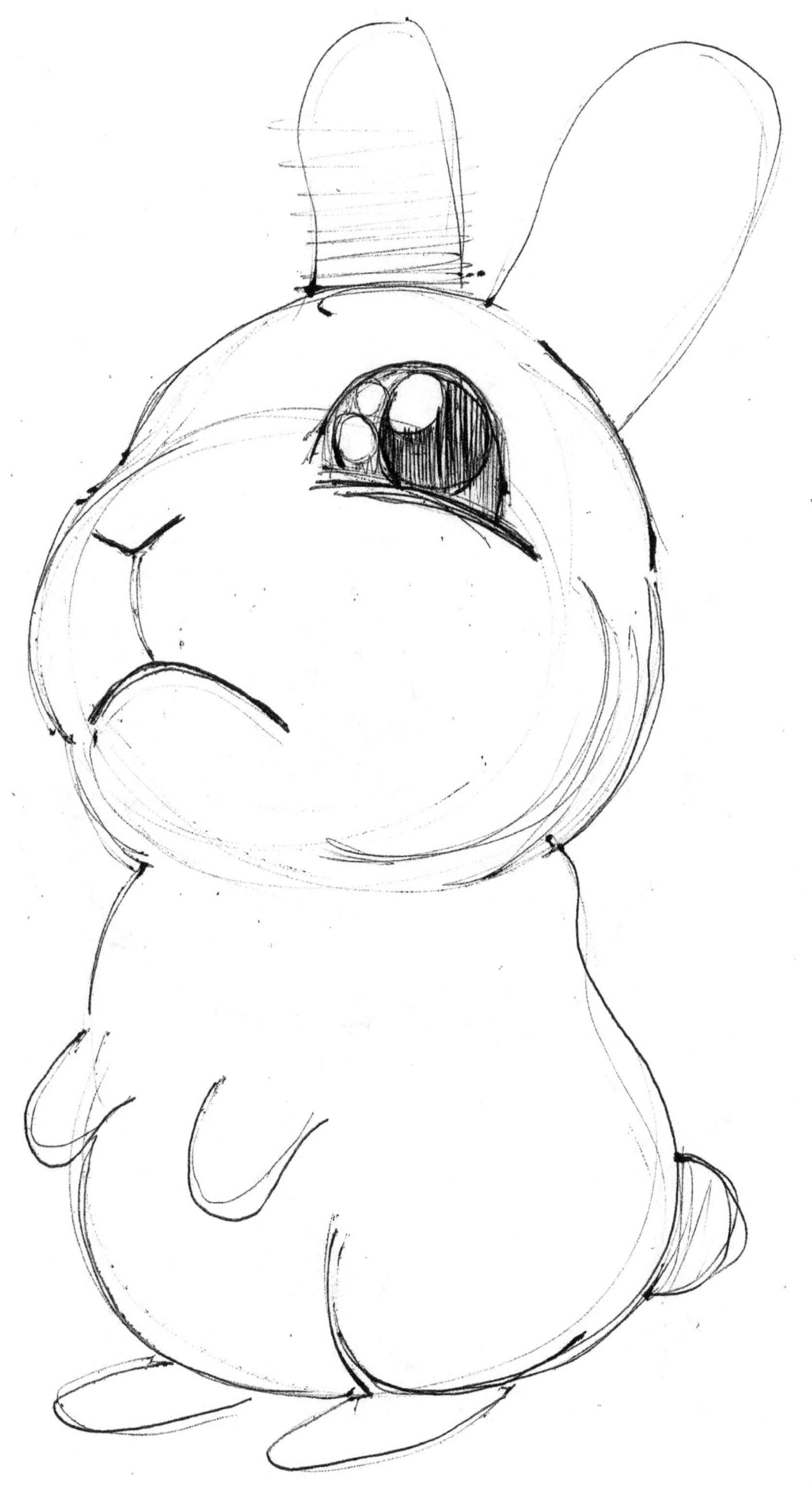

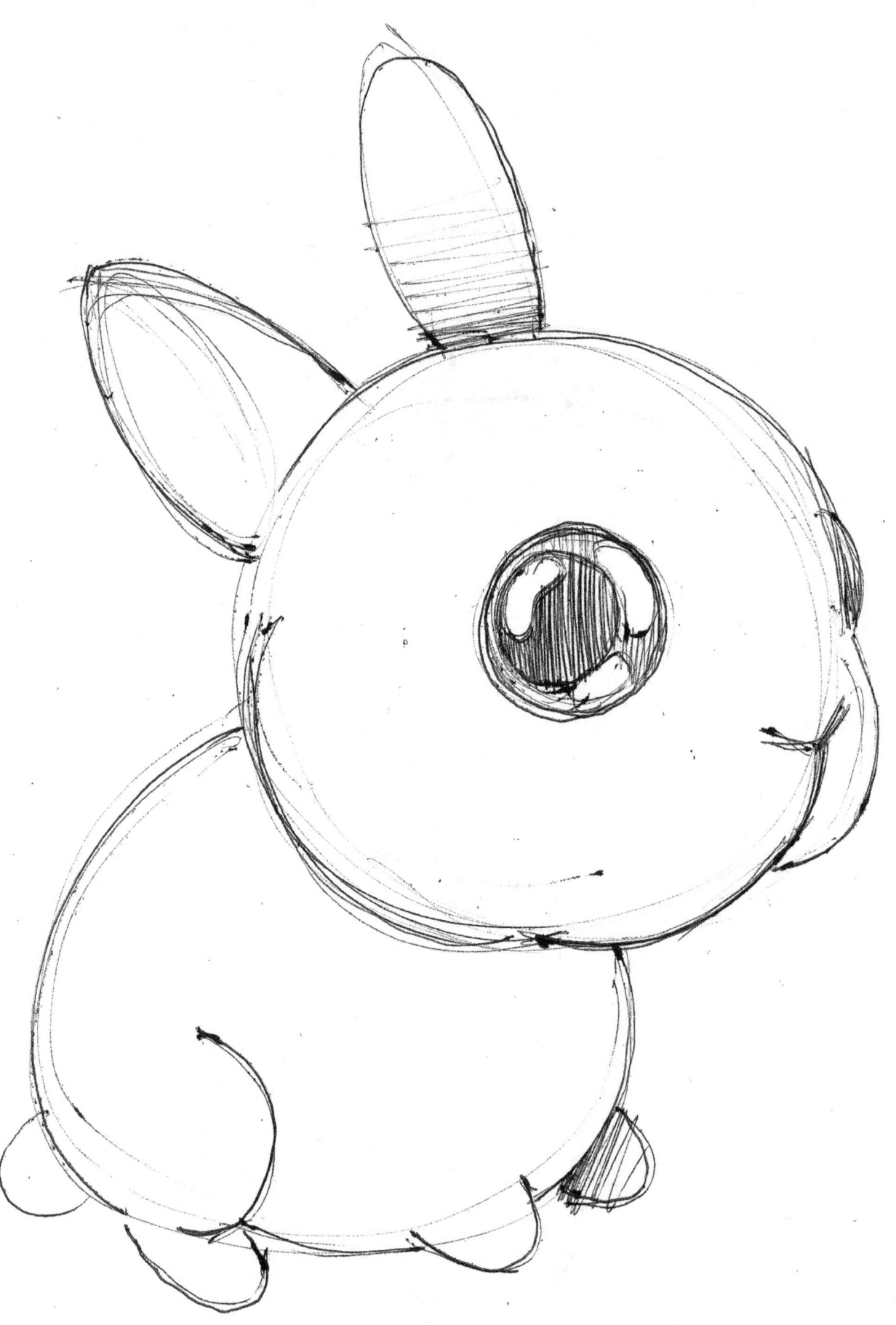

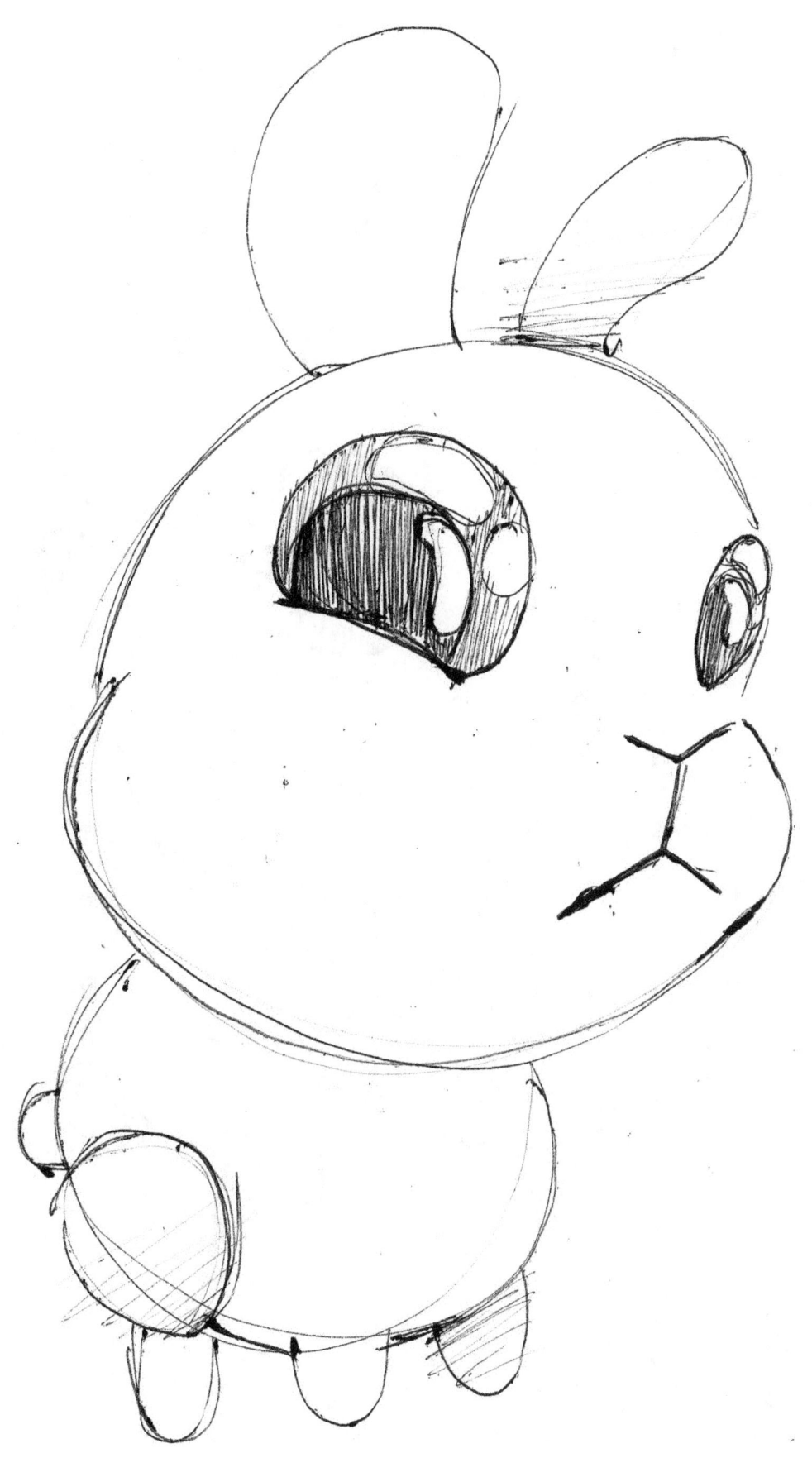

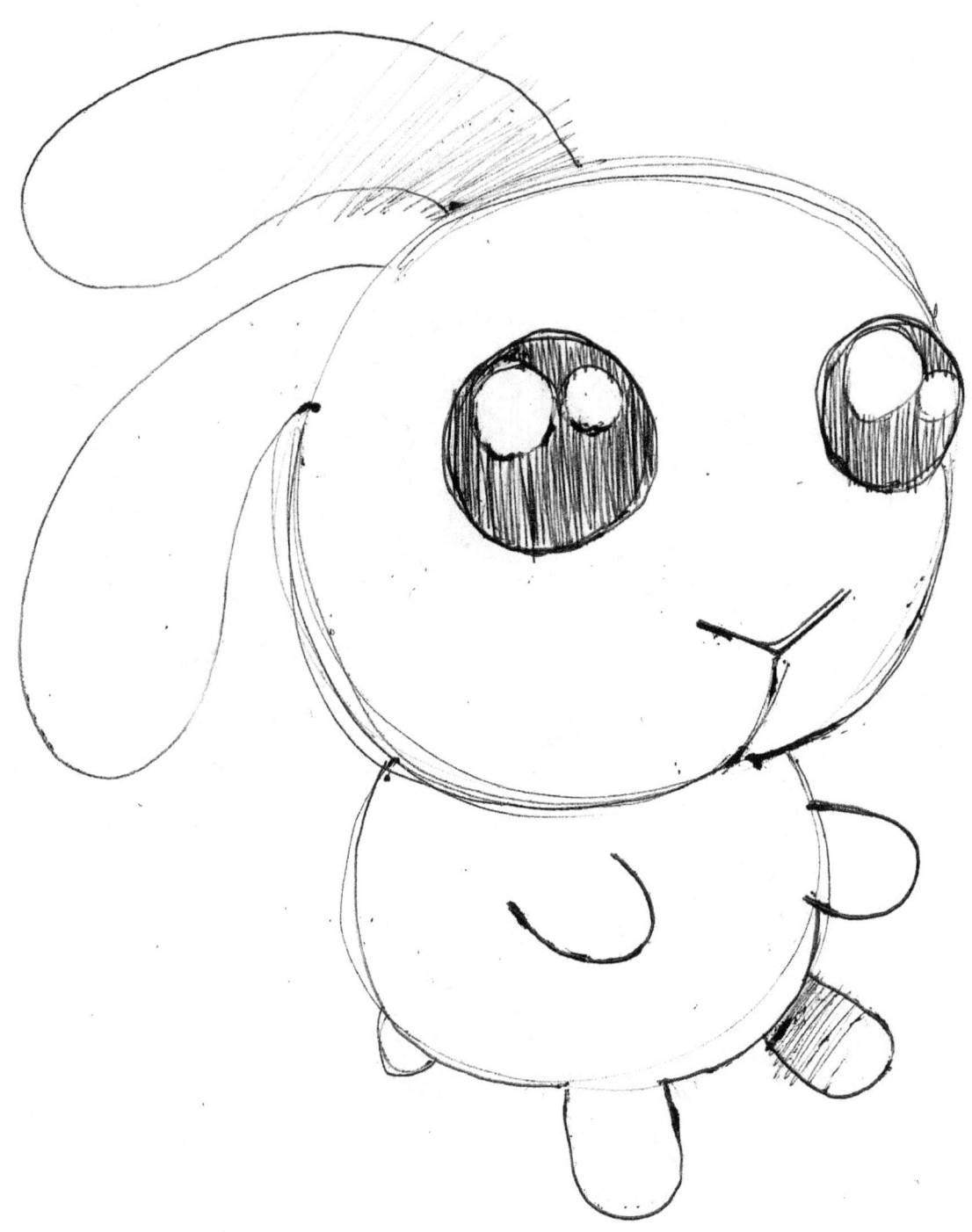

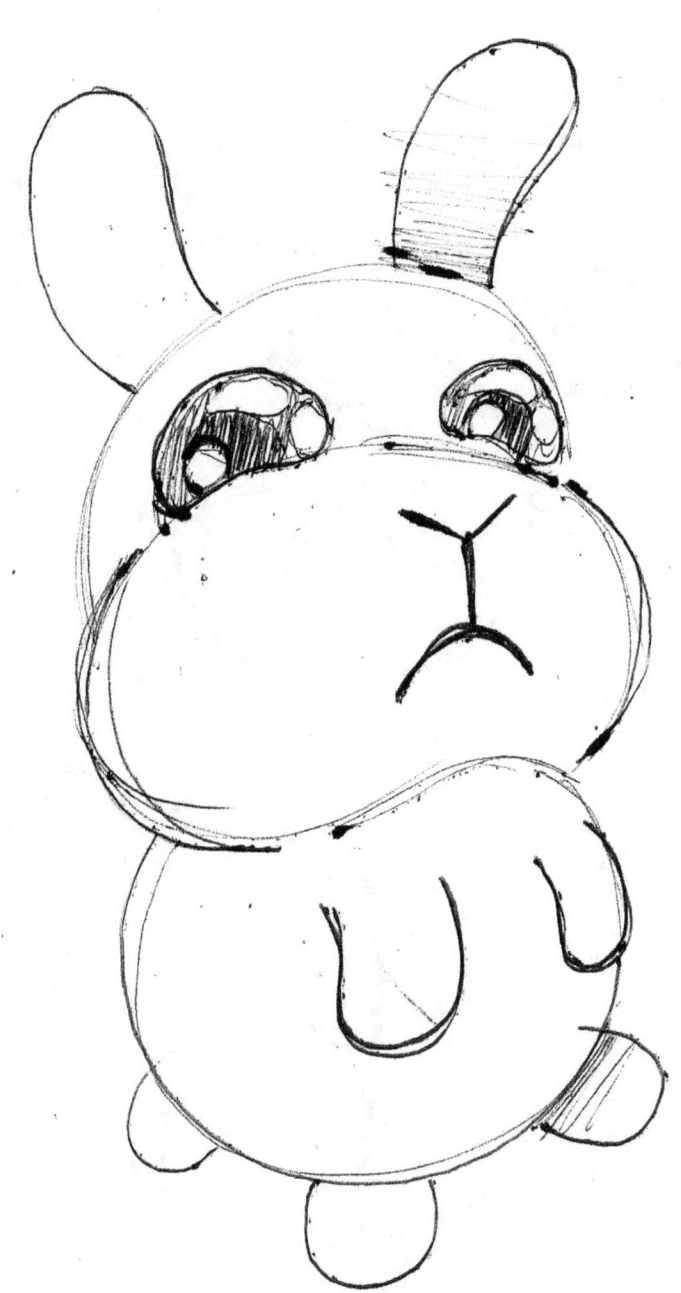

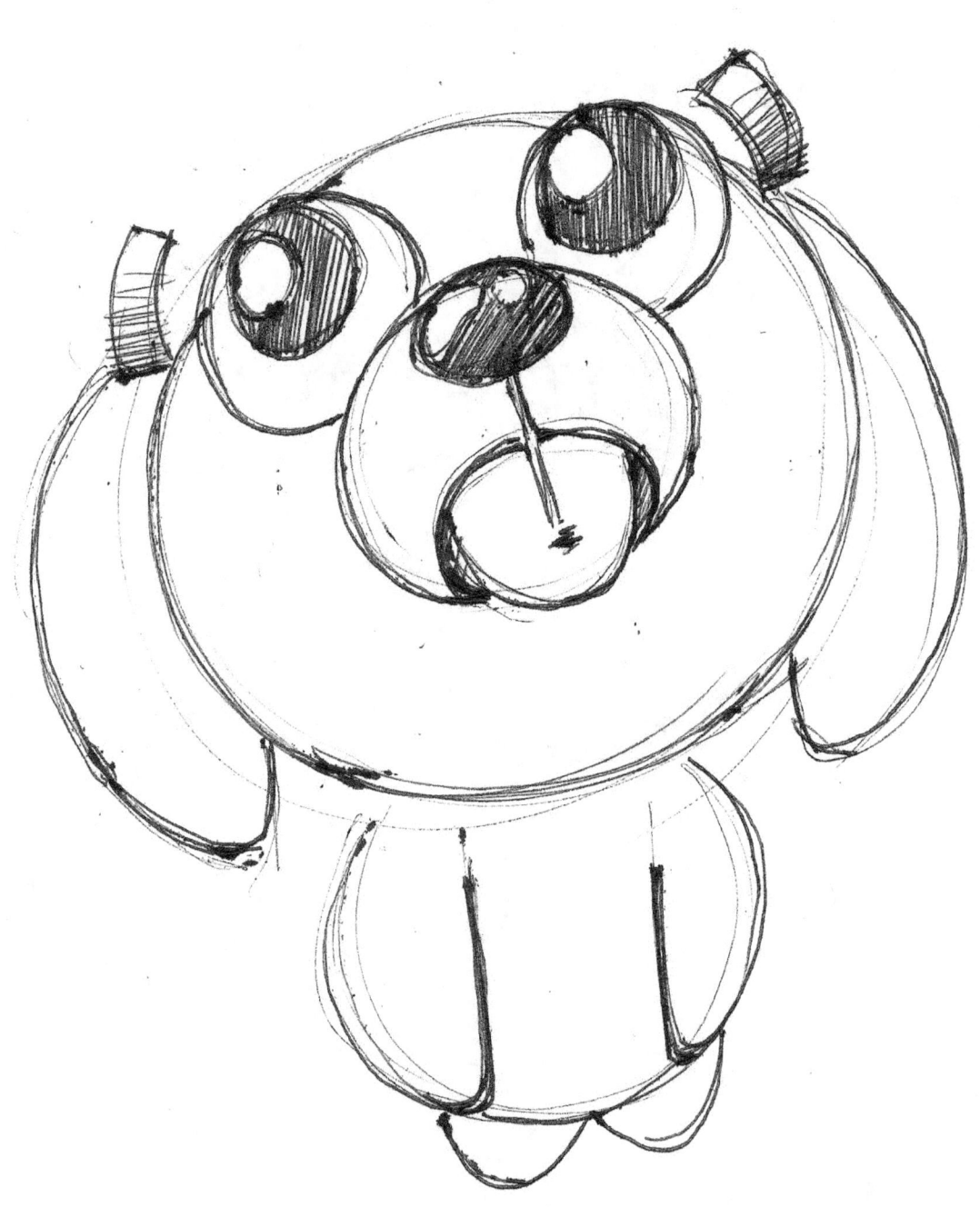

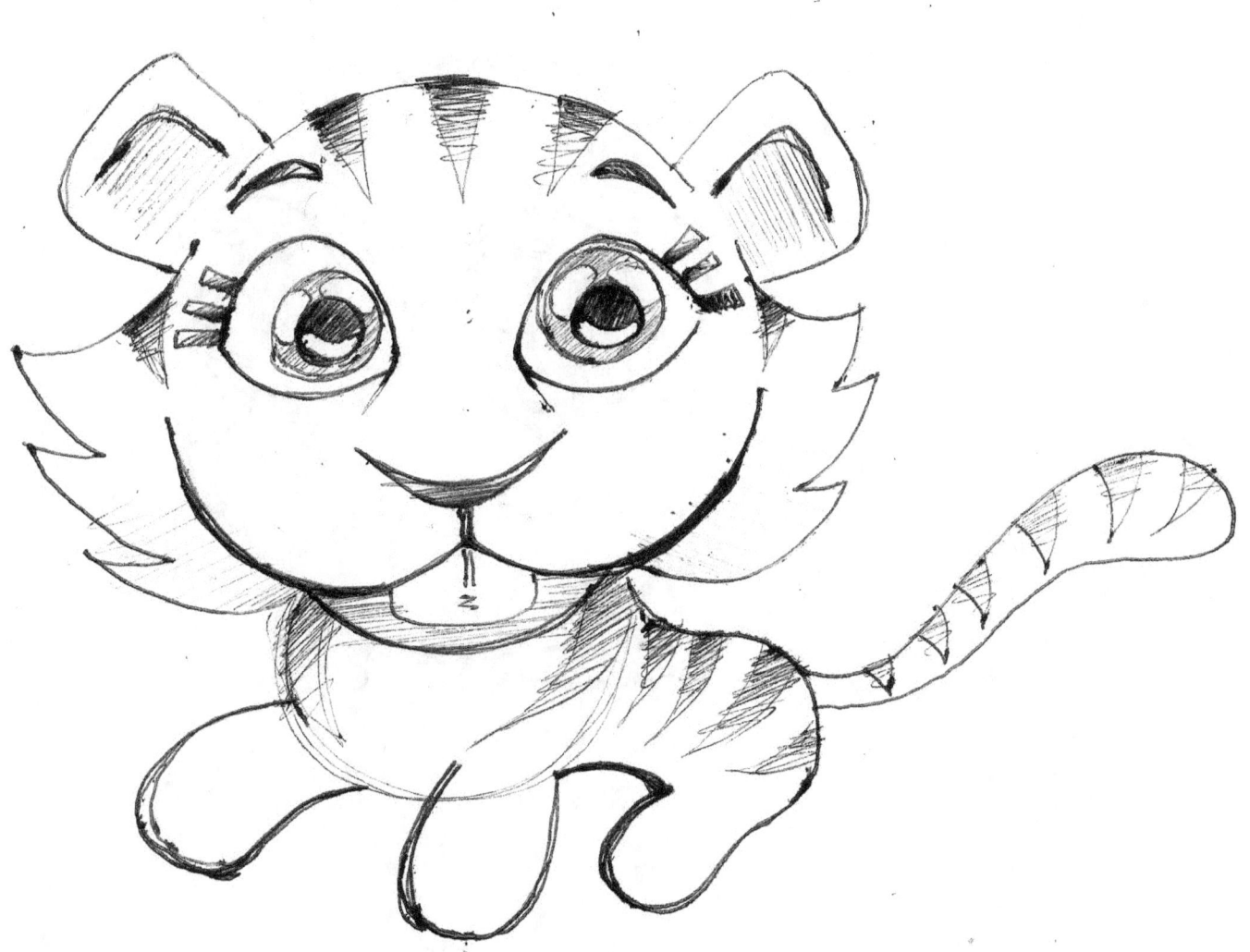

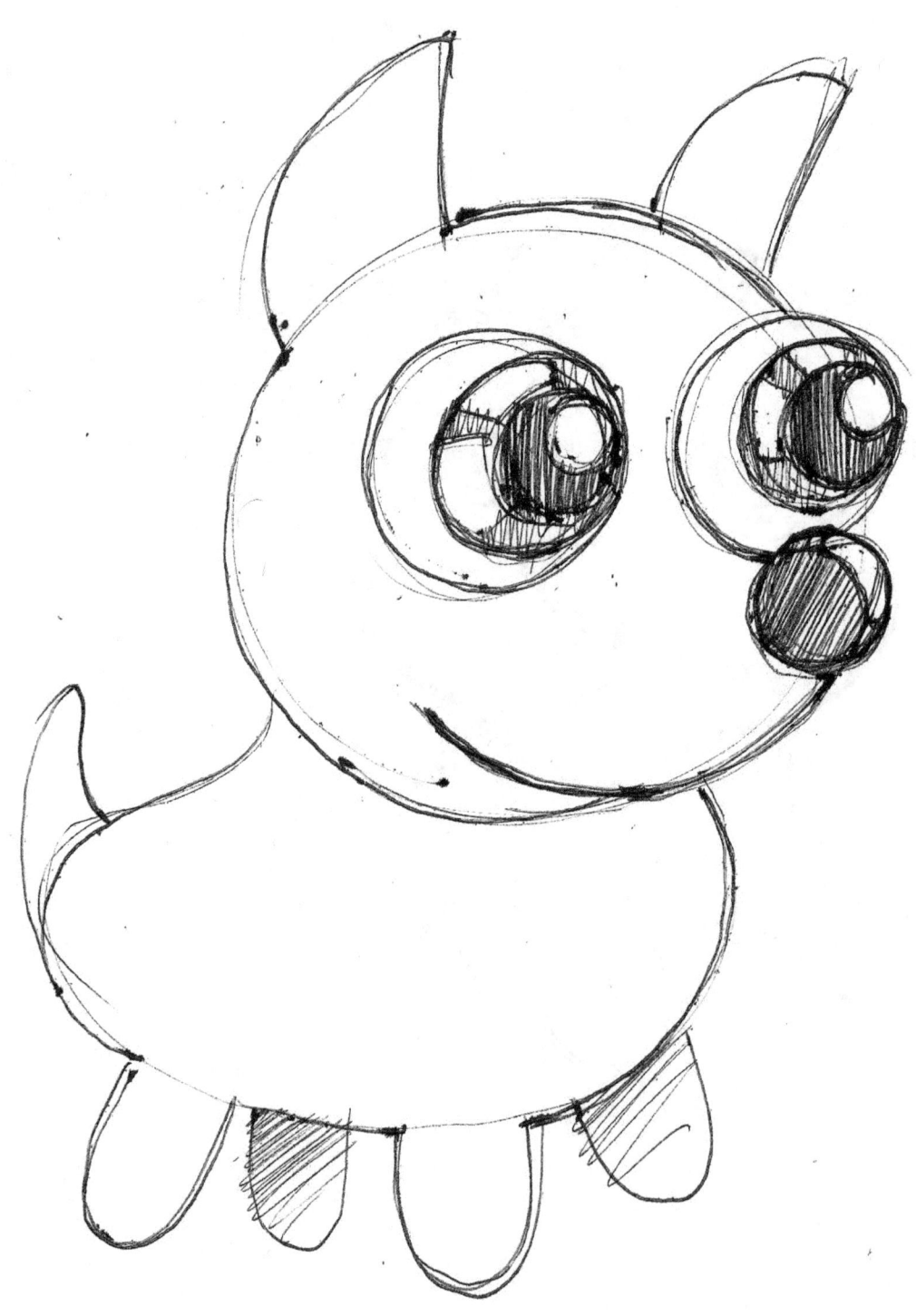

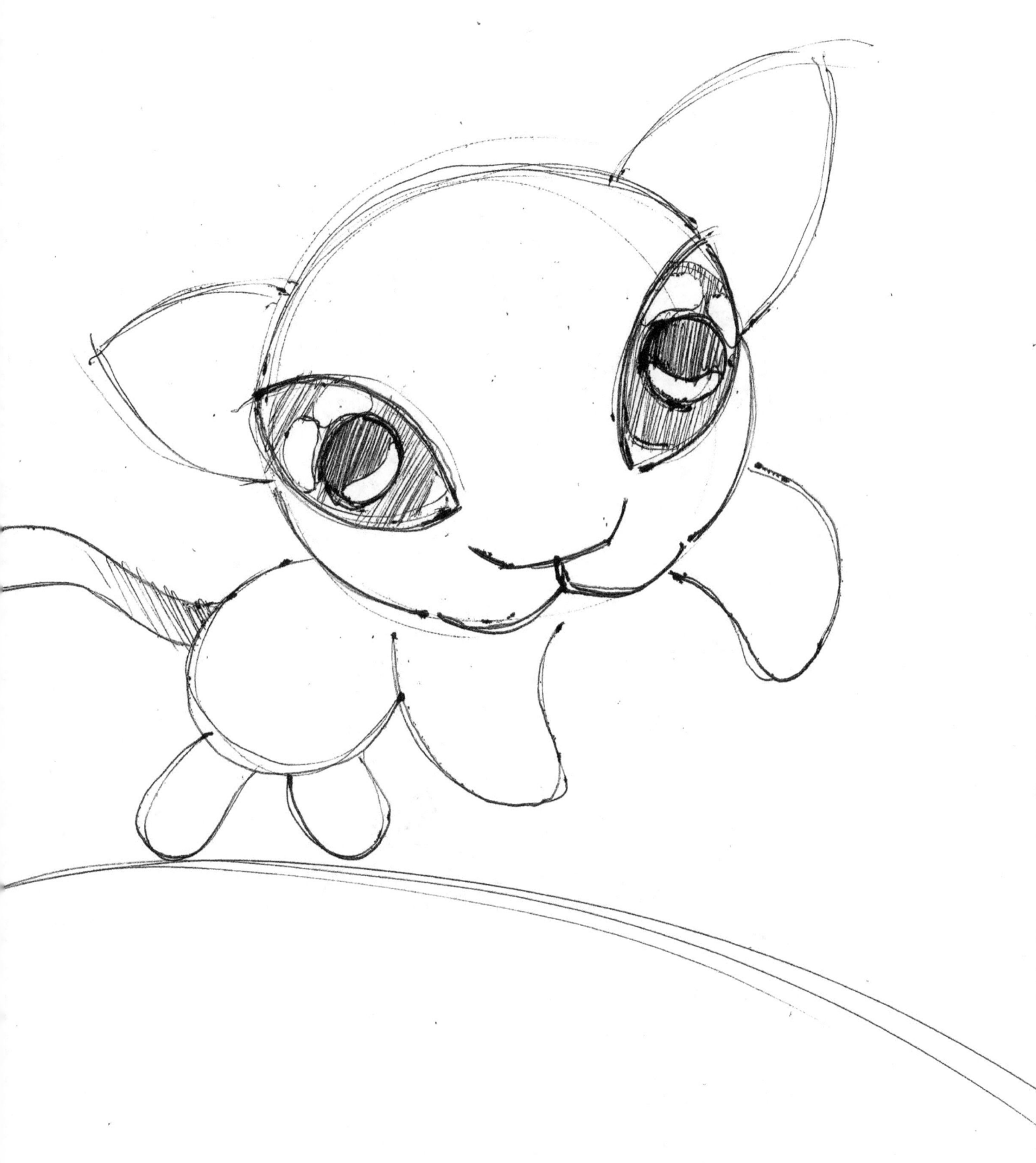

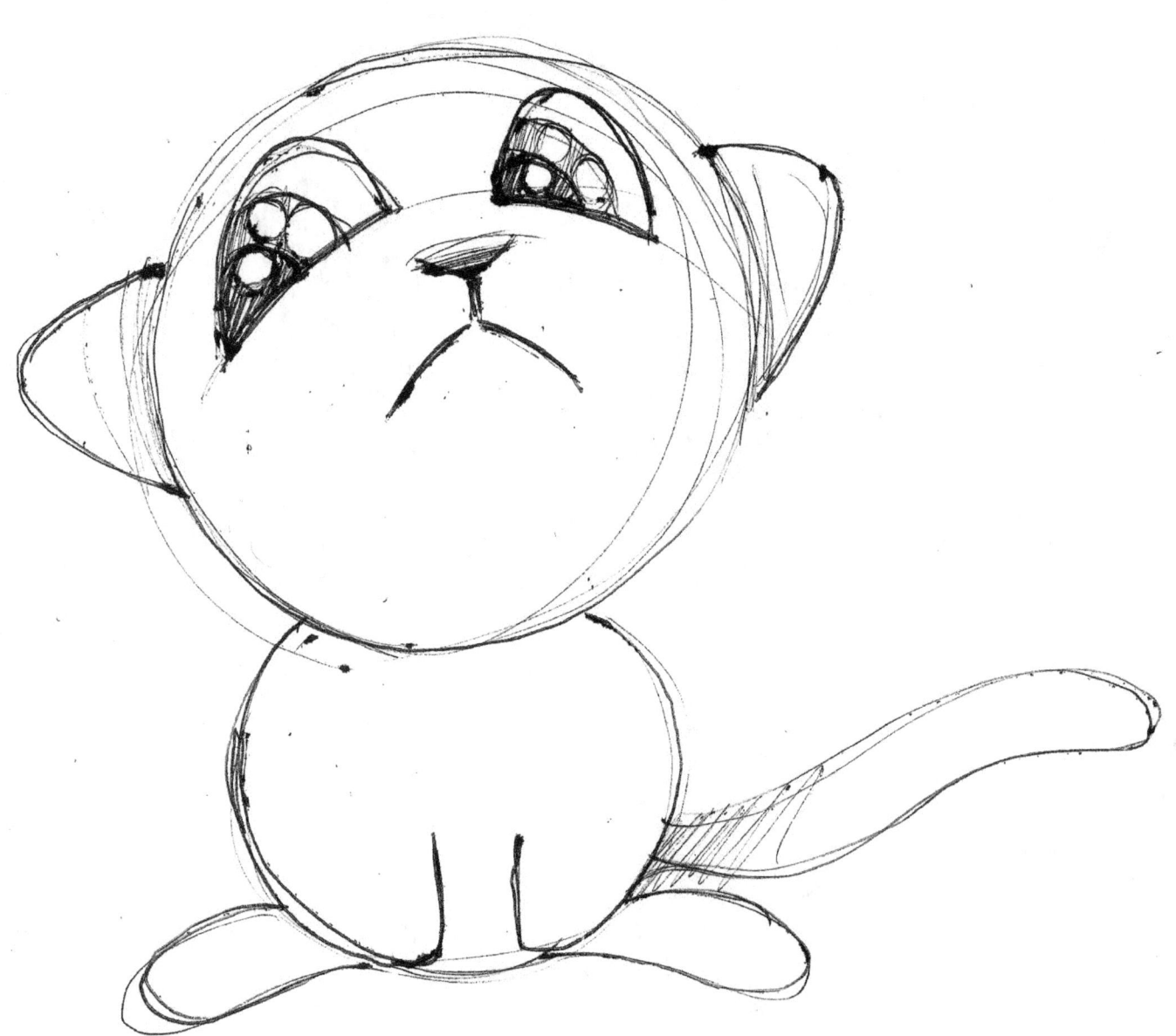

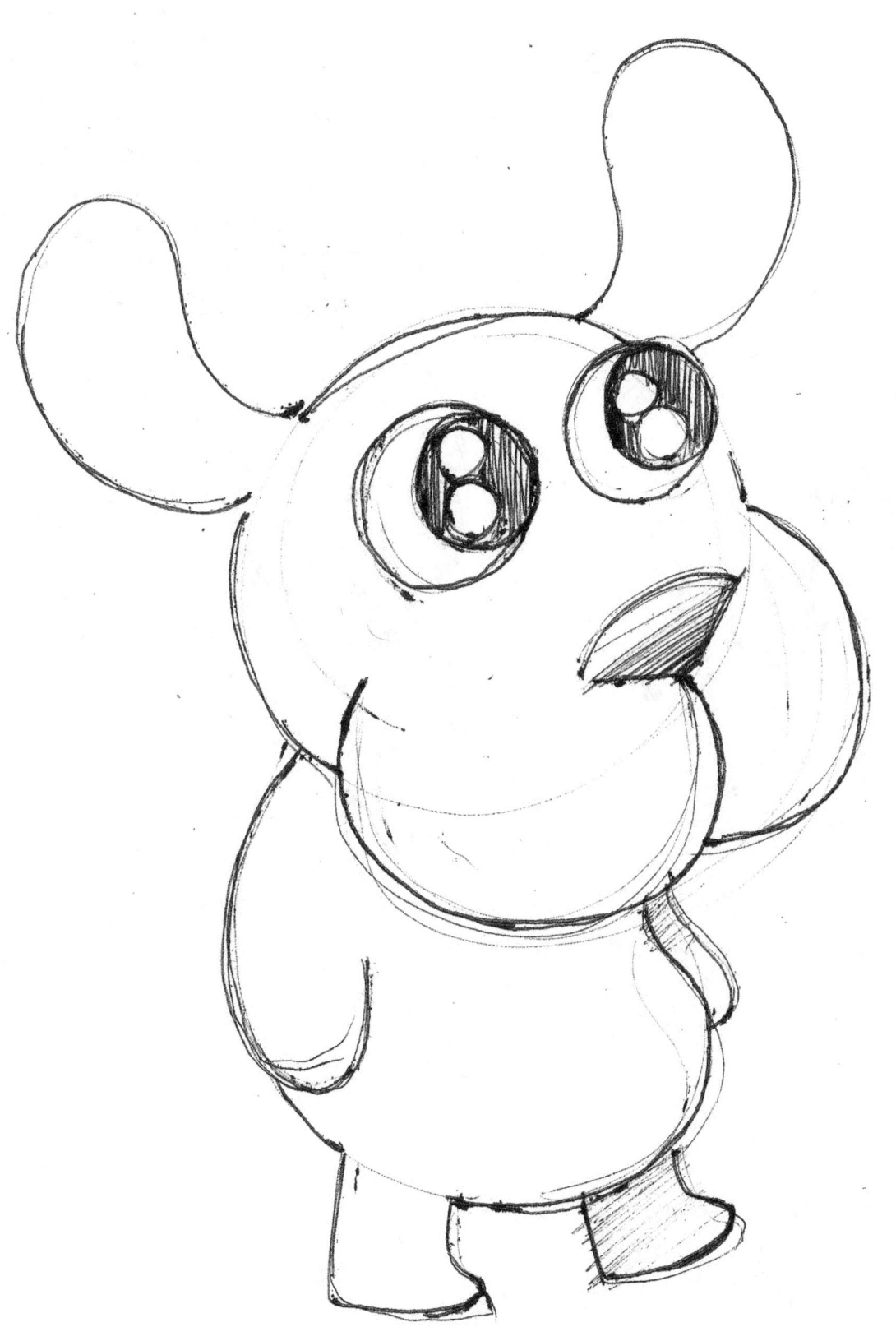

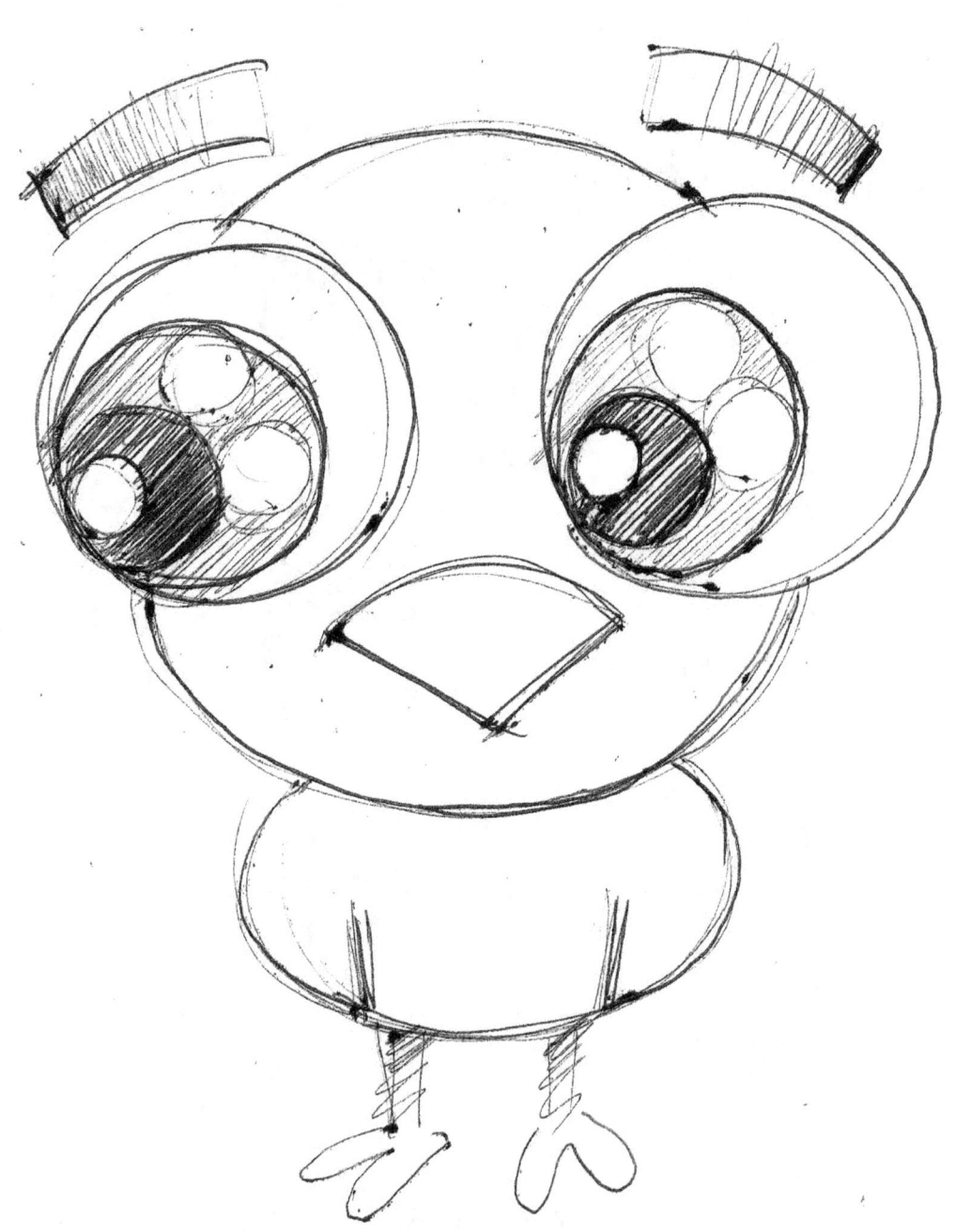

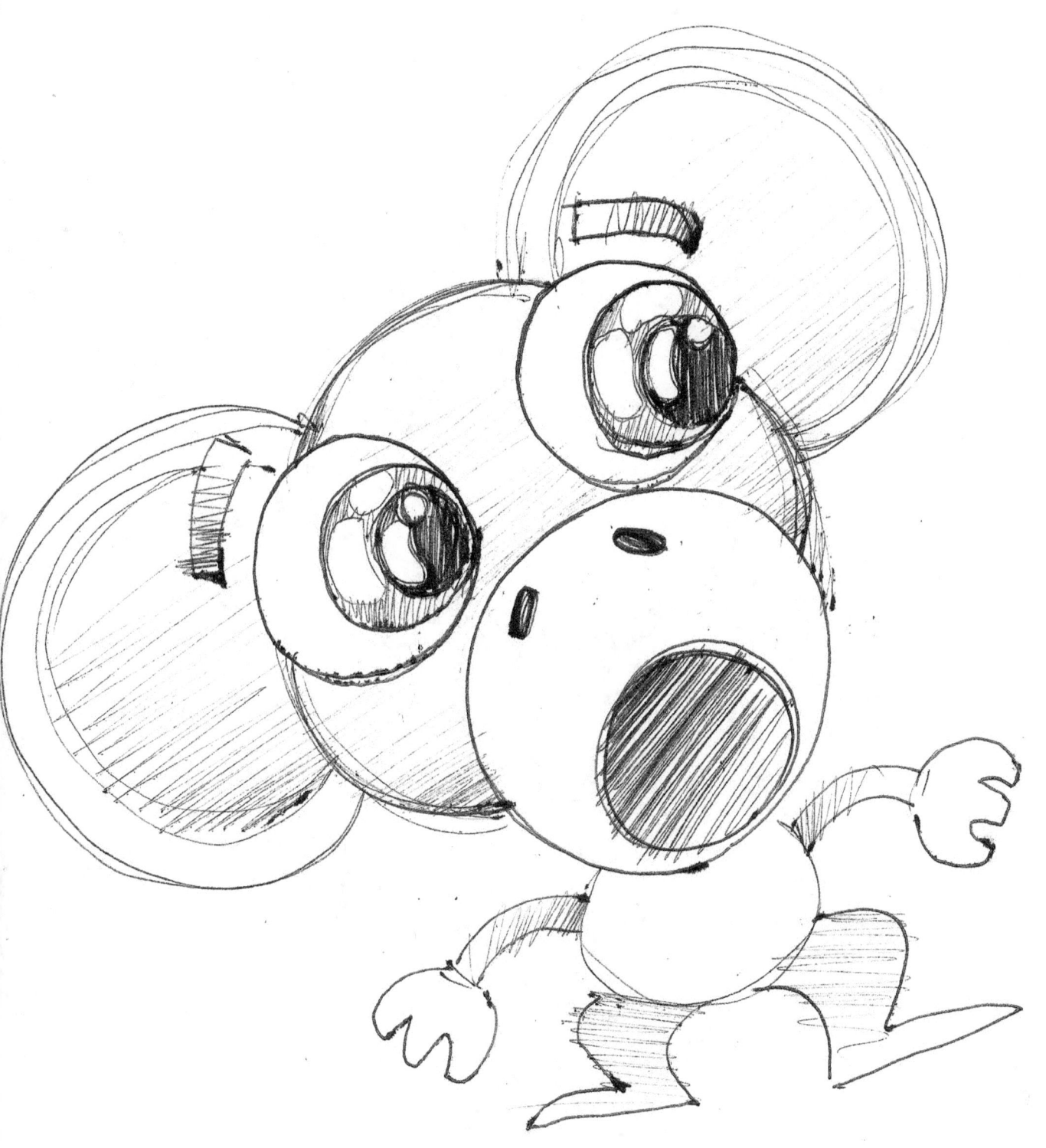

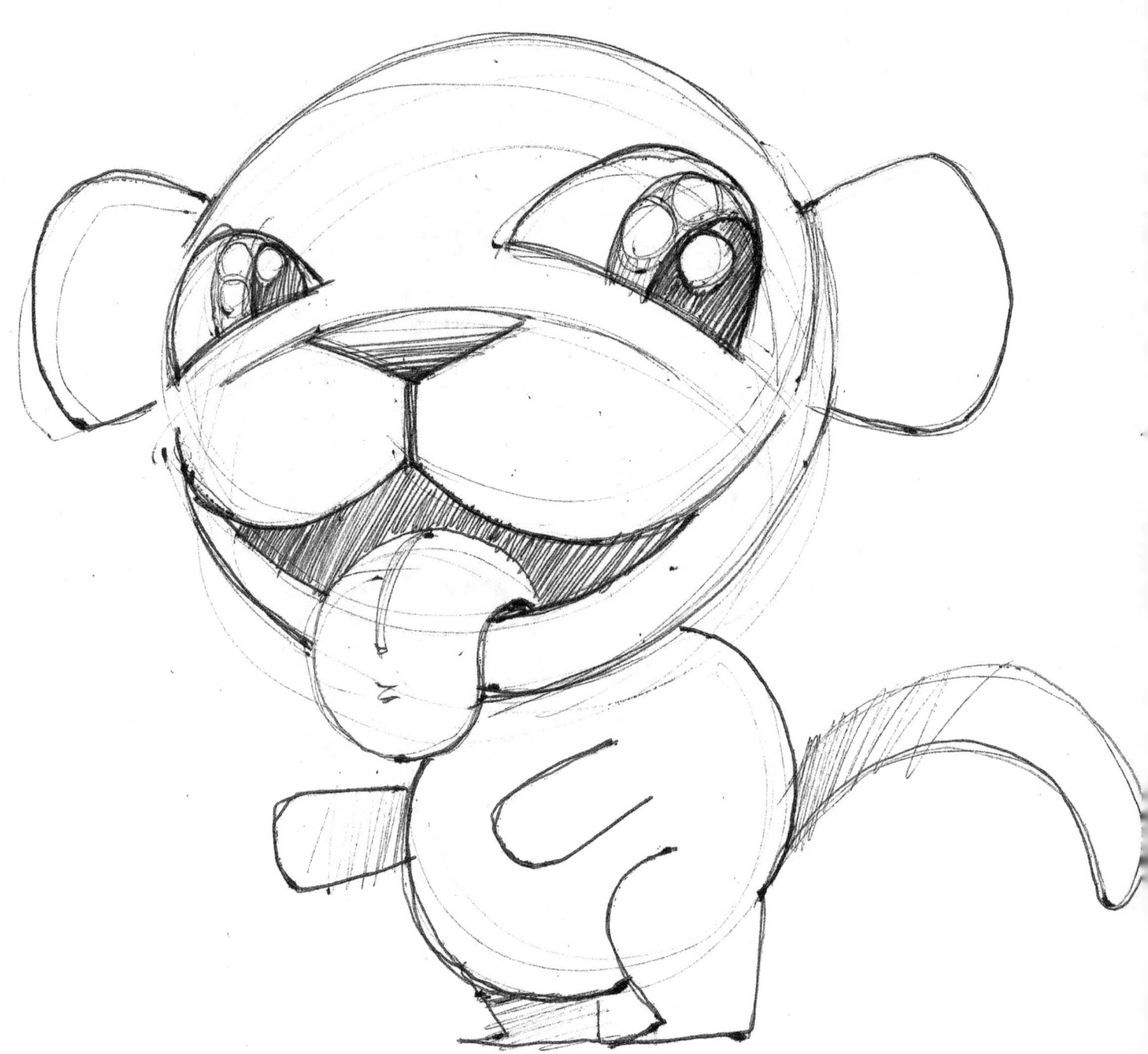

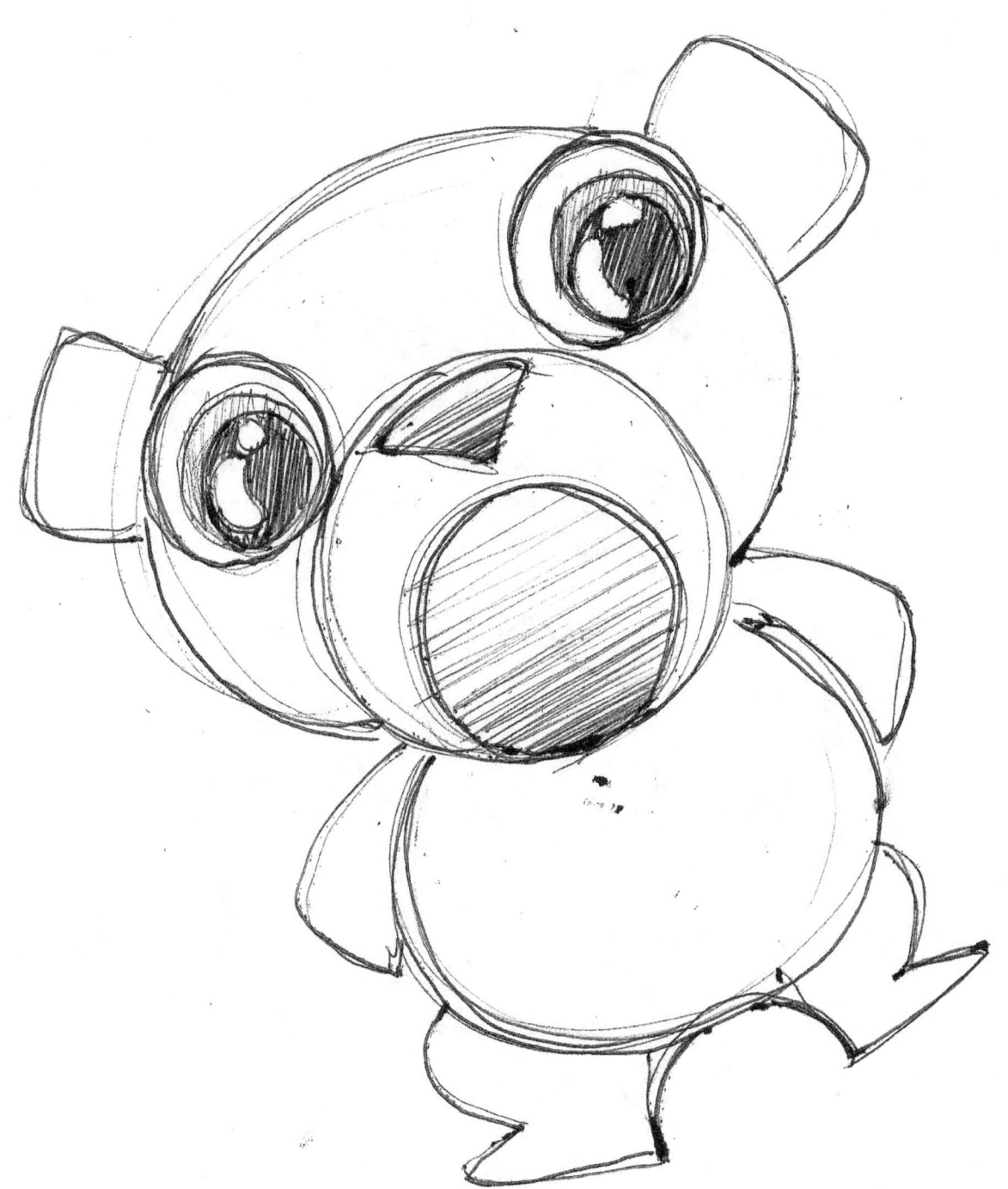

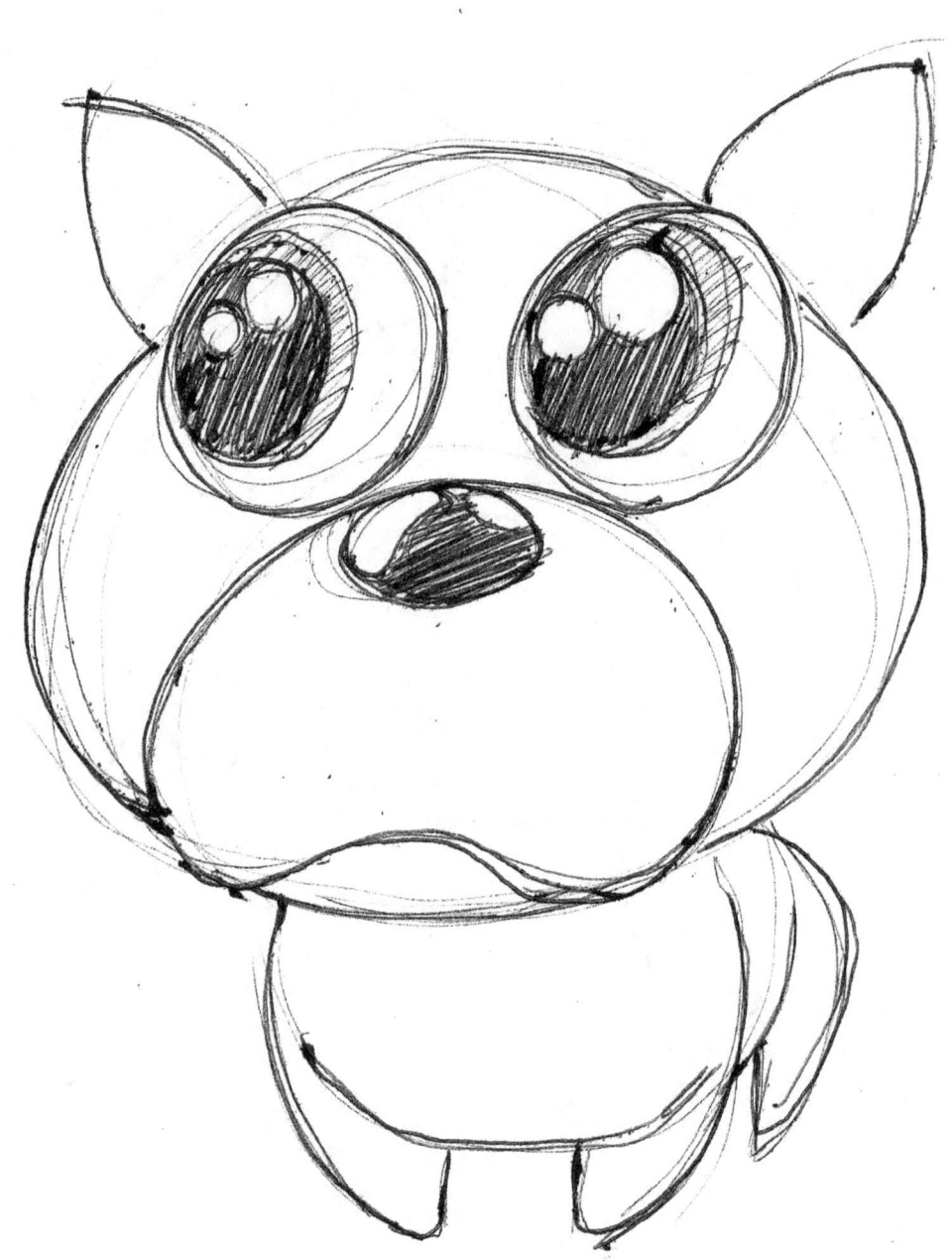

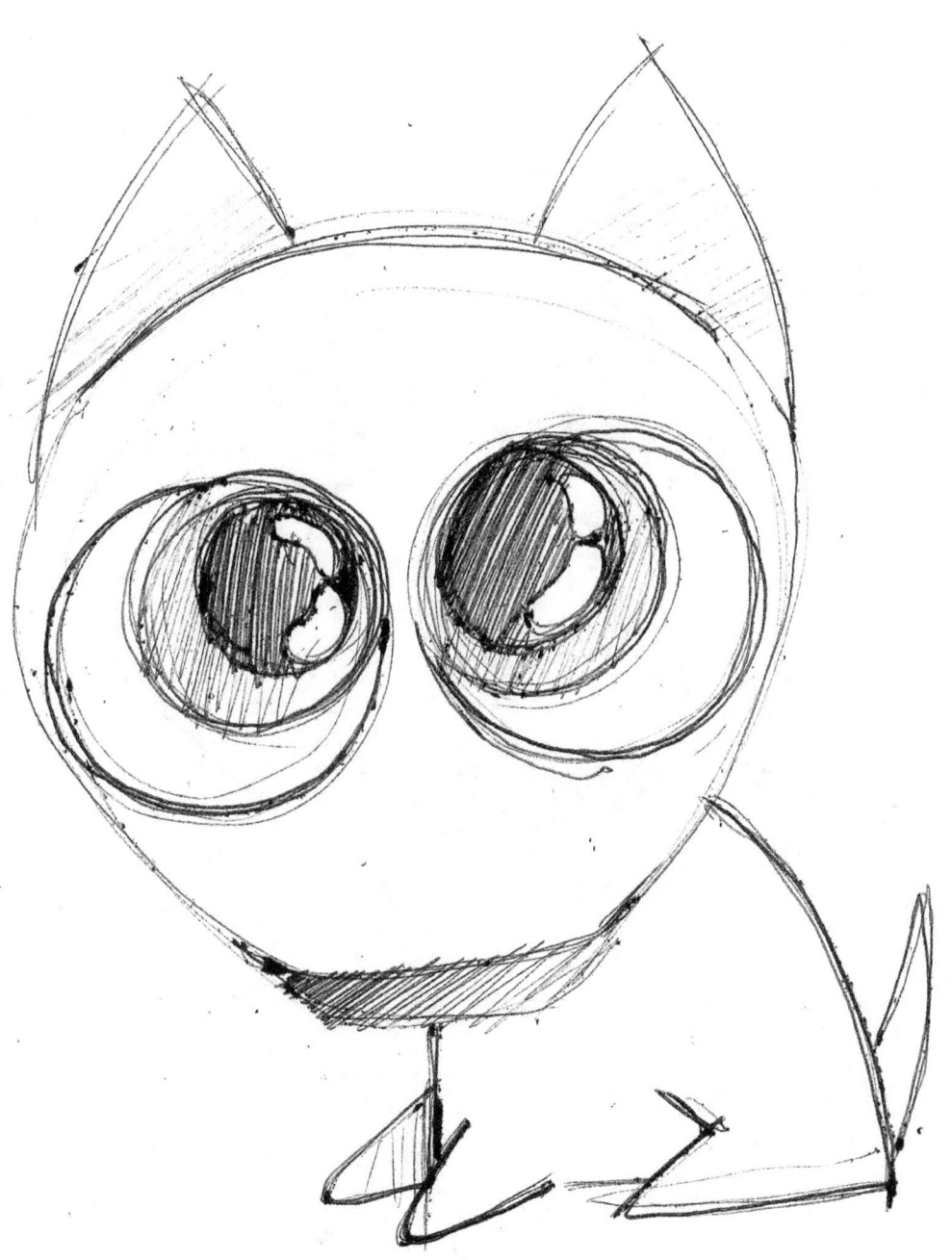

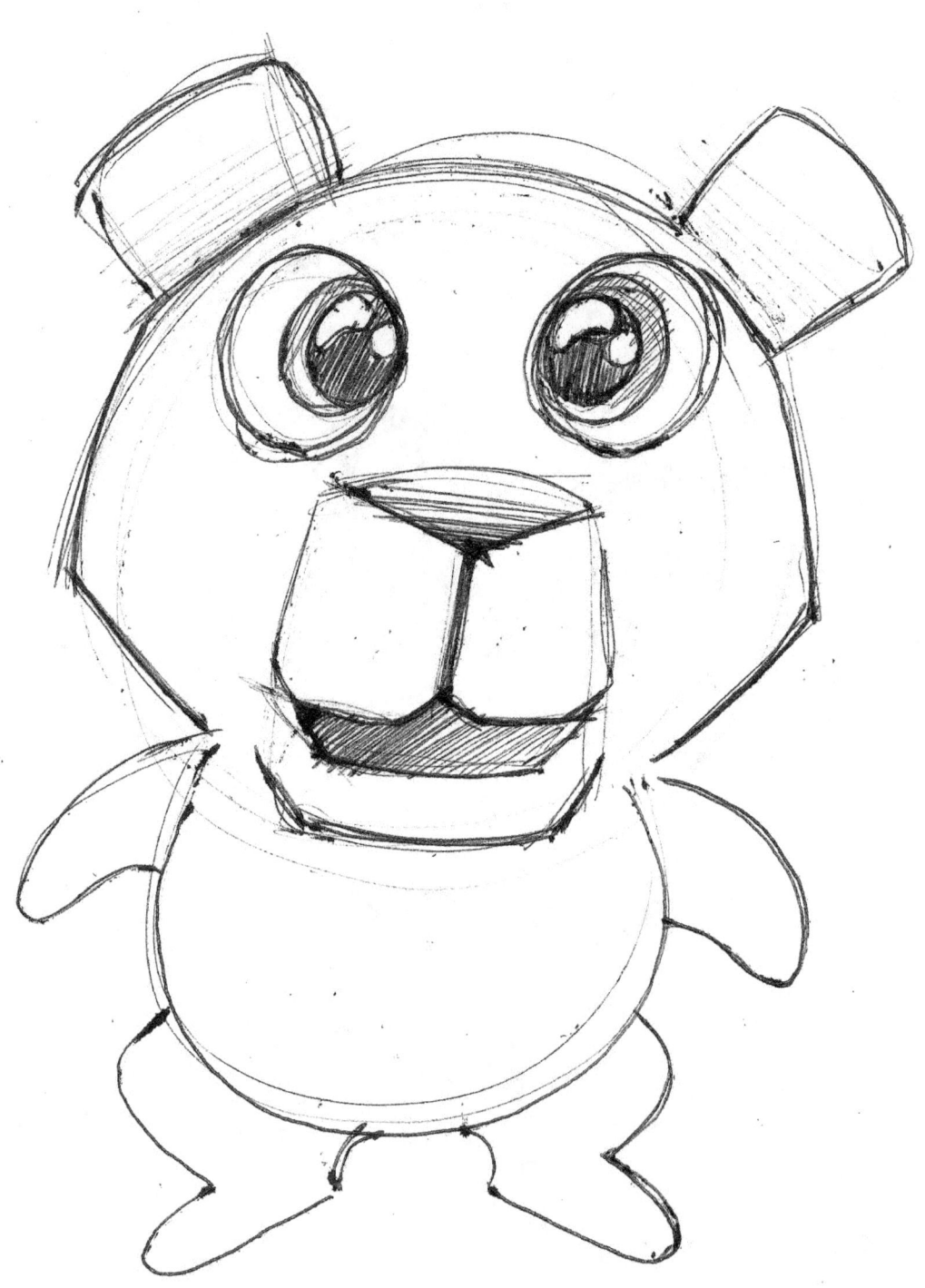

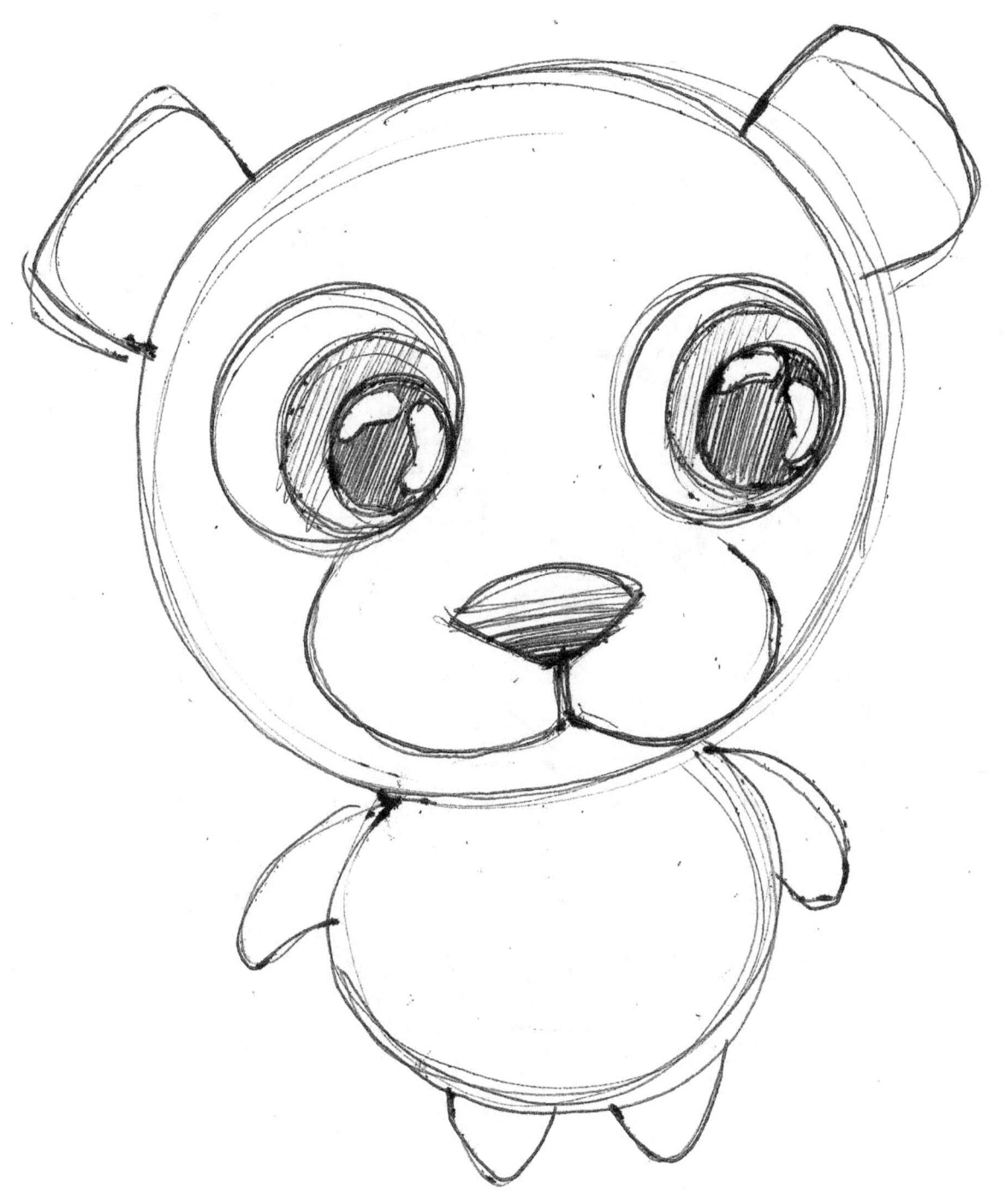

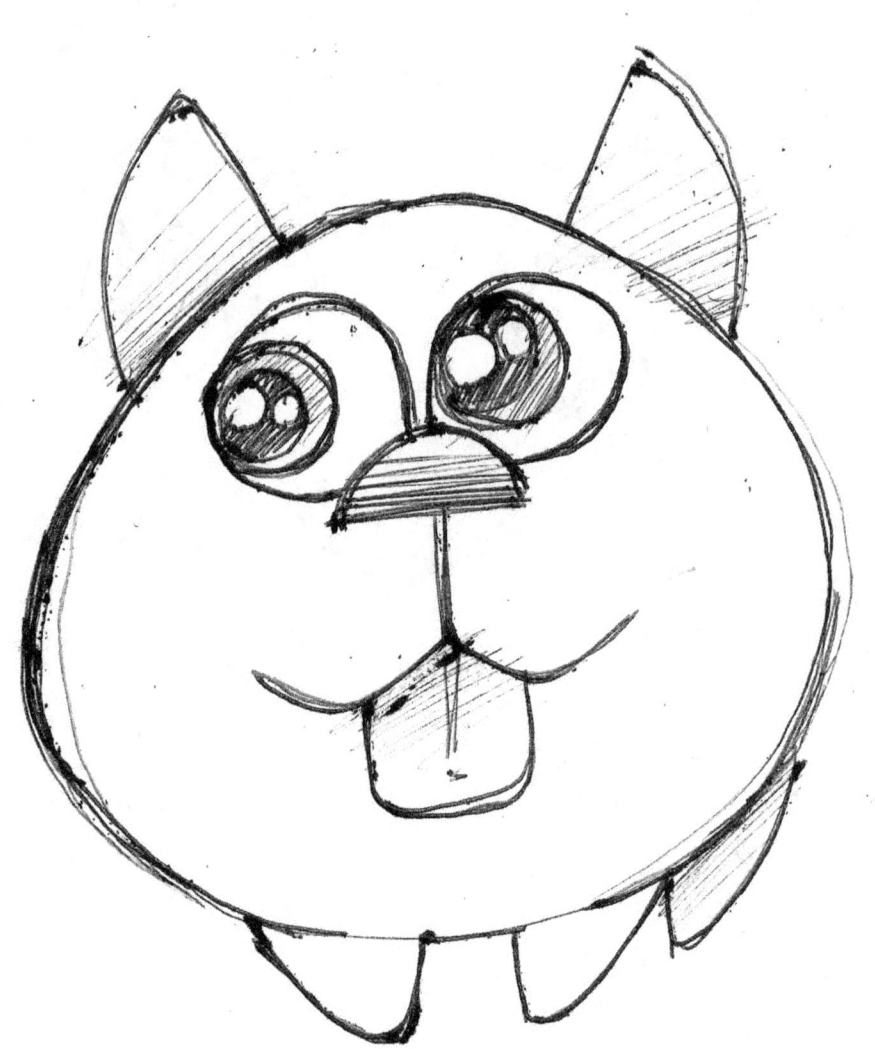

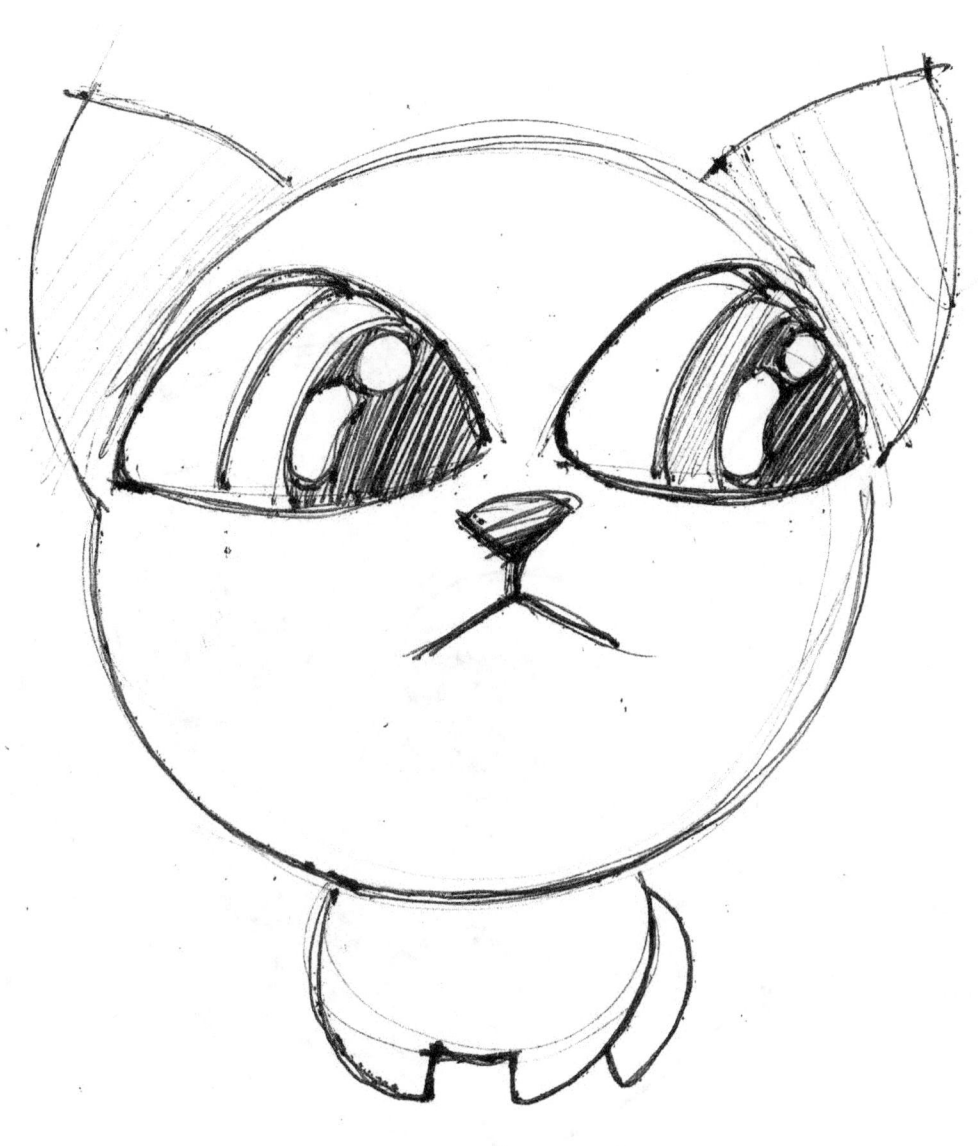

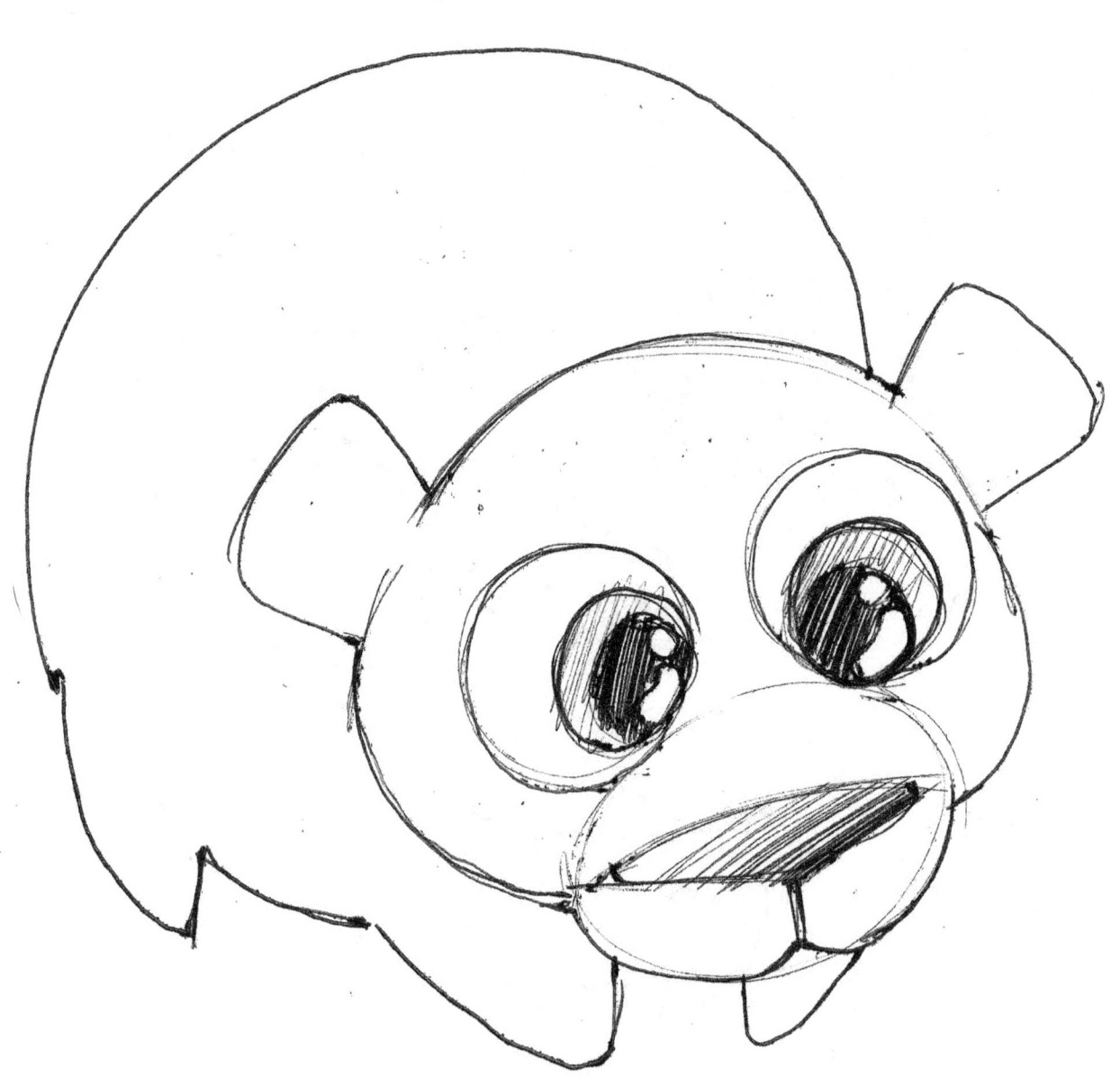

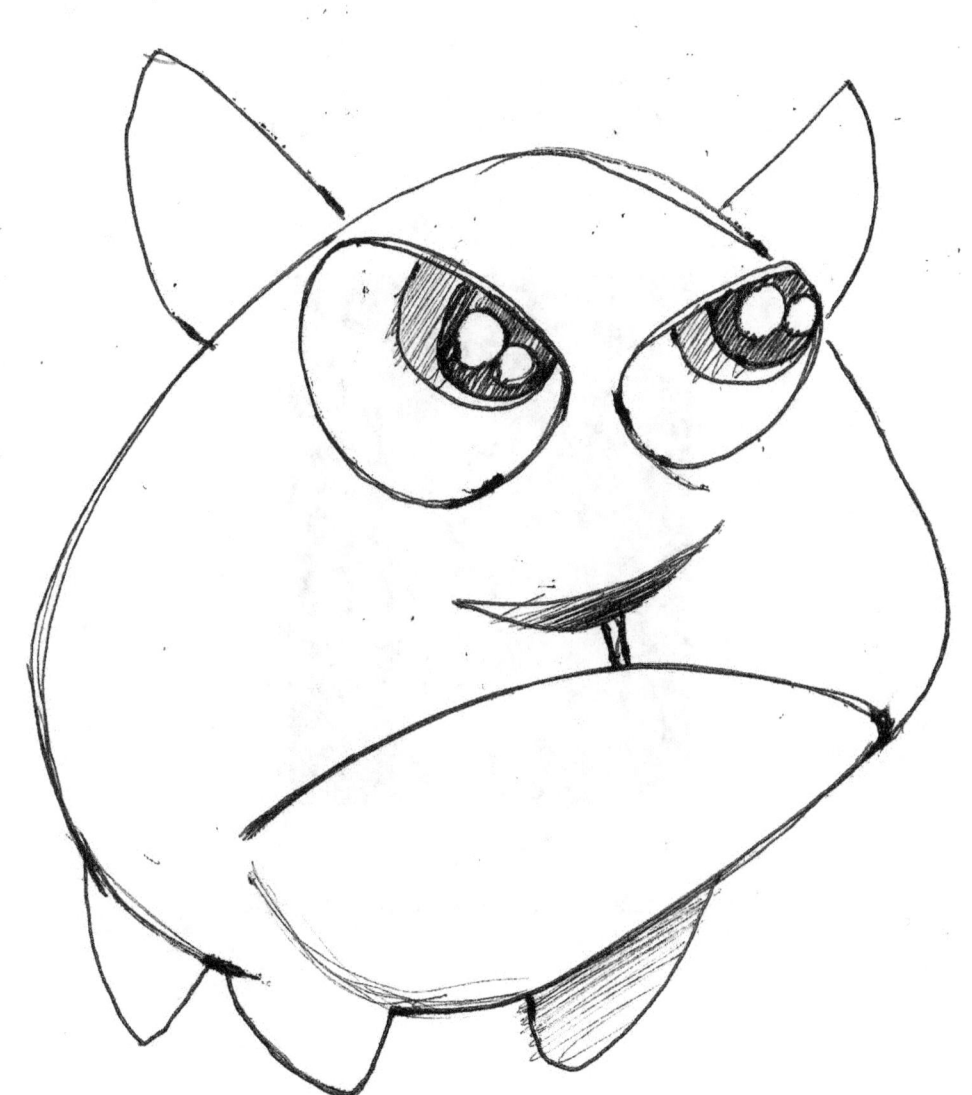

ABOUT THE AUTHOR

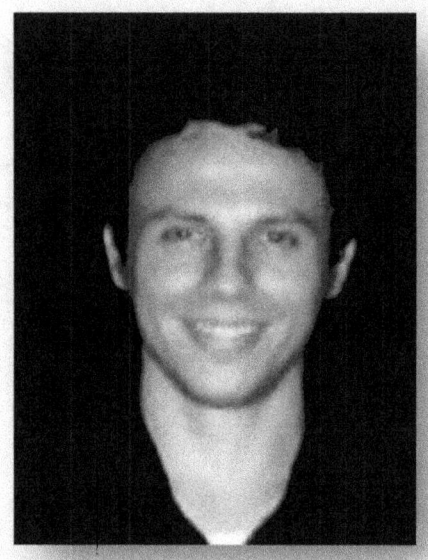

www.marcoaureliogalan.blogspot.com

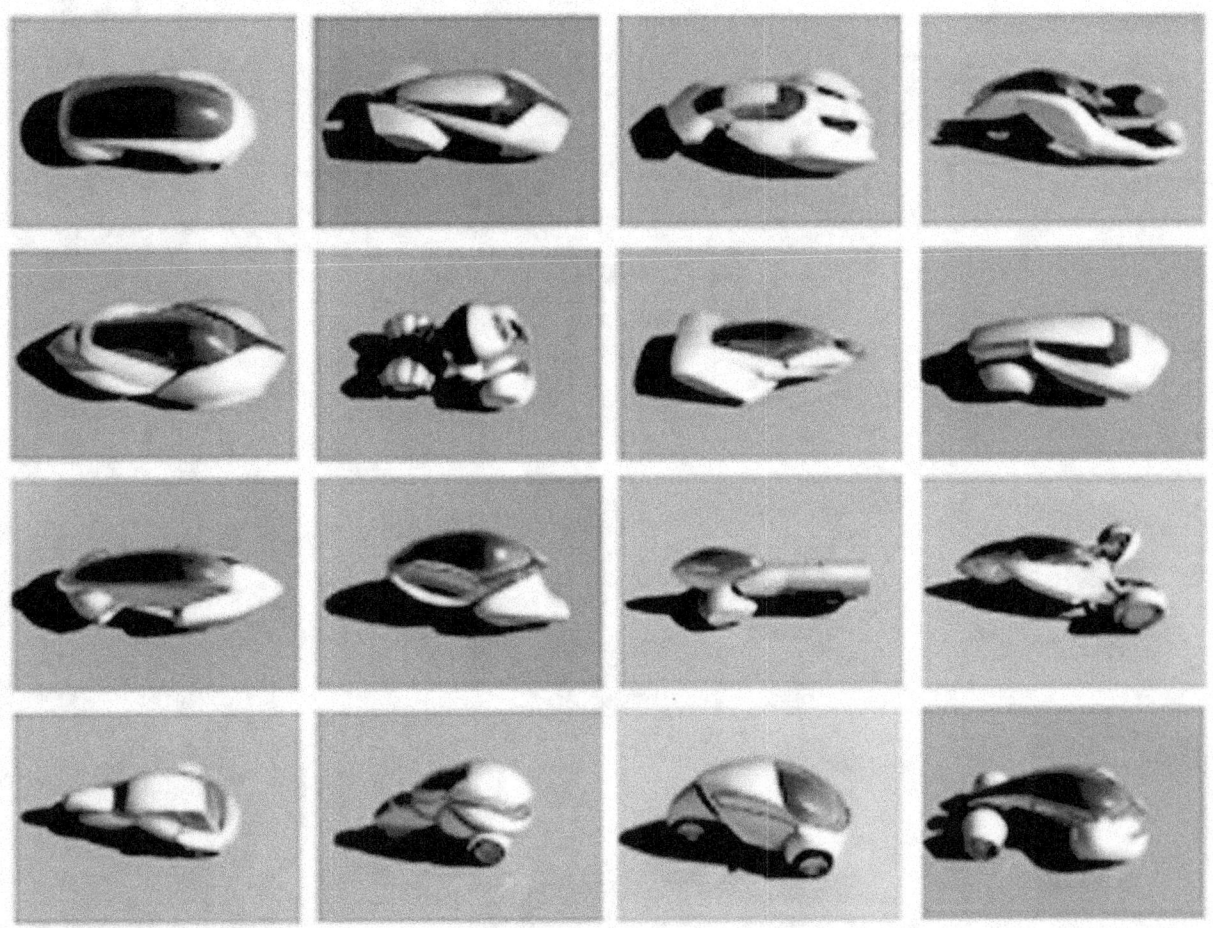

24 BIONIC CARS
MARCO AURELIO GALAN HENRIQUEZ

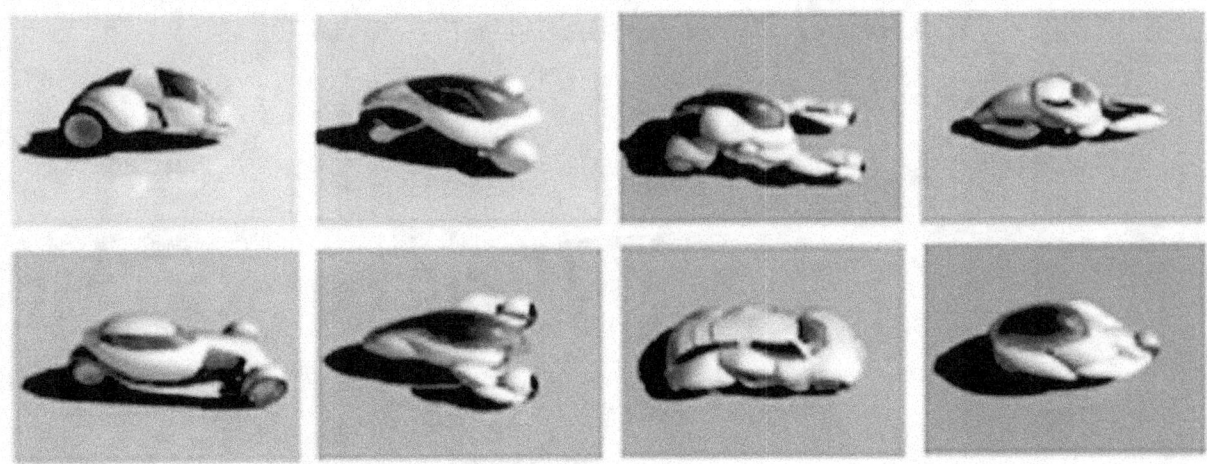

https://www.createspace.com/3942876

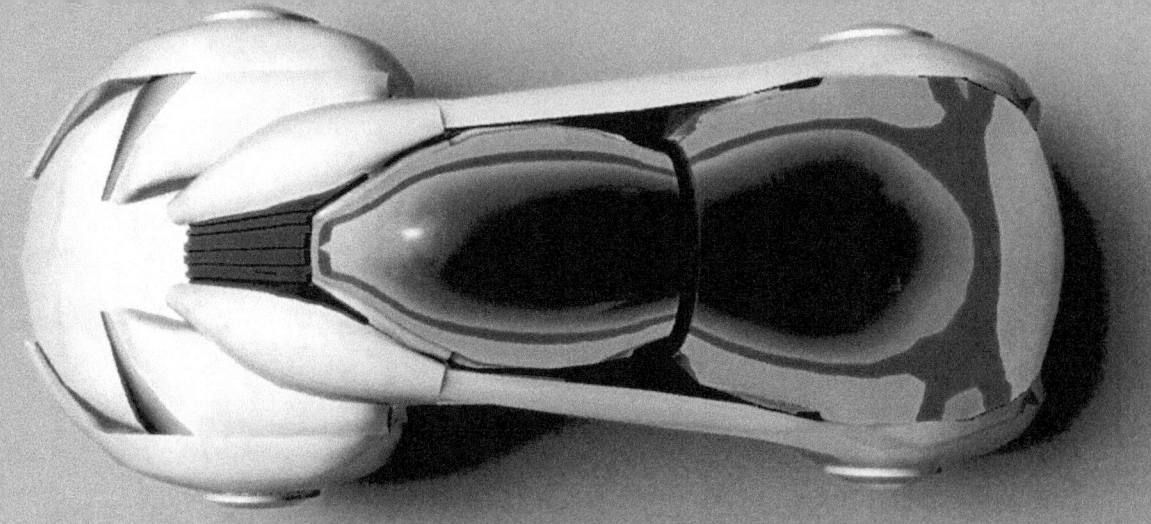

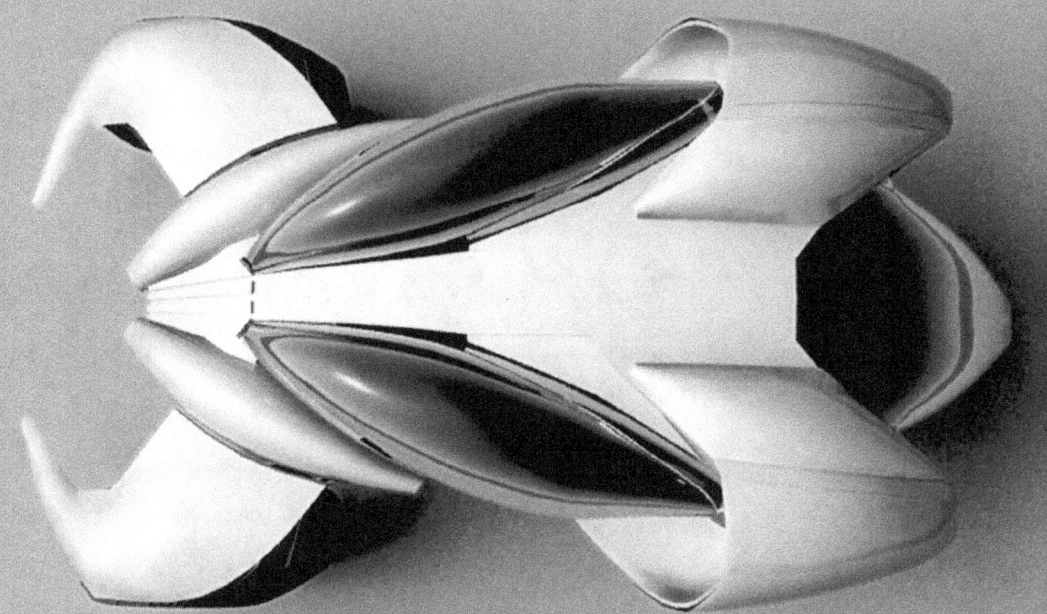

SUN CHARIOTS PROJECT
MARCO AURELIO GALAN HENRIQUEZ

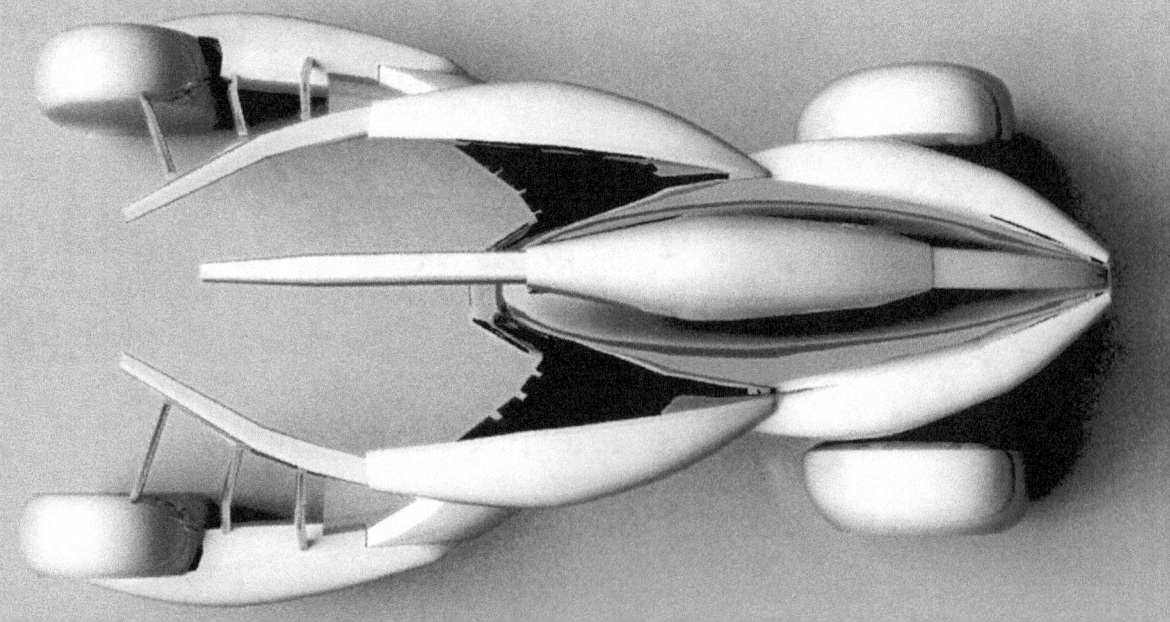

www.ingramcontent.com/pod-product-compliance
Lightning Source LLC
Chambersburg PA
CBHW080259180526
45167CB00006B/2599